CHEROKEE
National Forest

CHEROKEE
National Forest

A HISTORY

MARCI SPENCER

FOREWORD BY SENATOR LAMAR ALEXANDER

THE
History
PRESS

Published by The History Press
Charleston, SC
www.historypress.com

First published 2024

Manufactured in the United States

ISBN 9781467147705

Library of Congress Control Number: 2024937567

Notice: The information in this book is true and complete to the best of our knowledge. It is offered without guarantee on the part of the author or The History Press. The author and The History Press disclaim all liability in connection with the use of this book.

Dedicated to retired USFS Staff Officer Lewis Kearney,
who kept my resources coming, my spirits up and my pen moving.

To Bisco, who stayed one paw-step behind my right boot.

To my 150,000-mile-old Jeep for cruising backroads with me.

To Dad, Max Garland Lance, who would have enjoyed my books
about the mountains he loved.

Oh, Tennessee, my Tennessee
What Love and Pride I feel for thee,
You proud old state, the Volunteer,
Your fine traditions I hold dear…
I thrill at thought of mountains grand,
Rolling green fields and fertile farmland.
Earth rich with stone, mineral and ore,
Forests dense and wildflowers galore,
Powerful rivers that bring us light,
Deep lakes with fish and fowl in flight…
And, o'er the world as I may roam,
No place exceeds my boyhood home.
And, oh, how much I long to see,
My native land, my Tennessee.

Excerpt from Tennessee's state poem, designated in 1973.
Commander William Porter "Bill" Lawrence (1930–2005)—a Nashville native,
U.S. Navy vice-admiral and U.S. naval pilot—wrote this poem during his
sixty-day-long solitary confinement as a prisoner in the Vietnam War.

CONTENTS

Contents

FOREWORD

Marci Spencer's history of the Cherokee National Forest demonstrates that any Tennessean in public life has had plenty of opportunities to help those who want to conserve and enjoy this 650,000-acre outdoor playground. For example, when I was elected governor in 1978, among the first constituents to appear on my doorstep were the whitewater rafters of the Ocoee River, which runs along the edge of the Cherokee Forest. These rafters had discovered the wonders of the Ocoee only two years before. The Tennessee Valley Authority operates an unusual flume from a dam on the Ocoee that carries river water five miles down to a hydroelectric power plant. In 1976, TVA closed the flume for repairs. That allowed the river water to run free, creating whitewater rapids and an enthusiastic community of rafters. These rafters had big ideas—as did the state's tourism commissioner, Irving Waugh. Irving had an especially fertile imagination, having created Opryland and the annual televised Country Music Awards show. So, he and I invited Jerry Reed, the actor and Nashville musician, to join us, along with my wife, Honey, to raft the Ocoee. Irving turned our whitewater adventure into a television commercial. According to rafter David Brown, in his book *The Whitewater Wars*, the Ocoee, which had only seven thousand rafters in 1977, attracted fifty-six thousand in 1980. The "infectiously joyous" rafting journey in our TV commercial "opened the flood gates," Brown wrote.

But in 1983 came trouble. TVA had finished its repairs and was ready to reopen the flume. Rafters could see their outfitting and rafting businesses drying up, literally. That year, Howard Baker was U.S. Senate majority leader and I was a governor. We found a solution that allowed TVA ratepayers to be reimbursed for dollars that were lost on days the flume was closed. River recreation flourished. Tourism jobs were created. The Ocoee became so popular that it was the whitewater rafting site for the 1996 Summer Olympics. This Olympic rafting experience can still be enjoyed today—right there on the edge of Cherokee National Forest—the largest tract of public land in Tennessee.

The Cherokee lies on either side of its better-known sister—the Great Smoky Mountains National Park—and is larger than the Smokies by about 120,000 acres. The forest welcomes more than 3 million visitors per year, more than most national forests. As I found with the Ocoee rafters, the Cherokee National Forest has a legion of its own passionate advocates. Early in my time in the U.S. Senate, The Conservation Fund approached me about Rocky Fork, a 10,000-acre tract in Unicoi and Greene Counties. The fund wanted to make this private land part of Cherokee National Forest because of its bears and its streams and peaks that reach to 4,800 feet, as well as the 1.5 miles of the Appalachian Trail that wind through it. The U.S. Forest Service purchased about 2,200 acres, and The Conservation Fund bought the rest of the property from the landowners. Over several years, I helped secure more than $30 million in federal funds to buy the rest of the 10,000 acres from the Fund. Eventually, nearly 8,000 acres became part of the national forest, and thanks to Governor Bill Haslam, more than 2,000 were made into Tennessee's fifty-fifth state park. Another example: the Tennessee Wilderness Society wanted to designate 20,000 acres of the forest as wilderness land. Senator Corker and I introduced legislation for five consecutive Congresses before we were able to pass that bill in 2018. That "wilderness" designation means that you and I can roam and fish these areas but that their sensitive ecosystems and watersheds will be protected.

Toward the end of my time in the Senate, I asked the leaders of Sevier and Cocke Counties to take a look at thirty-three miles of unused National Park Service Foothills Parkway right-of-way to determine what could be done with it while we waited for Congress to appropriate funds to build the rest of the parkway. County leaders determined that the best use would be mountain bike trails. As it turned out, the best place to put most of the new trails was on Cherokee National Forest land. So, in 2020, we secured a $6 million Appalachian Regional Commission grant to create up to seventy-five miles of mountain bike trails—a significant step to helping grow the economy of Cocke County. Finally, Congress's passage of the Great American Outdoors Act in 2020 is the most recent opportunity those

Lamar Alexander,
Tennessee governor
from 1979 to 1987
and U.S. senator
from 2003 to 2021.
Lamar Alexander.

of us in public life have had to make sure the Cherokee National Forest is in good shape for future generations. For the first time, this act uses proceeds from energy exploration on federal lands to help national parks and forests and other public lands to reduce their $12 billion deferred maintenance backlog. The new law provides the largest such infusion of federal support since the Eisenhower years. The Cherokee National Forest has a $27 million deferred maintenance backlog, which, under normal budgets, would take years to reduce. This new law will speed up restoring its roads and trails for 3 million annual visitors.

All it takes is a climb to the top of Oswald Dome, a hike out to Benton Falls or to spend an afternoon of fly fishing on South Holston Lake, with the magnificent richness of the Cherokee National Forest spread out before you, to see why anyone in public life encounters so many passionate advocates of this forest—and has so many opportunities to help preserve and create new ways to enjoy it.

—U.S. Senator Lamar Alexander

ACKNOWLEDGEMENTS

M ore than one hundred people have contributed to this book. Retired USFS personnel with a commitment to the national forest they served provided personal stories, resources and reviews. Scientists, biologists, historians, land trust organizations, firefighters, educators, museum directors, recreational leaders, residents and others also enriched this history of the CNF and reviewed its content. The book would not be as thorough, accurate or entertaining without your knowledge and assistance. Whether you furnished information for the text or edited my words, I deeply appreciate every one of you. I offer heartfelt gratitude to my acquisitions editor, Kate Jenkins; my copyeditor, Ryan Finn; and The History Press staff for believing in me during the delays in completing this book project.

INTRODUCTION

In April 1996, the high priestess in Olympia, Greece, captured the sun's rays to ignite a flame that united the ancient and modern Olympic Games. The flame passed from torch to torch eight hundred times across Greece and then boarded a plane with members of the Atlanta Committee of the Olympic Games (ACOG) bound for Los Angeles.

At the Los Angeles International Airport, the 1960 African American U.S. Olympic decathlon gold medalist Rafer Johnson lit his three-pound, thirty-inch aluminum torch to begin its fifteen-thousand-mile cross-country relay. Escorted by Georgia state troopers, torchbearers passed the flame twelve thousand times along the three-month trip through forty-two states, traveling by foot, train, plane, steamboat and the Pony Express. In Florida, the torch (without its oxygen-consuming flames) took a space shuttle flight and then headed toward the Cherokee National Forest (CNF).

The flame left Blairsville, Georgia, and traveled to the state-line cities of McCaysville, Georgia, and Copperhill, Tennessee, where the Toccoa River becomes the Ocoee River as it enters Tennessee. Residents cheered as the flame passed, headed north to Ducktown and turned west on the Ocoee Scenic Byway (US-64/74).

"I was the next link," said now retired USFS National Accessibility Program Manager Janet Zeller. Wearing the official torchbearer's shirt, she received the flame from a motorcyclist beside the USFS Ocoee Whitewater Center. In her wheelchair, "jerry-rigged with a cup holder, created by a CNF employee to steady the torch," Janet explained, she carried the flame along a walkway through the native garden that volunteers, including CNF Forest Supervisor John Ramey, had completed the previous day. Most torchbearers were former Olympic athletes, Olympic committee members and sponsor-appointed individuals. Just 5,500 torch-relay ambassadors, however, were chosen from 40,000 nominated community leaders. Janet was chosen by the CNF to represent all USFS employees. She had turned her loss of mobility into a lifelong mission to integrate accessibility into outdoor recreation without changing the setting, for all people to recreate together.

After a stairway fall left the forty-one-year-old school librarian paralyzed as a quadriplegic, physical rehabilitation helped Janet adjust her life to move forward. Her personal goal was to return to outdoor recreation activities. In the 1980s, she studied the federal laws protecting the rights of persons with disabilities (the Americans with Disabilities Act applying to state government services was passed in 1990). In 1991, Janet worked with a national forest on a mediation case, involving a person with a disability who wanted to use an all-terrain vehicle (ATV) to access a federally designated wilderness area. The 1964 Wilderness Act designates some mandates that motorized use is prohibited in federally designated wilderness areas. After six months of mediation and team accessibility training, everyone understood and agreed that motorized access was not legal in federally designated wilderness areas; however, other accessibility options were possible.

That fall, the USFS hired Janet as its first Accessibility Program Manager in the Eastern Region. In 2001, she was hired as the first USFS National Accessibility Program Manager, building teams of Regional and National Forest Accessibility Coordinators and instructing and writing USFS standards for recreation areas.

In her personal life, between 1994 and 1998, Janet served as the president of the American Canoe Association (ACA), the first president with a disability. As a certified canoeing and kayaking instructor, she developed the ACA's Adaptive Paddling Instructor Certification program and, in 2009, authored *Canoeing and Kayaking for People with Disabilities*.

So, on July 16, 1996, Janet represented both the ACA and "my fellow Forest Service employees, who work daily caring for the land and serving the people on the national forests across the U.S." After an Ocoee River Olympic ceremony, Janet transferred her light to the next runner, a Ringgold, Georgia teen hero who provided home care for senior citizens. The torch continued west along the Ocoee Scenic Byway, passing the Tennessee Valley Authority (TVA) dams and Parksville Reservoir (also called Lake Ocoee or Parksville Lake). At US-411, the runners turned south to head toward Atlanta.

Janet Zeller, USFS 1996 Olympic torchbearer. *Janet Zeller.*

USFS Ocoee River Project Manager Paul Wright told a reporter, "Janet Zeller represented the strength and diversity of 30,000 Forest Service employees who have made direct or indirect contributions and sacrifices to assure that three billion television viewers will see a world-class facility worthy of the Olympic title."

THE 650,000 EAST TENNESSEE acres of the CNF, bordering North Carolina north and south of the Great Smoky Mountains National Park (GSMNP), celebrate its Olympic history as well as its recreation opportunities, natural resources, scenic views, watersheds, unique ecosystems and Native American history. Each ranger district's name pays tribute to the Cherokee people. The CNF protects ancient Cherokee burial sites and a section of the Trail of Tears. It partners with Oklahoma's United Keetoowah Band of Cherokee Indians of the United Youth Services Corps and offers conservation projects in their sacred, ancestral homelands.

The CNF's human history recounts the lives of explorers, loggers, miners, railroaders, pioneers, politicians, soldiers and dam builders. It tells the story of Civilian Conservation Corpsmen (CCC) earning money to send home to impoverished families by building recreation areas and fighting wildfires. The CNF supports researchers, like the American Chestnut Foundation and the University of Tennessee–Knoxville Tree Improvement Program, working to restore the American chestnut (*Castanea dentata*), lost to an early 1900s blight, by raising hybrid chestnut seedlings in a CNF seed orchard and transplanting them to the national forest. It celebrates land acquisition projects that protect vulnerable species and patch together non-contiguous public lands and Appalachian National Scenic Trail (A.T.) corridors. It supports volunteer trail maintenance teams and the Cherokee Hotshots, a highly skilled firefighting crew.

This tale of history through the CNF follows rivers, trails and scenic byways that, hopefully, will entice readers to explore, snorkel, paddle or dream in the outdoor world. Intriguing discoveries await.

PART I

Ocoee Ranger District

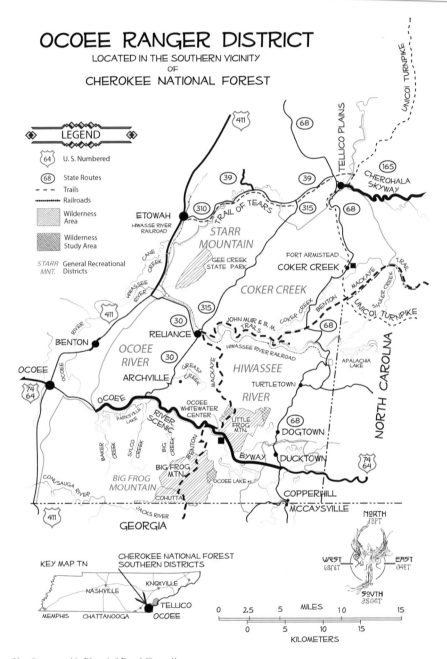

OCOEE RANGER DISTRICT
LOCATED IN THE SOUTHERN VICINITY
OF
CHEROKEE NATIONAL FOREST

LEGEND
- 64 U. S. Numbered
- 68 State Routes
- - - Trails
- Railroads
- Wilderness Area
- Wilderness Study Area
- STARR MNT. General Recreational Districts

UNICOI TURNPIKE

411

68

39 39

TELLICO PLAINS

165 CHEROHALA SKYWAY

310 ETOWAH
HIWASSE RIVER RAILROAD

TRAIL OF TEARS

STARR MOUNTAIN

315 68

GEE CREEK STATE PARK

FORT ARMISTEAD
COKER CREEK

CANE CREEK

HIWASSEE RIVER

COKER CREEK

MACKAYE TRAIL

SYLER CREEK

411

315

30 RELIANCE

JOHN MUIR & B. M. TRAILS

COKER CREEK

BENTON

68 UNICOI TURNPIKE

BENTON

OCOEE RIVER

30

GREASY CREEK

HIWASSEE RIVER RAILROAD

HIWASSEE RIVER

APALACHIA LAKE

NORTH CAROLNA

OCOEE

74 64

OCOEE

ARCHVILLE

OCOEE

MACKAYE

TURTLETOWN

PARKSVILLE LAKE

RIVER SCENIC

OCOEE WHITEWATER CENTER

LITTLE FROG MTN.

68 DOGTOWN

BAKER CREEK

SYLCO CREEK

BIG CREEK

BENTON

BYWAY

DUCKTOWN

74 64

CONSAUGA RIVER

BIG FROG MOUNTAIN

BIG FROG MTN.

OCOEE LAKE

COPPERHILL

COHUTTA

411

JACKS RIVER

MCCAYSVILLE

GEORGIA

NORTH

WEST EAST

SOUTH

KEY MAP TN

CHEROKEE NATIONAL FOREST
SOUTHERN DISTRICTS

KNOXVILLE
NASHVILLE
TELLICO
MEMPHIS CHATTANOOGA OCOEE

0 2.5 5 MILES 10 15

0 5 10 15
KILOMETERS

Ken Czarnomski, Phoenix2Reach@gmail.com.

OCOEE SCENIC BYWAY/ OCOEE RIVER AREA

Parksville Lake

The twenty-six-mile-long Ocoee Scenic Byway, the first national scenic byway designated in a national forest, roughly follows the Old Copper Road along today's US-64/74 beside the Ocoee River and extends seven miles up Chilhowee Mountain via Forest Service Road (FSR-77). In the mid-1800s, John Caldwell paid Cherokees from Turtletown Village to construct the Copper Road for teamsters transporting copper ore from the mines at Ducktown, Tennessee, to the railroad station in Cleveland, Tennessee. Copper haulers traveled for two days over the rugged road, stopping overnight at the Halfway House. To provide more efficient freight travel, the Marietta and North Georgia Railroad built a rail line from the Copper Basin south to Marietta, Georgia, and the Knoxville Southern Railroad built a line north to Knoxville in the 1800s. A CNF hiking trail follows a portion of the Old Copper Road.

At the west end of the Ocoee Scenic Byway, Sugarloaf Mountain Park is located beneath its namesake peak and beside the tailwaters of today's Ocoee Dam No. 1, owned by the Tennessee Valley Authority (TVA). Near this site in 1855, Samuel Parks purchased the Shields Brothers gristmill and later sold it to Julius Raht, the owner of Copper Basin mines, who operated a mill and store here in the mid-1800s for Copper Road travelers. Around 1911, about 1,500 workers and their families moved into Parksville Village—with its dining hall, store, machine shops, bathhouse, medical services and employee barracks—to construct the dam. Gertrude Karaivanoff Matlock, dressed in a "French serge suit, ostrich feathers on my hat, [and] low cut shoes," she wrote, arrived with her husband, an engineer, but learned quickly that she only needed "the plainest clothing and high boots, since we did plenty of walking." Each day, men walked up to fourteen miles from their homes to work. Gertrude's husband traveled to St. Louis to hire Italians, Hungarians, Irishmen and Bulgarians to help build the dam. The Parksville Village Hotel was perched on a hill above the current byway. Villagers traveled to a hotel at Benton Springs on Bean Mountain (or Chilhowee Mountain) to escape hot summers. Remnants of a 1911 Louisville and Nashville (L&N) spur line, used to haul construction materials and Sugarloaf Mountain rocks to the dam site, remain on the river's southern bank. Trains traveled on L&N Railroad's spur line to Ocoee, Tennessee, to connect with its mainline between Louisville and Atlanta.

Claude Clifford (CC) Card (1880–1946) operated a taxi service for power company dignitaries. "He drove Model T and Model A Fords from his Cleveland, Tennessee dealership [now listed in the National Register of Historic Places] to Parksville Village," said his seventy-seven-year-old granddaughter, Amy Card-Lillios. CC bought Cleveland's first Model T from Henry Ford. It arrived by rail to the city's train depot.

After eighteen months, the Eastern Tennessee Power Company (eventually absorbed by the Tennessee Electric Power Company, or TEPCO) filled its Parksville Reservoir. Around 1912, the company rehired some workers to build Ocoee Dam No. 2, its flume line and powerhouse. Gertrude and others moved upriver to the company's Caney Creek Village, on the south bank of the Ocoee River.

The company built its 450-foot-wide, 30-foot-tall Ocoee Dam No. 2 upstream from its powerhouse to divert water from the Ocoee River into a five-mile-long wooden flume perched high on a rock shelf cut into the walls of the gorge. "This ingenious flume system allowed the amount of power generated by the 30-foot dam to equal that of a 250-foot-high dam," reported TVA's website. For the next sixty-three years, the siphoned waters generated electrical currents rather than riffles, rapids and eddies—created by a natural tumble down the geographical gradient through the gorge.

The power company transported construction materials for Ocoee Dam No. 2 on the Parksville rail line. From the railroad terminus, a boat pulled a barge loaded with the supplies across the Ocoee River to a wharf at Caney Creek. From the wharf, crews built a rail line past Caney Creek Village to

Ocoee No. 2 flume. *Tennessee State Library and Archives.*

the construction site for a "dinky" (small locomotive) to transport freight and laborers to the dam project. As Copper Basin sediments washed down the Ocoee River and accumulated near Caney Creek, workers moved the wharf downstream to deeper waters. Remnants of the wharves are visible today.

At Caney Creek, the company provided ice, grocery and newspaper deliveries; indoor plumbing, electricity and water chlorination; outdoor lighting; fire hydrants; and a one-room church/schoolhouse. Youngsters swam in the Big Creek swimming hole, families picnicked in a field above the powerhouse and tennis players challenged Etowah, Cleveland and Copperhill visitors on tennis courts near the hotel. Later, it replaced its freight train with a trolley car, providing passenger service to a swinging bridge over the Ocoee River, east of the village.

Officials transferred Gertrude and her husband to Copperhill to collect environmental data for a lawsuit when they suspected that the copper industry's discarded acidic wastes and byproduct fumes had damaged powerhouse machinery. By 1918, the couple had moved back to Parksville for Gertrude's husband to work at Ocoee Powerhouse No. 1. Gertrude reveled in the luxury of residential electrical power. At Copperhill, a lady had washed the family's clothes in a spring twice a week, charging two cents per garment. "The washing machine in Parksville was a God-send!" wrote Gertrude. One husband became alarmed at his summer power bill, though, later learning that his wife would prop the refrigerator door open to cool their home.

In 1933, President Franklin D. Roosevelt formed the Tennessee Valley Authority (TVA) to provide flood control, hydroelectric power and navigation for the people in the Tennessee River Valley. Around 1939, TVA acquired TEPCO's Ocoee Dams No. 1 and No. 2, its property and villages. TVA closed Caney Creek Village after workers completed Ocoee Dam No. 3. Don Curbow paid fifteen dollars for the boat used to pull barges across the Ocoee River to Caney Creek, but it sank overnight in a storm, near today's USFS Mac Point Beach Recreation Area on Parksville Lake (also known as Parksville Reservoir and Lake Ocoee).

Around 1943, James Webb of Athens, Tennessee, purchased Caney Creek structures and hauled the dismantled materials over the swinging bridge. Jerry Hamby, owner of the Lake Ocoee Inn and Marina, grew up in one of the restored homes. Jerry and his family moved from Tampa, Florida, to Athens around 1945. In 1972, Jerry; his wife, Reita; his brother-in-law, Randy Wattenbarger; and Randy's wife, Brenda, purchased the marina business from Ed and Mable Lowe. Lowe had leased the property from TEPCO to build the inn and marina. Troye Linginfelter, a retired schoolteacher, worked for Jerry at the inn as a cashier/hostess and mentioned that she grew up in Caney Creek Village. They compared the layout of their childhood homes and learned that they grew up in the same house, she in Caney Creek and he in Athens. Fifty years later, Hamby, his daughter Stephanie and son-in-law, Ryan Cooke, operate the marina under a USFS Special Use Permit.

Today, the forest has reclaimed the site of Caney Creek Village. In 2019, Jack Callahan led eleven Cherokee Hiking Club members on the unmaintained, 7.5-mile USFS Caney Creek Trail to the old village, fording Big Creek and backtracking repeatedly to locate the overgrown footpath. "We made it all the way," reported Richard (Rick) Harris, the hiking club webmaster, "but the trail was in horrible condition. We got temporarily discombobulated twice and used a GPS to get back on the trail." The hikers located foundations, water systems and concrete fishponds and found dishware fragments, pots, oil cans, 1920s farm radio batteries and other relics.

In 2020, eighteen-year-old Kevin Fryar, a member of the Boy Scouts of America (BSA), Troop 44 in Cleveland, Tennessee, renovated the Caney Creek Trail as an Eagle Scout Project. He received permission from the USFS and Boy Scout Council and worked with Rick Harris and assistant Scout leader Jennifer Shroll to develop a rehabilitation plan. Harris gave a trail maintenance presentation at a meeting with Fryar's troop and the all-female Troop 444. Now retired from the Cincinnati Children's Hospital

Jack Callahan explores Caney Creek foundations. *Jack Callahan.*

pediatric bone marrow transplant center, Dr. Harris leads volunteer CNF and Benton MacKaye Trail maintenance crews.

Kevin, the grandson of the former CNF silviculturist Roger D. Fryar and the son of Michael (Mike) Fryar—an assistant Boy Scout troop leader, nurse practitioner and former USFS wildland firefighter—became interested in conservation and outdoor adventures through his scouting experiences. A reconnaissance hike with his dad convinced Kevin to tackle this Caney Creek Trail project. Even with a GPS, "we had a difficult time finding the trail," said Mike.

In November 2020, Kevin and crew leader Harris held a tailgate meeting for twenty-five Scouts, Scout leaders and members of the Tellico/Ocoee District Volunteer Trail Maintainers. They discussed equipment, safety gear, weather, health and hydration. Scouts grabbed handsaws and joined Crew no. 1, the "Big Boys Club" (adults skilled in chainsaw use), who cut about seventy trees off the trail. Crew no. 2 cleared trailside vegetation with loppers and swing blades. Crew no. 3 repaired the treadway.

"My confidence grew as the project developed," said Kevin. When the crew realized that they were no longer on the obscured pathway, Kevin demonstrated his leadership skills by directing a few workers to backtrack, said seventy-two-year-old U.S. Air Force veteran Wilfred (Will) Dostie, "to locate the correct trail. I was impressed with his calm manner." At the end of the workday, the team crossed Big Creek, explored the former settlement and returned to the trailhead at 7:00 p.m., two hundred man-hours later. "I'm insanely proud of my project," said Kevin. "Mr. Harris said the trail looked the best that he'd ever seen and was surprised that we completed it in one day."

The CNF housed the Ocoee Ranger Station in one of the Sugarloaf Mountain Park buildings until its offices moved to the juncture of Ocoee Scenic Byway and FSR-77, explained retired USFS Law Enforcement Officer Russ Arthur. "During the Olympic Games on the Ocoee River, law enforcement officers occupied one of the historic buildings as a base headquarters," but during the construction of the whitewater competitions channel, the Ocoee Project Team had held its offices in that building between 1993 and 1996.

In 1992, at Sugarloaf Mountain Park, TVA engineers formed a 320-foot-long, 30-foot-wide model of the proposed Ocoee River competitive course. The 1:10 scale model—contoured with shelving wire, gravel and concrete—matched the Upper Ocoee's gradients, depths and topographical features. When a calibrated flow of water was discharged from Ocoee Dam No. 1 to flow through the model, TVA engineers and the USFS course design team

Rick Harris maintains CNF trails. *Rick Harris.*

moved sandbags, rocks and pebbles in the model to experiment with river behavior, flow rates, wave heights, eddy formations and hydraulic changes. Kayak manufacturers Perception and Dagger built nine-inch-long kayaks to run the rapids in the practice model. For years, the Olympic channel model remained a commemorative structure, where children imagined a wild river ride around its curves and obstacles. Today, a playground and exercise equipment have replaced it.

Driving east on the Ocoee Scenic Byway, an overlook provides a view of Ocoee Dam No. 1 at the base of Sugarloaf Mountain. Big Frog Mountain looms in the distance above TVA's 1,900-acre Parksville Reservoir. Tiny Goat Island (or Treasure Island) lies in the foreground. In 2005, a gentleman floated a grand piano on a barge out to the island and proposed to his lady. The CNF manages most of the lake's 417-mile-long shoreline. Along the byway, motorists leave busy highway traffic at boating access ramps, overlooks, picnic tables and other recreation stops, like the swimming area at Parksville Beach.

———•———

In a predominantly Virginia pine forest, rooted on a Parksville Lake peninsula, CNF and Tennessee Wildlife Resources Agency (TWRA) biologists attempted to save the last known population of an endangered species in Tennessee. For more than a decade, the USFS spent more than $100,000 and countless hours in conservation efforts to manage and restore a small cluster of Red-cockaded Woodpeckers (RCW) (*Picoides borealis*) in their critical habitat.

Unique among North American woodpeckers, these black-and-white beauties, smaller than the Northern Mockingbird (*Mimus polyglottos*), Tennessee's state bird, not only carve nesting cavities into live trees but also share parental responsibilities with other family group members. According to the U.S. Fish and Wildlife Service (USFWS), an estimated 250,000 family groups of Red-cockaded Woodpeckers once inhabited more than 90 million acres across the Southeast. Land development, agricultural projects and logging have reduced the population to around 4,700 family groups on less than 1 million scattered acres. The USFWS has listed it as an endangered species. RCWs prefer mature longleaf and loblolly pine trees seventy to one hundred years old. With the loss of its preferred habitat, they adapted to older forests of shortleaf, slash, pitch,

Virginia and other pines. Beside Parksville Lake, the woodpecker struggled to survive in Virginia pine (*Pinus virginiana*) forests along the northern margins of its distribution range. Unfortunately, the Virginia pine's life history and growth characteristics only offered a second-rate housing substitute to the deep-rooted, fire-resistant longleaf pine (*P. palustris*), native to the Piedmont and coastal plains. Unlike longleaf pines that often live three hundred years and reach a height of over one hundred feet, the less hardy Virginia pines reach about half that height, topple easily in strong windstorms and only live sixty-five to eighty years.

In 1986, TWRA officer Craig Watson camped with his wife; twin brother, Keith; and his brother's companion on a peninsula where the waters of Indian Creek join those of Baker Creek. One morning, Watson heard the squeaky chatter of an energetic avian family. The avid birder, who had been identifying bird species for ten years since his University of Tennessee–Knoxville graduate studies, had discovered the last documented group of Red-cockaded Woodpeckers in his home state.

He and CNF Wildlife Biologist Joe Dabney monitored the activities of three healthy RCW adults. "Craig and I complemented each other," said Dabney. "I am a self-proclaimed 'hook and bullet' biologist, meaning I got interested in the field through my love of hunting and fishing. Craig was a more ecological-minded biologist." In the spring of 1989, Dabney and Watson noted that a female laid her eggs in a nesting cavity. About four weeks later, two fledglings departed the three-inch-diameter cavity and joined the family group. Dabney and Wilson helped protect the nesting/roosting area from predators by cutting midstory vegetation. They also fastened metal plates, or restrictors, around the birds' cavities to prevent Pileated Woodpeckers (*Dryocopus pileatus*) from enlarging the tennis ball–sized entrances to the RCW homes into gaping rectangles. They took squares of steel, cut an inverted U-shape on one side and placed them around the top of the cavities. The cut-out at the bottom of the plate allowed the woodpecker to perch on the pine bark and enter its home. Watson and Dabney waited until dark to observe the woodpeckers' response to the restrictors and learned that the opening was too small for the birds to enter.

The problem? "Bergman's Rule," said Dabney, "which states that the body size of any given species increases as you go north within its range. Our Tennessee Red-cockaded Woodpeckers obviously had slightly larger bodies than their southern relatives that the restrictors had been made to accommodate." He had them enlarged at a machine shop. The team also attached sheets of aluminum around the base of cavity trees to discourage the gnawing interests of Parksville's beaver population. To give the RCW family a cavity-carving head start, the pair drilled holes in the tough bark to speed up the RCWs' normal, ten-year-long excavation endeavors.

In 1989, Dabney and Watson left the five-member RCW family group in CNF to pursue career paths that offered greater involvement with RCW recovery efforts. Dabney became the USFS team leader in Atlanta's Southeast Regional Office, establishing RCW management guidelines. "It was the highlight of my biology career," he said. "I take great satisfaction in knowing that the number of RCWs on national forest lands have increased to the point that they have been proposed for downlisting. I moved to a small town in Arkansas and retired there as a District Ranger. Shortleaf pines were on my district, and every time that I would see older, flat-topped trees, I halfway expected to see a Red-cockaded's cavity."

Watson left the TWRA and worked with USFS Research Biologist Bob Hooper on RCW conservation/recovery projects at the Francis Marion National Forest in South Carolina. When Hurricane Hugo killed hundreds of Red-cockaded Woodpeckers and destroyed 90 percent of their cavity trees in Francis Marion in 1989, Watson developed a restoration plan and installed man-made cavities. By 1990, he had transferred the artificial cavity technology to CNF biologists, who cut holes in the pines at Parksville Lake and inserted these imitation nesting boxes. Around 1999, Watson began working as a USFWS migratory bird biologist in Charleston.

In the CNF, biologists found two eggs in a nesting cavity in 1989. After a storm toppled dozens of pine trees, however, they could locate only one Red-cockaded Woodpecker. To determine its sex, they placed a net across its roosting cavity overnight, trapped it as it took flight the next morning and attached two identifying leg bands. They named the male "Sad Sack" and set out to find it a mate.

In December 1990, two Florida biologists arrived with a chosen female and joined CNF staff to place her in a cavity near Sad Sack's roosting tree. The next morning, they watched the male fly out and then "tugged a string attached to a miniature screen," wrote TWRA education coordinator Doug Markham, to remove the cover over the female's cavity. They tapped the tree with a stick as if to send "the female a Morse code to come out." She flew to a nearby pine and later disappeared.

In 1993, an ice storm damaged more Virginia pines, but CNF officials planned another matchmaking project. In November 1994, a playback of RCW calls helped Sad Sack locate an introduced female from Talladega National Forest. The Alabama native "immediately took off across Parksville

Lake with him in close pursuit," wrote Markham, but within minutes, he returned without her. The next month, Sad Sack also slipped into avian history. Perhaps the deserted tree cavities have served as shelter for flying squirrels, frogs, screech owls or wood duck families. If feathered companions bond emotionally with others in their community, like *Homo sapiens* do, Sad Sack spent some lonely last days in Tennessee, but this printed memorial honors his life in the pines of the Cherokee National Forest.

———— • ————

BIG FROG, SUGARLOAF AND Chilhowee Mountains tower above Parksville Lake like majestic mansions overlooking a valley domain, while the CNF cloaks its edges, hiding privately owned lakeside cabins on Forest Service lands. In 1915, the government passed the USFS Term Occupancy Act and offered citizens who owned cabins on federally managed lands a Special Use Permit. From 1930 to 1950, commercial businesses began leasing USFS land to build campgrounds, lodges and inns, but the USFS ended private construction on national forests in 1968. Today, the USFS Recreation Residence Program manages about fourteen thousand cabins nationwide, including about sixty-two resident structures in CNF's Parksville Lake area and about seven in the Tellico River corridor.

Around 1939, the USFS began purchasing tracts of land originally leased to cabin owners by TEPCO and later TVA. "One summer cabin on TVA's land did not have direct access to the lake," said Robert E. Lee, a former CNF Recreation Residence Manager. In 2009, Jerry Hamby, who operates his business under a USFS Special Use Permit, purchased this cabin (no. 14), located near the marina north of US-64, and rents it to visitors as the "Falling Water Cabin." Hamby also purchased "Ocoee Cabin" (no. 12), a four-bedroom unit built by the Hargess Lumber Company.

"The Forest Service traveled to each cabin's dock for annual inspections by pontoon boat," said Lee. "Structural alterations, tree cutting, and cabin additions had to be covered under the Special Use Permit." Lee implemented an organized numbering system for Parksville Lake cabins during his twelve-year tenure. When Lee began working with CNF's residence program in 1991, "there was much confusion and frustration about what improvements could be made, so I initiated an annual cabin owners meeting. Forrest Lee Preston, founder of the Life Care Centers of America, hosted the first meeting. We bridged gaps in the chain of communication."

Cabin owners renew USFS Special Use Permits every twenty years. Families often pass their cabin from one generation to another. The Parksville Lake Cabin Owners Association, the local chapter of the National Forest Homeowners (NFH) organization, has developed a collaborative relationship with CNF's recreation residence managers. "As a recreation residence permit holder," one USFS project leader wrote, "you are a partner with the Forest Service in the stewardship of these historic resources."

Amy Card-Lillios owns "Tall Timbers Cabin" (no. 47) near Baker Inlet, built between 1935 and 1937 by her father, Bob Card Sr. William Wallace Jacobs (1894–1968), Amy's uncle and a power company executive, obtained permission for Bob to build the cabin at his former campsite. As a youngster, Bob saved his newspaper delivery earnings to order a red Old Towne canoe from Maine. After it arrived at the Cleveland train station, he explored the lake's sinuous shoreline and often camped at this site. A corn field free of stumps and stones, now under water, provided a gentle slope and easy access to the lake. Bob purchased wood from the Conasauga River Lumber Company and gathered stones for a chimney at Baker Creek. The cabin had no electricity or indoor plumbing but was framed with a vaulted ceiling that rose above natural pine flooring. Card Spur Road, built with hand tools in the 1930s, leads to Amy's cabin and seven other lakeside residences, each one painted green, gray or brown to blend into the landscape, per USFS requirements. After five generations of cabin upgrades, Amy's five-bedroom main lodge and ten-person bunkhouse hosts seven- to seventy-year-old birthday parties and events. The family have found snakes in the bedrooms, bears at the back door and "a variety of other creatures to keep life interesting," said Amy.

On Card Spur Road, Pryor Newman, a founding member of Cleveland Bank and Trust, built cabin no. 44 in 1940. "Some in the family call it 'Puddleby-on-the-Marsh' from Dr. Doolittle," said eighty-seven-year-old Sally Dooly Newman. Pryor's son and Sally's husband, Tommy Newman Sr. (1934–2018), was the first person known to ski barefooted and backward on Parksville Lake. In the cove near the USFS Kings Slough Boat Ramp, Sally's father, Weyman Isaac Dooly Sr. (1899–1973), the general manager of the Conasauga River Lumber Company, built the Dooly Cabin (no. 39) in 1956 from scrap lumber for his wife, Louise, and eight children: Tupper, Noble, Rosalind, Marjorie, Weyman Jr., Sally, Warnie and Phillip. During family reunions, the group gathered around a table made from a fourteen-foot-long piece of poplar. In the early 1900s, the logging company built a mill and village near the L&N Railroad. Eventually, Sally's brother Weyman

Conasauga River Lumber Company. *Jenny Rogers.*

Jr. managed the company. Many of the seventy thousand acres owned by the logging business in Tennessee and Georgia now lie within Cherokee and Chattahoochee National Forests.

"My earliest childhood memories include 'Daddy Jim' [Weyman Sr.] piling us all in the boat to motor over to Lake Ocoee Inn for their famous Sunday brunch," said his granddaughter, Jenny Rogers. "I'll always remember their buttermilk and lemon icebox pies." In 1945, the Conasauga River Lumber Company built a bridge across the Ocoee River to haul timber from the Caney Creek area. It collapsed in a storm and floated into the lake. Dooly and Ed Lowe rescued the bridge lumber to build the restaurant and marina, now owned by Hamby, and the logging company built a new wooden bridge across pontoons to continue its operations. Mabel Lowe was as famous for her pies as for her inexpensive salads. In 1958, a honeymoon couple rented the inn's smallest cabin. After paying for gas, the cabin and a justice of the peace, the newlyweds had thirty-five cents left to split a salad for breakfast. For sixty-one years, they returned to Lake Ocoee Inn for their anniversary salad.

In Baker Inlet, J.T. Lemons owns "Maypops Place" (cabin no. 59). In 1977, Lemons and his business partner opened Ocoee Outdoors, the first whitewater outfitter on the Ocoee River. In the 1970s, inspectors in a railcar traveling across the top of the Ocoee Dam No. 2 flume system noticed aging defects in the line. Officials chose to repair rather than remove the "monument to early hydraulic engineering," reported the TVA. While the TVA repaired the structure, the Ocoee River flowed through its riverbed below the dam and got its wild waters back. Paddlers took notice of the exciting whitewater challenges.

When the TVA finished its flume repairs in the mid-1980s, the agency negotiated a contract with the State of Tennessee and the Ocoee River outfitters to provide about 114 annual water releases for recreational use below Ocoee Dam No. 2 (Middle Ocoee). "I joined the battle to keep the Ocoee flowing," said Hamby. "TVA turned the river off and on like a faucet, giving us the ideal amount of water needed and the cubic-feet-per-second flow rate" for thrilling whitewater adventures. Hamby added rafting services

Warnie Dooly Finnell (1937–1994), born at Conasauga mill village, taught school there. *Jenny Rogers.*

to his inn and marina business around 1981. A honeymooning couple from Texas were Lemon's first customers. For more than forty years, his staff has provided river-guided experiences for thousands of outdoor enthusiasts, including country music singer/actor Jerry Reed, former U.S. Tennessee senator and vice president Al Gore, Tennessee governor and U.S. senator Lamar Alexander, U.S. Tennessee senator Jim Sasser and Texas governor and U.S. president George W. Bush.

On the northern shores of Parksville Lake, "Twigs" (cabin no. 9), owned by Anne and Sammy Feehrer, is one of four cabins occupying a quarter-acre tract of CNF land on a peninsula, providing a fair-weather sunrise greeting from the east and a farewell sunset salute from the west. In 1940, Sammy's grandfather, Lieutenant Colonel Charles Francis ("C.F.") Kelly (1893–1980), a World War I and World War II army veteran and a Cleveland, Tennessee banker, built "Timberlane" (cabin no. 10), now owned by Sammy's brother, Kelly. A CNF ranger initially chose Timberlane's site at the end of the peninsula but moved away from the Ocoee region before building a cabin there. C.F.'s wife, Margaret Sugg Kelly (1896–1983), graduated from Maryville College in 1917, continued English and music studies at New York's Columbia University and taught high school English and history for thirty years in Cleveland, Tennessee. Margaret penned more than two hundred poems, many featuring the CNF/Ocoee region.

"She was my high school history teacher," said Maryl Elliott of "Stony Point Cabin" (no. 7). "We would distract Mrs. Kelly from our lessons by asking her to give us a bird call. Worked every time." Maryl and her sister, Katie Torrence, own Stony Point, built in the 1930s by their grandfather Charles Stanwix Mayfield Sr., a TEPCO attorney.

Sammy and Kelly spent their summers at Timberlane with their father, Wayne Feehrer, and mother, Alice Grant Kelly Feehrer. In the 1960s, Wayne placed a twelve-horsepower Buccaneer outboard motor on their first homemade barge. "It had barrels for pontoons, a galvanized rooftop and a plywood deck, surrounded by steel piping and chicken wire, so the kids wouldn't fall off," said Sammy. As a teenager in the mid-1970s, Sammy pumped gas, washed boats and waited tables at Lake Ocoee Inn and Marina to earn gas money for his family's boats.

Eighty-seven-year-old L.C. (Buddy) Rhodes Jr. owns "Rhodes End" (cabin no. 11), built in the 1930s on the peninsula and purchased by his father, Leonard (Clyde) Rhodes Sr. (1905–2007), in the 1950s. As a youngster, Buddy learned to swim in Parksville Lake at YMCA's Camp Ocoee, located on CNF's western shoreline.

Weyman I. Dooly Sr. *Jenny Rogers.*

In 1916, floodwaters stranded Glenn (Chick) Ellis (1893–1992) and a friend at the YMCA Blue Ridge Conference Center in Black Mountain, North Carolina. After crews repaired the damaged railroad, the men rode the train through Western North Carolina and then hiked two hundred miles for eight days toward their home in Chattanooga, hitching a railcar ride on the flume line in Ocoee River Gorge. Their campsite beside Parksville Lake's tranquil waters inspired Ellis to establish a lakeside YMCA camp.

Around 1923, YMCA leaders and TEPCO officials negotiated a land-lease contract for sixty-five wooded acres with a one-mile shoreline. Later, TEPCO deeded the YMCA property to TVA, now owned and leased under a Special Use Permit by the CNF. In the 1930s and 1940s, CCC F-4 Camp Ocoee worked with the USFS to improve the access roads.

After serving in World War I, Ellis became Camp Ocoee's director for thirty-six years. Campers developed self-confidence, spiritual growth and appreciation for nature in their forested classrooms. They slept in tents, caught bullfrogs to cook on wood-burning stoves and carried water from a nearby spring. Sugarloaf Mountain berries became huckleberry pies. They bathed in the lake, and "since campers were male," wrote a camp historian, swimming trunks were not required "for those who could not afford them."

The Cloud family on Cookson Creek Road provided vegetables and dairy products to the YMCA camp. In the 1860s, Dr. Warren Copeland Jr. (1835–1916) built the current Copeland-Cloud House, a brick house with an adjacent white frame hospital, on his one-thousand-acre farm. The L-shaped structures provided two light sources in the hospital's ground floor surgical wing. The walls were three bricks thick, with the bricks kiln-fired on the property. His brother, Alexander Tillman Copeland (1822–1901), designed an Englewood, Tennessee frame home with an identical floor plan. Born in McMinn County, Tennessee, Dr. Copeland taught school, studied medicine under Dr. N. Pendergrass of Cookson Creek, attended Philadelphia's Jefferson Medical College and married his mentor's widow, Onie Pendergrass.

"My great-grandmother Winona Copeland Cloud [1860–1913] was Alexander's daughter," said the seventy-eight-year-old present owner of the home, Kenneth (Ken) Winston Cloud. After Winona married Andrew Johnson Cloud (1853–1935) in 1879, the couple managed the Halfway House, near the Rock Creek Community at the confluence of Greasy Creek and the Ocoee River on the Old Copper Road. George and Dorinda Archer Cloud also worked at the inn, explained Ken, holding a photo of Winona's father sitting in a window in the Halfway House. Built midway between Ducktown and Cleveland around 1859 and purchased in 1866 by Julius Raht, the inn and surrounding fields provided food and overnight accommodations for copper-hauling teamsters and other travelers. Dorinda bought supplies for the Halfway House in Benton, Tennessee. Teamsters blew bugles as they approached the inn to let the managers know how many guests to expect. Around 1900, Andrew Cloud renamed that area "Bonnie" and became its first postmaster. In the Rock Creek Cemetery on a nearby mountain, Winona and Andrew buried several unnamed infants near Andrew's parents. Later, the couple moved to a home that caught fire shortly after Andrew's death in 1935. Near the juncture of TN-30 and the Ocoee Scenic Byway, a Tennessee Highway Historical Marker commemorates the historic inn.

In 1935, Winona and Andrew Cloud's son, Winston (1887–1980), and his wife, Pearl Elizabeth Lowery Cloud (1897–1995), acquired Dr. Copeland's former home and opened a store in the old hospital. Local legends claim that the Clouds repainted the bloodstained ceiling of his surgical suite and discovered a Civil War–era skeleton in a closet. Ken only confirmed that his grandmother did find a skeleton that the doctor kept for patient educational purposes. Winston and Pearl demolished the deteriorating hospital in 1967. On April 5, 1984, officials listed the Copeland-Cloud House in the National Register of Historic Places.

Pearl, a widow, lived in the home until she died at age ninety-eight. At a public auction, Ken, a retired school principal, superintendent of Georgia's Walton County Schools and Loganville, Georgia city manager, and his wife, Ginger, a retired school counselor, acquired the Copeland-Cloud House, where he was born in 1942. Over the decades, the family have sold hundreds of acres to help fund the upkeep of the large home. Ken now maintains forty cows and 120 acres of orchards. He encased the barn, built in the 1860s with hand-hewn boards and wooden pegs, with a metal framework for structural support. Visitors traveling Cookson Creek Road en route to the USFS King Slough boat ramp or the YMCA camp pass massive oaks behind a rock wall, sheltering the historic home.

Ellis added weeklong camps for girls and underprivileged youth at Camp Ocoee and invited Cherokee leaders to offer experiences in cultural diversity. Older boys backpacked on CNF trails near the Sylco area and across Big Frog Mountain to the YMCA building at Copperhill. They hiked the A.T. from Springer Mountain, Georgia, to Wesser, North Carolina; paddled the Hiwassee and Nantahala Rivers; and conquered the cliffs on Starr Mountain.

Dr. Warren Copeland and family. *Kenneth Cloud.*

Parksville Lake. *Tennessee State Library and Archives.*

During a five-day adventure, camp leaders and teens launched canoes below Ocoee Dam No. 1 and paddled the Ocoee and Hiwassee Rivers to join the Tennessee River. They then canoed south to pass through the 1939 Chickamauga Navigation Locks near Chattanooga's Ross Landing, the trading post named for Cherokee leader John Ross and the site of the river crossing for Cherokees forced west on the Trail of Tears.

B.J. Davis is Camp Ocoee's current executive director, a Middle Tennessee State University graduate who was a homesick camper as a boy. In his office/mini-museum, Davis preserves a 1938 TEPCO land-lease contract, a 1945 YMCA camp scrapbook and a 1956 USFS Special Use Permit. The greatest treasure is Ellis's World War I Army and Navy Service Record, its frayed book covers bulging with military memorabilia, French postcards, letters, news clips, photos, hospital records and leadership certificates.

"We have a great working relationship with the USFS," said Davis. The YMCA collaborates with the USFS to remove trees and upgrade camp facilities. In 2012, the USFS condemned the outdated 1938 dining hall, and contractors demolished it. The supports for the building were sitting in baskets poured with concrete. Hundreds of summer resident camps exist across the country, but "you'll find us nestled in a breathtaking setting on the shores of Lake Ocoee in Cherokee National Forest," touts a Camp Ocoee brochure.

Sylco Creek

Forty years ago, few fish could survive in Parksville Lake due to the toxic upstream runoff from copper mines, but restoration efforts in the Copper Basin and environmental regulations improved the water quality after the mines closed in the 1980s. It is "one of Tennessee's most dramatic water quality success stories," reported the Tennessee Department of Environment and Conservation (TDEC) in 2020. The lake now supports populations of trout, catfish, crappie, bass and yellow perch. TDEC officials regularly analyze fish tissue samples and identify contaminants that could threaten public health.

Orange buoys at the eastern edge of Parksville Lake warn boaters of sandbars created by silt deposited by the Ocoee River. A pair of mallards drift in the shadows of a sheltered cove. A great blue heron silently stalks for a sudden strike. The shallow waters to the south also prevent a motorboat journey into Sylco Inlet, but a canoe with two and a dog could paddle it, gliding over the site of a former church, post office, general store and a road to the Sylco Community. In the 1930s, the CCC recovered steel rails from Conasauga River Lumber Company's train track on the lake bottom. Near the head of Sylco Inlet, the USFS issued a Special Use Permit to the Boy Scouts of America around 1949 to build a camp on forty-four acres at the site of a former sawmill. Since the 1970s, the First Baptist Church of Cleveland, Tennessee, has operated the site as Camp Cherokee. On a hill above Sylco Inlet, some of the region's earliest settlers now rest in peace.

Before the CNF acquired the Sylco region in the late 1930s, dozens of families had settled in the area and built a flourishing community with gristmills, schools and country stores. Around 1847, Edward Bayer of Brooklyn hired a Frenchman, Napoleon Guerin, to persuade Catholic citizens of Germany, France and Italy to come to America to form a colony on thousands of acres that he had purchased in the region. On Dutch Creek, a tributary of Sylco Creek, they arrived by horse-drawn wagons on a rugged road along Big Creek to "Bayer's Settlement," later called "Vineland" for its vineyards and, eventually, the "Old Dutch Settlement." Guerin and his assistant, the Frenchman Alphonso A. Chable, managed the community for Bayer. Later, Chable served as a Civil War Confederate captain, acquired his own property on Sylco Creek and operated a post office there. His son, Will Chable, and Leland Fouts became early CNF officials for the Ocoee/Hiwassee Ranger District.

An early CNF project adopted by Will Chable, the 1916–19 district ranger stationed at the Sheeds Creek Warden Station near Sylco, was the construction of the Big Frog Mountain Trail and a forty-foot-high chestnut log lookout tower platform on the mountain. Chable left the USFS to work as a Conasauga River Lumber Company surveyor. Fouts and his staff held offices in a two-story McFarland hotel on the Hiwassee River.

In 1852, Bayer, his wife, Adele, and her sister, Rosine Parmentier, traveled from New York to visit the Sylco region. After disembarking a ship in Savannah and traveling by train to Cleveland, Tennessee, Rosine and her party enlisted a gentleman to take them by wagon to the settlement. "The mountains were towering one above another," she wrote in her diary, "the nearer ones covered with verdure, the more distant ones [with a] bluish cast." They visited a Cookson Creek farm, forded the Ocoee River and, miles later, crossed it again, where the peaks "reminded Edward of the mountains of Switzerland." After dark, a pine knot torch provided light as they crossed Sylco Creek twenty-seven times before reaching their destination. During their three-week visit, Alphonso Chable and Guerin led a hike up Big Frog Mountain, where they emerged from a heavy mist "and beheld white fleecy clouds at our feet [like] waves of the sea…the tops of the high mountains… look[ed] like islands." In the late 1800s, Bayer deeded his lands in East Tennessee to Rosine. She sold some of the acreage but bought other tracts in the area. Before she died in 1908, she sold a major portion of her holdings to George Peabody Wetmore, who sold it to the Ocoee Timber Company. Much of the land is now part of the CNF.

On October 15, 1852, Rosine wrote that she crossed "the interminable and winding Sylco Creek on logs and reached Mr. Arthur's house." In the early 1800s, Lewis Arthur built his home beside Sylco Creek. Today, the rock foundations are hidden, but Arthur's descendants know where it was.

"His homeplace was up in that holler," said retired USFS official Russ Arthur, a fifth-generation grandson. Most of his Arthur ancestors, except for his father, were born in the Sylco region. His grandfather Grover Cleveland Arthur attended a Sylco school in the early 1900s. At age seventeen, he walked to Gaston, Alabama, to work in the steel industry. When Grover learned about a steel company's lucrative overseas employment opportunity, he caught a train to Gary, Indiana, and boarded a ship to India. On the return voyage to America three years later, the well-paid twenty-year-old met the only non-steelworker onboard, Alfreda Palmer, the seventeen-year-old daughter of a wealthy Bostonian family. Thirty days later, the couple married in Gary, Indiana, where Russ's father, James Russell Arthur (Jim), was born in 1928. With the hefty salary Grover earned in India, he purchased a farm on the Conasauga River just south of the Tennessee border.

"I've hiked almost every trail south of the Ocoee River, but my heart's at Sylco," Russ said. Since age fifteen, his Sylco heritage and outdoor experiences fostered his ambition to work for the Forest Service. "Other kids went to parties and played sports, but I found entertainment outdoors. I kept asking CNF staff, 'What do you need to do to work for the Forest Service?' 'Get some education, son,' they would say. 'Then come talk to us.'" Russ earned a forestry degree from Chattanooga State University, accepted a stipend volunteer position surveying CNF campground use and moved to North Carolina and then Arkansas to work in USFS law enforcement. Twelve years later, Russ returned home to Tennessee to help the USFS manage the Ocoee River Venue Law Enforcement Committee for the 1996 Olympics. Even a noteworthy career in USFS law enforcement—overseeing historic events such as interrogating the 1996 Olympic Centennial Park bomber Eric Rudolph, capturing one of the nation's worst serial arsonists and traveling to Cambodia and Vietnam to train new law enforcement rangers for the International Forestry Program—did not compare to the passion Russ had for Sylco.

"It's where I've spent much of my life," he said. Annual family reunions, extended camping trips and weeklong gatherings with turkey hunters were spent at Sylco. Russ and his dad were members of the Cherokee Chapter of the National Wild Turkey Federation (NWTF) in Chattanooga. As a founding member of the local chapter, Jim organized projects in collaboration with the CNF and helped establish the Hogback Ridge Restoration stewardship initiative to restore habitats for deer, turkey and other species.

By the 1920s, human expansion and overharvesting had caused the numbers of Eastern Wild Turkeys (*Meleagris gallopavo silvestris*) to plummet. In the 1930s and 1940s, attempts to raise turkeys in captivity to restock Tennessee habitats proved unsuccessful. When 1950 surveys revealed alarmingly low numbers, biologists adopted a new turkey recovery plan. They used a rocket-like device to fire nets, attached to weights, over the heads of turkeys foraging at corn-baited sites, such as CNF's Ocoee Wildlife Management Area between Sylco Campground and Big Frog Mountain. They transported the captured turkeys to other forests across the state. With the help of volunteers like Jim Arthur, the NWTF assisted with trap-and-relocate efforts, provided financial support and contributed cardboard boxes for shipping. In the early 1900s, officials estimated that Tennessee had a few thousand turkeys. By 2017, the TWRA was reporting about 300,000 of them.

Arthur, a World War II veteran who retired from the DuPont Company after thirty-five years, volunteered as a USFS Sylco Campground host each summer, welcoming first-time campers, frequent regulars, church groups, wedding parties and Boy Scout troops from North Carolina, Tennessee and Georgia. He told stories about Sylco, such as the history of CCC Camp Cleota, which occupied the campground area in the 1930s. Near Sylco Creek, foundations of the CCC encampment are silent reminders of their work building trails and fish rearing pools. The Sylco CCC men also carved FR-221 (Sheeds Creek/Peavine Road) from the west to meet the Tumbling Creek CCC men cutting the route from the east. Today, this Forest Service Road is a primary route to CNF trails, primitive campsites and historic areas. As of 2021, boulders block the entrance to the unmaintained Sylco Campground. At one time, the agency considered updating the facility or converting it to a group campground, but the picnic tables, pit toilet and fire rings are now gone.

The USFS granted Russ and his dad permission to maintain the Arthur Cemetery near the Sylco Campground. Lewis Arthur (1798–1872) rests there alongside his wife, Kisiah Arthur (about 1814–1889). In 2008, the pair noticed a leaning tree threatening to fall and break the headstones, so the USFS sent an expert to cut it down. He yanked on the cord of his chainsaw, steadied his grip for a clean cut and watched as the tree fell right across Kisiah's headstone. After the CNF district ranger acquired $2,000

Hunters at Sheeds Station, Sylco Creek region. *Russ Arthur.*

in funding, he ordered a replacement for the shattered marker from Hartford, Connecticut.

"Dad walked the lands of his ancestors in the Ocoee region until the day he died." Around 2009, Russ and his dad built a cabin, called "Sylco South," on five acres of land they bought a half mile south of the confluence of the Jacks and Conasauga Rivers. Annually, they went to Sylco South during turkey hunting season and the day after Christmas. But in December 2013, Jim said, "I'm going to skip this one, son." Russ sent him a wishing-you-were-here text from the cabin, but the eighty-eight-year-old did not reply. Jim had suffered a stroke. After his passing, Russ found a box prominently placed on a bench in his dad's workshop. Inside the box, dozens of thick, identical notebooks lined the interior. Russ pulled one out and flipped to a page marked "April 25, 1972."

"It was my dad telling me the story of the first time he left me in the woods by myself. I teared up and squalled like a baby. I closed the notebook and said, 'Well, old man, you left me again.'" One of these years, when forecasters predict a two-week winter storm, Russ plans to head to Sylco South with his wooden box.

CONASAUGA RIVER

Way down south of Sylco near the Georgia border, the 3.3-mile-long CNF Conasauga River Trail leaves FSR-221 near the mouth of Sheeds Creek and Jacks River and follows an old logging railbed beside the river. Conasauga River begins its journey in Georgia's Cohutta Wilderness. In 2015, the Georgia Board of Resources designated an eleven-mile river section of its headwaters as an outstanding national aquatic resource under the federal Clean Waters Act. The river courses north through Alaculsy Valley, crosses the state line and flows toward the CNF.

"There are 75 native fish in the Conasauga," said retired CNF Wildlife Fisheries Biologist Jim Herrig, "90 in total." In 1981, the USFS hired Herrig, a former army captain and biology graduate from South Dakota and Colorado State Universities, to manage Colorado's San Juan, Rio Grande and Grande Mesa National Forests. "There were only 10 fish species, mostly trout, in the watersheds of those three national forests," he said. "Can you imagine transferring from Colorado to the CNF with its 150 species of fish in its combined north and south districts?" Biologists claim that the Conasauga River is one of the ten most biologically diverse rivers in the nation. Some of its aquatic species exist nowhere else on the planet.

Conasauga's mussels, one of the most threatened species worldwide, are in great danger. Streamside agricultural projects, forest canopy changes, increased sedimentation, pollution and dam construction have led to the decline in these bivalve, soft-bodied invertebrates. The harvesting of mussels for the button industry also led to this decline. Before the production of plastic buttons began in the 1940s, the industry collected freshwater mussels to produce its product from the mussel's nacre (or mother of pearl), the shiny inner layer of its hard shell. The Center for Biological Diversity, whose conservation efforts have protected twenty-two species of mussels under the Endangered Species Act, reports that the Tennessee and Mobile River Basins support more species of mussels than anywhere else on earth. In the 1970s, researchers identified about forty species of mussels in the Conasauga River, but today, about twenty-five species are reported, many listed by the USFWS as endangered or threatened.

Most southeastern freshwater mussels use their single, muscular foot to burrow in a sandy riverbed and move about fifty feet along its gravel substrate. "It has an interesting life-history," said Herrig. After the male releases its sperm into the river, the female siphons the water containing the sperm into the reproductive chambers of her gills and fertilizes up to a thousand eggs. After a brooding period, the eggs develop into tiny larvae, called glochidia, that may be released to float downstream in one mass bundle. Some mussels, however, have developed a clever way to repopulate a greater distance along a watercourse. The female converts part of her soft mantle into an imitation lure, such as a wiggling insect, snail, small fish or worm. When a fish takes the bait, the "lure" ruptures, releasing glochidia into the water. The larvae hitch a ride on the gills of the fish and travel as much as one hundred miles. After several weeks of feeding and growing on their host, the mussels drop to the bottom of the stream to filter algae and bacteria and eat plankton in their mussel bed. Biologists believe that some mussels have formed a host-specific relationship with fish or salamanders. In clear, flowing aquatic environments, mussels can live from seventy to one hundred years.

After a yearlong natural resource analysis of the 500,000-acre Conasauga watershed, a 1995 grant funded a study to determine the best management options. By 1999, the chief of the USFS had chosen the Conasauga River as one of the agency's major watershed restoration projects. CNF and Chattahoochee National Forest officials joined the Conasauga River Alliance and nearly thirty-six partners—including The Nature Conservancy (TNC), USFWS, Southeastern Aquatic Research Institute, private property owners and others—to improve and sustain the basin's water quality. Their combined knowledge developed strategies that would not only preserve critical watershed habitats but also meet the water source needs of farmers, recreationists, communities and businesses, such as a Georgia-based carpet dyeing industry supplying nearly 50 percent of the world's carpets. To help reduce erosion and streambed sedimentation, the Conasauga River Alliance promoted a fifty-foot riparian buffer zone of native plants. It urged landowners to install fencing to keep livestock out of the river. The Southeast Tennessee Resource Conservation and Development Council (Southeast TN RC&D) provided state funds to repair failed septic systems in Conasauga River tributaries. TNC began monitoring the macroinvertebrate health in the river at eleven sites to help determine the cause of the continued decline in mussel populations. Both the USFS and TNC evaluated the toxins found in the stream's sediment. Through the USFS Southern Research Station, scientists launched studies to determine the best vegetation to replant more than 10,000 forested acres killed by southern pine beetles, to evaluate the effects of forest fires and thinning projects on water quality and to help design forest roads and trails that reduced runoff and sedimentation. TNC and the USFS also provided program funds to engage Dalton Middle School students in the maintenance of the Conasauga River Alliance website. When CNF staff learned that mechanics were washing cars, draining transmission fluids and changing engine oil on the banks of the Conasauga River, the agency placed public education and campsite restoration as high priorities to protect the watershed.

"In 2000," Herrig said, "Lewis Kearney formed a CNF team with the TWRA and TNC to determine what could be done to make improvements to the Conasauga River area." That year, the team participated in a Conasauga River Alliance educational program, targeting watershed landowners. The public's enthusiastic response was overwhelming. "The USDA Natural Resource Conservation Service (NRCS)," said Kearney, "was a major sponsor of that two-day field conservation event held at a conference center just below the Tennessee state line." NRCS collaborates with private landowners to foster voluntary conservation measures that improve land use activities for healthy, sustainable soil and aquatic landscapes. Participants rotated between exhibits about river habitats, sensitive aquatic species, buffer strips, poultry waste management and other resource protection issues. "We offered our first guided public snorkeling in the Conasauga at that event," said Herrig. For years, the CNF fisheries team had conducted fish surveys using seine net, electrofishing, scuba diving and snorkeling techniques in its waterways, like the Hiwassee, Tellico and Conasauga Rivers and the Citico and Spring Creeks, but now the agency provided a means for the public "to see the freshwater aquarium at their feet. They needed to know what we wanted to protect." At the popular two-day snorkeling event, said Herrig, "eighty-year-old farmers who had lived their entire lives on the shores of the Conasauga River told me they were astounded when they saw what was in their river."

CNF began hosting aquatic ecology snorkeling tours for tourists, school and church groups, scout troops and hiking and conservation clubs, providing masks, snorkels and wetsuits. After the staff presented information about aquatic and riparian systems, species identification and conservation measures, the group waded in. Masked-up, underwater views of the astonishing

Jim Herrig discusses aquatic resources. *Jim Herrig.*

array of Conasauga inhabitants awakened minds, young and old, to new acquaintances, previously overlooked and undiscovered. The underwater world brimmed with a self-absorbed life energy, tending to its survival needs in the body of a river. Eager visitors shuffled in without hesitating. Reluctant ones held the hands of lifeguards and river guides, contracted by the USFS. The TVA, Southeast TN RC&D and the World Wildlife Fund sponsored snorkeling opportunities for underserved, at-risk youth in urban areas. "Kneel face down and breathe," Herrig instructed a snorkeling group, ready to explore the river from a fish's point of view. "Then, pull your feet up and float as you push yourself around." Six to eight fish species thrive in the steep-sloped headwaters of the Conasauga River, but in the CNF, a snorkeler can identify dozens of fish in a day in the wider, slower-moving water over the relatively flat terrain. Sharing the waters with beavers, snails, salamanders, crayfish, snakes and freshwater mussels, the dazzling sunfish, the algae-scraping stonerollers and the fast-moving darters steal the show. A timid, solitary Coosa bass hovers close to a large boulder and then bolts away to find a more secluded cover. The drum and redhorse suckers click a metallic greeting from deep waterholes. In shallow waters, a hogsucker extracts algae from the riverbed. An empty mollusk shell offers shelter for small fish evading a hungry predator. River cooters, snapping turtles and striped-neck musk turtles prefer time alone. At other CNF snorkeling sites, like the Hiwassee River, the stone-a-minute, mound-building river chubs entertain their inquisitive visitors. So do friendly schools of Tennessee shiners spawning in the spring, when dozens of silvery gray bodies turn a blazing orange and inspect the masked, surface-floating guests up close. In the Conasauga River, spotting the rare freckled-belly madtom (a small catfish) or the Conasauga logperch is a winning prize. The madtom is sensitive to poor water quality and thrives in clear, free-flowing water. In slow currents or riffles, the logperch spawns in the river's gravelly substrate and flips over stones to feast on invertebrates. In 1985, this endangered species and its critical environment prevented the Army Corps of Engineers from constructing a dam near Dalton, Georgia.

Around 2010, the nonprofit Conservation Fisheries Incorporated (CFI), founded by University of Tennessee graduates Patrick Rakes and J.R. Shute in 1986, collected Conasauga logperch specimens and raised hundreds of offspring in their laboratory in Knoxville. Dedicated to preserving aquatic biodiversity, CFI was the first southeastern enterprise to develop propagation techniques to restore rare nongame fish to regional waterways. In cooperation with the USFS and USFWS, CFI released fluorescent tagged Conasauga logperch back into their native waters. By 2014, however, the propagated logperches stocked in the river at Conasauga's snorkeling site and in the Alaculsy Valley had disappeared, reported Pat Rakes.

"It appeared that the habitat in CNF was insufficient," he said, "even though adult waifs occasionally appeared around the mouth of Jacks River. The main reproducing population appear to reside downstream of CNF around Highway 411." For thirty years, the organization has snorkeled the rivers of eleven states and propagated at least seventy-seven species of fish. In the CNF, the organization has collected eggs for propagation in its facility with USFS and USFWS support, reintroducing the captive-bred fish into Citico Creek and the Tellico and Conasauga Rivers. In addition to the endangered Conasauga logperch, CFI also propagates endangered smoky madtoms and Citico darters, threatened yellowfin madtoms and spotfin chubs and other fish listed under the Endangered Species Act. Mussel propagation facilities enlist their help to provide the specific fish host species required for the parasitic mussel larvae. Lack of funding and river access on privately owned property create challenges, but so does lack of knowledge.

"Most nongame fish have never been propagated by anyone," said Rakes. "So, it's a challenge figuring out how to do it. Few knew that darter larvae are pelagic, phototropic [attracted to light] and require a water current to feed and thrive." Due to nonexistent or limited commercial sources for supplies, CFI self-designed some of its fish-propagating equipment and cultured its own zooplankton to feed the fish larvae.

On Facebook in 2021, former USFS snorkeling guide Casper Cox posted, "Bright blue skies played shimmering prismatic havoc with my photographic attempts [at the Conasauga snorkeling hole]. A multitude of spawning species in the cold, crystal-clear water was highly motivating: bridled, greenbreasted, speckled, bronze, and holiday darters. Ever present Alabama, tricolor, and blue shiners in a feeding flurry. I dampened a crushed saltine into a ball and placed it under a stone. Soon minnows were swarming in for a bite. Male Alabama shiners were sparring in rapid plunges. The little drab female Coosa darter was followed relentlessly by the colorful and much larger male."

When the Tennessee Aquarium at Chattanooga canceled a Conasauga snorkeling trip twice due to inclement weather, Cox asked for driving directions. After snorkeling in Florida and the Virgin Islands, he was eager to snorkel in a river. "I dipped down into that liquid AC [air conditioner] of the Conasauga River, where life comes to you, and the experience changed my life," said Cox. He joined the North American Native Fishes Association (NANFA), studied the book *Fishes of Tennessee* and met Herrig, leading a Conasauga USFS snorkeling trip. For the next ten years, from

May to September, the sixty-three-year-old Chattanooga resident worked as a CNF snorkeling guide, dropping sculpins into the masks of students and introducing novices to the unseen sights of aquatic depths. With scheduled back-to-back USFS events, he and friends camped at primitive Conasauga campgrounds, snorkeling at night by flashlight. Cox also organized "Tennessee River Rescue" events, snorkeling to collect underwater trash, where people could witness "the impact of man's heavy hand in the rivers."

The British Broadcasting Corporation (BBC) hired Cox to help it film "Tales of Tennessee" about the area's unique aquatic wildlife, as part of its *Seven Worlds, One Planet* series, which included episodes about Asian snub-nosed monkeys, Antarctica southern right whales and Australian cassowaries. Cox wanted to reserve the historic Watchman's House beside the railroad on the Hiwassee River for their stay, but the crew needed internet service. At Lottie's Diner in Benton, Tennessee, home of cat-head biscuits, Cox introduced the Brits to a southern meal of okra, mashed potatoes and country ham.

"Two decades ago, when Jim Herrig started popping snorkeling gear on kids at the Conasauga River," said Kim Winter, PhD, the USFS NatureWatch national program leader in Washington, D.C., "he became the grandfather of the USFS national educational snorkeling program." Forest Service leaders learned about Jim's snorkeling events through his "show and shine" reporting in its databases, where staff share stories about what they are offering at national forests across the country. Before Jim retired, Winter and Nat Gillespie, USFS Assistant Fisheries program leader, hired a writer "to do a brain-download to learn what Jim did to get people energized about snorkeling." By 2006, Executive Director Keith Williams had begun offering river snorkeling in the outdoor activities program at Maryland's NorthBay Education Foundation.

Between 2016 and 2018, the Forest Service and NorthBay found each other through mutual friends at Freshwaters Illustrated, partnered to publish an organized educational curriculum plan and began traveling the country to train Forest Service staff in implementing freshwater snorkeling programs. After Winter, Williams and Craig Roghair, fisheries biologist with the USFS Southern Research Station's Center for Aquatic Technology Transfer (CATT), developed successful pilot projects at four locations in the East, the USFS launched its snorkeling program throughout the National Forest System. Today, USFS aquatic education/snorkeling events connect people with nature's life in rivers in about nine states, including programs for wheelchair users, the hard of hearing and other people with special needs. In June 2021, the Cleveland-based See You at the Top (SYATT-Cle), the National Association of Black Scuba Divers (NABS) and the Tennessee Aquatics Program teamed up with the USFS to offer "Get Black Outside," an inaugural freshwater snorkel and camping trip in George Washington/ Jefferson, Ocala, Monongahela and Cherokee National Forests, designed to welcome people of color to safe, character-building experiences in nature.

"Here in the D.C. area," said Winter, "we've offered a bilingual snorkeling program during Latino Conservation Week in July for the past four years." Since the impaired Potomac River prevents a healthy snorkeling experience, the group drives an hour and a half to Virginia's George Washington/ Jefferson National Forests to snorkel in the creeks feeding the Shenandoah River. Identifying five to six species of fish is not the main goal, however. On the riverbank, half of the students study macroinvertebrates while the other half snorkels, and then they switch activities. The purpose of aquatic education projects is to not only educate the public about USFS management efforts to protect the watershed, Winter explained, but also to "emphasize the role that everyone plays in stewarding water clean enough for us to swim, drink and enjoy. Water clean enough for us is clean for fish."

"This whole movement came out of the CNF," Kim said. "Jim's passion about snorkeling kept us motivated. His legacy has expanded as a model for other programs across the country."

———————•———————

BORN IN 1774, CAPTAIN David McNair, an early white settler in the Conasauga region, received 640 acres from the U.S. government for his service in the War of 1812. McNair was Conasauga's postmaster, provided portage services on the river and married Delilah, a relative of Cherokee chief Vann. His grave site is surrounded by a rock wall near today's Conasauga community. Delilah died on the Trail of Tears at Charleston, Tennessee. Her Cherokee family returned her body to Conasauga to bury her next to her husband and then returned to the Forced March. In 1846, they placed a marker inscribed:

> *Sacred to the memory of David and Delilah McNair, who departed this life, the former on August 15, 1836, and the latter on November 31, 1838. Their children being members of the Cherokee Nation and having to go with their people to the west, do leave this monument, not only to tell of their regard for their parents, but to guard their sacred ashes against the unhallowed intrusion of the white man.*

After the mid-1800s, Simeon E. Browder and descendants owned substantial property in the Conasauga region. In the mid-1900s, Dr. James Lowe of Cleveland, Tennessee, acquired some of the property from Browder family members in payment for medical debts. John Simpson's father, Joe, bought three hundred acres of former Browder land around 1980 that bordered the CNF to the east, Conasauga River to the north and private property to the south and west. Its limited road access and other issues thwarted Joe's plans to build a cabin there.

In the early 1900s, according to John, a lumber company logged walnut trees on the property for gunstocks in World War I. "In the 1980s, my father leased the land to hunters and contracted it out to the Conasauga River Lumber Company." The lumber company's spur rail line from the L&N Railroad crossed Simpson's property. Rail bed depressions and embankments built to support the Conasauga River railroad bridge are evident today. Browder Spring, where loggers placed a pipeline for a water source, still flows from the side of a ridge.

Joe Simpson replanted many trees after the logging operations ceased. By 1998, however, when John and his family inherited the property, southern pine beetles and, later, a 2002 drought had killed them. Loggers harvested about two hundred acres of the damaged timber, and John planted oaks, poplars, pines, black walnuts and other species. He leased five to ten acres of the river bottom to soybean farmers. "It's an incredibly beautiful place," John said.

The Conservation Fund and TNC purchased a boot-shaped 305 acres from the Simpsons to protect a half-mile section of the Conasauga River. "To date, over 8,000 young snorkelers on over 1,000 snorkeling trips have visited the river upstream of the Simpson tract," said Gabrielle (Gabby) Lynch, director of protection for the Tennessee Chapter of TNC. After the tract is transferred to the CNF, it may offer an additional "river access point and staging area."

BIG FROG MOUNTAIN/BENTON MACKAYE TRAIL

In 1986, Congress designated about 8,000 acres as the Big Frog Wilderness. About 100 of its acres are in Georgia. It borders the 37,000-plus acres of Cohutta Wilderness, designated by Congress in 1975 and expanded in 1986. About 1,700 Cohutta acres lie in Tennessee. Polk County's highest mountain, 4,224-foot Big Frog Mountain, straddles the border of the two wilderness areas.

In April 1958, the county held its first annual Ramp Festival on Van Arthur's 1800s potato patch on the southwest side of the mountain. By the 1970s and 1980s, *Southern Living* magazine and the TV show *Good Morning America* were promoting the event, celebrating the region's wild onion (*Allium tricoccum*). Jeep drivers hauled supplies up the mountain to cook meat, potatoes, eggs, cornbread and ramps for the festival. After Congress passed the Wilderness Act, its mandates prevented vehicle access, so helicopters delivered pots and pans to the mountaintop until a one-thousand-pound-net with cooking supplies got hung up in a tree. After a gentleman climbing the mountain to attend the festival had a heart attack, the event moved to the Sylco Campground and, later, to the Polk County 4-H Camp, formerly CCC Camp McCroy at Greasy Creek on TN-30.

"Why just hike a trail when I can help improve and protect it along the way?" said seventy-two-year-old Bobby Mitchell, president of the Southern Appalachian Backcountry Horsemen (SABCH). That morning, he had gathered with the USFS, SABCH, the Tellico-Ocoee Trail Maintainers and other volunteers behind Ocoee Powerhouse No. 3 for a safety meeting before the planned trail maintenance project in Big Frog Wilderness. Nearby, fishermen, paddlers and families camped at the USFS Thunder Rock Campground. Benton MacKaye Trail (BMT) hikers passed through the campground, circled by the powerhouse, crossed the bridge over the Ocoee River and continued northeast toward Little Frog Wilderness.

"Without volunteer help," one USFS official commented, "the CNF trails wouldn't stay open." Year-round trail maintenance projects barely keep pace with storm-generated blowdowns, surface erosion, mudslides and washouts. Trails and roads become hazardous and impassable. Bridges, clogged drainages and trail signs need reconstruction and repair. The Wilderness Act requires managers to conduct trail maintenance in wilderness areas without mechanical equipment, such as chainsaws and ATVs. In 2010, the Southern Appalachian Wilderness Stewards (SAWS) formed in CNF's Coker Creek area to help the USFS maintain wilderness trails in CNF's Citico and Big Laurel Branch Wilderness areas. Today, the organization helps preserve seventy-five wilderness areas in ten national forests across eight states. It hosts annual workshops on crosscut saw techniques, conservation, first aid and other topics.

Balanced over his shoulder, Mitchell's covered crosscut saw bounced in rhythm with each step as he led a crew toward the northwest section of

Big Frog Wilderness. At the trailhead, ten Chattanooga-based Southeast Conservation Corps (SECC) youth members joined the crew. During six-week-long, labor-intensive conservation projects, they learned discipline, teamwork and leadership skills. The vegetation hung wet and heavy from a thunderstorm the previous afternoon. Old beech trees sprouted new life into clusters of healthy shoots. "They're called suckers," someone said, "but I call them 'sons of beeches.'" Bear claw scratches on a trailside tree reminded the crew that natives share this trail.

"Hold up, everybody," said Mitchell. "Need to move a big tree." Like a backcountry hiker studying a map before entering new territory, he studied the lay of the land and the angle of the fallen trunk. He identified the species, estimated its age, evaluated its trunk diameter and observed the character of the bark. Stringy bark catches on crosscut saw blades, he said, and shredding bark gets tangled in the teeth. A shot of WD-40 helped saw blades glide through pine resin and wet logs.

The tree had fallen down a hillside. Its bushy crown held the trunk above the trail, creating a "top bind" that required "under-bucking," said Mitchell. He removed the saw's canvas cover, attached two wooden handles, cut a groove underneath the trunk to lessen its strain and placed a wedge in the groove to prevent a trapped or twisted saw blade. Lining up the blade across the grain of the wood, a crewmember at each end held a handle and moved the blade in a rhythmic, rowing-like motion, pulling and then riding it back. "Don't rush to push," coaxed Mitchell. "Keep it level. Pull evenly without stopping."

"Five more strokes and we've got her done!" he cheered. And he was right.

That day, Ken Jones, a seventy-two-year-old retired TVA engineer and SAWS Wilderness Skills Institute graduate, joined the Big Frog trail project with his wife, Phyllis, a retired schoolteacher. Jones replaced a handle on a crosscut saw that his grandfather Marvin W. Walker (1890–1956) used in the CCC in Alabama. Jones uses the saw for CNF trail maintenance projects and has cut more than one thousand trees.

Twenty-five years ago, Clayton Pannell, the then Benton MacKaye Trail Association (BMTA) president, approached Jones about cutting the BMT route through the CNF and maintaining it. In 1975, after discovering an original copy of Benton MacKaye's map showing his suggested A.T. route through Georgia's Cohutta Wilderness, David (Dave) Sherman suggested building a trail that roughly followed MacKaye's route, said eighty-five-year-old George Owen, a founder of the BMTA in 1980. In the 1970s, Sherman was the Office of Planning and Research director with the Georgia State Department of Natural Resources and section-hiked the A.T. over ten

Left: Marvin W. Walker used a crosscut saw in the CCC that his grandson Ken Jones uses now to maintain CNF trails. *Ken Jones.*

Below: In 1975, Dave Sherman hiked Ocoee No. 2's flume railbed with Bob Johnson, hired by the TVA to document it for nomination to the National Register of Historic Places (approved in 1979). *Dave Sherman.*

years (1973–83). He became an admirer of the regional planner, Benton MacKaye, who had proposed the construction of the A.T. fifty years earlier. In Washington, D.C., in the 1980s and 1990s, Sherman was the Land Acquisition Special Projects Coordinator for the National Park Service and, eventually, the USFS. "I coordinated with parks, national forests and regions on many different high-profile and politically sensitive projects," he said, "such as the acquisition of New Mexico's 100,000-acre Baca Ranch in a volcanic crater and Yellowstone National Park's New World Gold Mine acquisition." His most personally rewarding project continued for thirty years: the acquisition of thousands of acres to protect the A.T. corridor. In 2013, Sherman was inducted into the A.T. Hall of Fame.

By 1987, volunteers, in partnership with the USFS, had completed the construction of the BMT from its intersection with the A.T. on Springer Mountain, Georgia, to the Georgia/Tennessee border. By 1992, the CNF and volunteers had extended the BMT over Big Frog Mountain to the Ocoee River. Around 1996, Pannell sketched the proposed Tennessee/North Carolina BMT route to the Great Smoky Mountains National Park (GSMNP) and discussed it with CNF staff. For nine days, Jones joined botanists conducting environmental impact surveys on the planned route. By 2003, the USFS had completed archaeological and biological assessments and a second botanical study. Pannell and Jones flagged 22 miles of new trails and 65 miles of existing ones and constructed their first 2.5-mile BMT section on Sugar Mountain in the Tellico Ranger District. Volunteers worked with them three days a week for fifteen months. In the CNF, Jones, Owen, BMT members and others continue to help maintain the trail. Rick Harris serves as CNF's BMT maintenance director. For more than forty-five years, Dave Sherman has followed BMTA's progress. He attended the club's annual meeting in 2021. In 2022, bipartisan Congressional sponsors from Georgia and Tennessee introduced a bill in Congress to designate the 300-mile-long BMT as a National Scenic Trail.

———————————•———————————

ONE MILE PAST THE USFS Parksville Beach, the Ocoee-Hiwassee Ranger Station sits at the junction of the byway and FSR-77 (Oswald Dome Road). Like a loose ribbon draped from the southern base of Chilhowee Mountain to the USFS Chilhowee Recreation Area, this byway spur curls nearly two thousand feet in elevation past the Sugarloaf, Parksville Lake and Gazebo

Overlooks. The roadway passes the former sites of the 1840 Jacob Clemmer (1808–1871) roadbed; the late 1800s, forty-two-room Benton Springs Hotel; and a marker near the site of a Civil War conflict. The CCC built rock walls and other structures in the camping and day-use areas of the Chilhowee Recreation Area. It also constructed an earthen dam, creating the seven-acre McKamy Lake for swimming, fishing and canoeing.

Each year at McKamy Lake, children and their families attend a fishing rally coordinated by the USFS, TWRA and the Wild Turkey Federation. In 2016, on National Get Outdoors Day, a former nonprofit organization, Partners of Cherokee National Forest, joined the USFS and the national Kids in Parks program to celebrate Tennessee's first "Kids Track Trail." They formed a figure-eight trail by combining the McKamy Lake and Forest Walk Trails and erected numerical markers along this family-friendly footpath that corresponded to numbered narratives in a brochure.

The CCC built a spur road to the Oswald Dome Lookout Tower on Chilhowee Mountain's highest peak. Its workers removed the wooden 1922 tower, replaced it with a new structure and served as fire tower wardens

Gazebo along FSR-77. The CCC had built a similar one nearby. *Tennessee State Library and Archives.*

The CCC built FSR-77 across Chilhowee Mountain from the Ocoee River to the current TN-30 at the Hiwassee River, 1941. *Tennessee State Library and Archives.*

until the Corps disbanded in the 1940s. Motorists drive the graveled, often rough road to the 3,022-foot-high Oswald Dome on the northern end of Chilhowee Mountain. About a quarter of a mile beyond the gated road, transmission antennas have replaced the tower. The CNF moved it to the Ocoee Whitewater Center around 2004. A steep trail to Oswald Dome from the USFS Quinn Springs Picnic Area on TN-30 offers beautiful wildflowers in the spring.

Hikers can access twenty-five miles of trails in the Chilhowee Trail System, including a trail to Rock Creek Gorge Scenic area, where the creek tumbles about sixty-five feet into Benton Falls. Beyond Benton Falls, hikers and bikers follow Clemmer Trail to a trailhead on TN-30, near the USFS Parksville Lake Campground. In the 1800s, Clemmer family members, James McKamy and others owned a sawmill, grazed sheep and built a hotel in the area.

In January 2020, Camcore, a North Carolina State University (NCSU) tree breeding organization, joined the USFS and other partners to transplant eastern hemlock (*Tsuga canadensis*) and table mountain pine (*Pinus pungens*) to the Chilhowee Genetic Resource Management Area. In the future, seeds collected from the trees at Chilhowee and its sister seed orchard in North Carolina's Nantahala National Forest will provide resources for NCSU tree breeding programs and USFS forest restoration and research projects.

OCOEE RIVER PROJECT / OLYMPICS

An early morning blaze in April 2022 destroyed the 7,660-square-foot USFS Ocoee Whitewater Administration Center on the Ocoee Scenic Byway. The Tennessee Bureau of Investigations and the USFS launched an investigation to determine the cause of the fire. In the 1990s, the USFS constructed the architectural treasure because the Atlanta Committee of the Olympic Games (ACOG), formerly known as the Atlanta Olympic Committee, planned to host its 1996 Olympic whitewater events on the Ocoee River. Initially, the ACOG, environmentalists, local groups and federal agencies responsible for the management and construction of the Ocoee River venue did not support the competitive paddling community's push to stage Olympic whitewater events on the Ocoee. After political powers muscled their influence and the ACOG approved the decision, however, the USFS, TVA, State of Tennessee, Polk County government and other stakeholders became involved.

The USFS, managers of the Ocoee region's natural resources, became responsible for constructing the competitive whitewater channel. The TVA contributed water releases for the channel's conceptual design phase, as well as the testing, training and competition on the river. The State of Tennessee accepted the responsibility for the planning and operation of Olympic and pre-Olympic events. The Tennessee Ocoee Development Agency (TODA) formed to organize, finance and manage the events. CNF Forest Supervisor John Ramey served as its ex-officio member of the board of directors; Parker Hardy its executive director; and Nantahala Outdoor Center's Ellen DeCuir its director of operations. Since ACOG only permitted Olympic whitewater events at no cost to its organization, Hardy's goal was to raise an estimated $12 million to cover expenses. DeCuir developed staffing and operational plans within ACOG standards and worked within the mandates of a USFS Special Use Permit to stage the event on national forest lands. "TODA was a major player," explained a retired Paul Wright, the Southern Region's Olympics Liaison Officer and the CNF Ocoee Whitewater Project Manager. "They were given an almost impossible task." Stress led to strife and heated discussions, "but I never failed to respect the challenges they faced."

The USFS planned to design and build a permanent Ocoee River recreation site, enjoyed by the public long after the Olympians had moved on. "The project had to promote long-term rural economic development," said Wright, "and it could not cause irreversible harm to the environment. In other words, it had to be consistent with and contribute to the agency's greater mission." The USFS designed the administration building, whitewater channel and adjacent area "for long-term social and economic benefit to the surrounding, forest-dependent communities."

Joellen Dickey, a marketing specialist and avid paddler at the Atlanta Center for Excellence, moved to the Ocoee region in 1992 to promote support for the Olympic event, develop a base of trained volunteers and serve as the executive director of the Ocoee River Canoe and Kayak Association (ORCKA). Her economic development activities, fundraisers, hospitality trainings and cultural programs stimulated enthusiasm and personal involvement. To introduce 150 athletes from thirteen countries to the Ocoee River, she launched a successful campaign to host the 1993 International Canoe Federation's (ICF) World Cup finals on the Middle Ocoee. The competitions not only became a rehearsal for the main CNF event in three years but also welcomed the world to the culture and cuisine of Tennessee. Communities in the Ocoee region organized picnics and festivals. "Joellen Dickey was the visionary, the optimist, the relationship builder," said Wright, and "the tireless worker who built the foundation for the success of the final Olympic event."

With encouragement from the U.S. Canoe and Kayak Team (USCKT), the Forest Service sent a credentialed team to Spain to study the physical and operational aspects of the 1992 Olympic whitewater competitions in La Seu d'Urgell. For a week, Joellen and the USFS team met whitewater course designers, international athletes, scorekeepers, judges and paddlesport professionals, including Bill Endicott, the Olympic canoe and kayak team coach. They learned about security measures, telecommunications and housing. As a bonus, they witnessed a historic event. In the men's double-canoe competition (C-2), Joe Jacobi and Scott Strausbaugh performed two penalty-free runs to capture America's first gold medal in the history of the sport. USA's Dana Chladek took home the bronze medal in the women's single kayak (KF-1).

The CNF, in cooperation with the TVA and the Tennessee Department of Environment and Conservation (TDEC), initiated biological, geological and cultural resources studies of the Middle Ocoee River, below TVA's Ocoee Dam No. 2, and the Upper Ocoee River, above Ocoee Powerhouse No. 3, to determine the best location to perform a feat never attempted in paddlesport history: building a competitive slalom course in the middle of a river. Officials had included Olympic whitewater competitions only twice—in Munich in 1972 and in Barcelona in 1992, both on a man-made water course.

The Middle Ocoee, early proponents believed, was the obvious location for holding the events. Paddling clubs had sponsored regional competitions on that river section. Members of the Ocoee River Outfitters Association, however, voiced concerns that the project construction, team trials, athletic trainings and international competitions would affect their guided rafting trips down the Middle Ocoee. The USFS's primary concerns were the potential impacts on the historic Old Copper Road and on the endangered Ruth's golden aster (*Pityopsis ruthii*) that grows in the dry crevices of midstream boulders. They also were concerned about the release of acid from Anakeesta rock formations that could exacerbate the already toxic condition of the river following years of copper mining upstream. The curvy, two-lane highway through the narrow Middle Ocoee section of the gorge—where nearly three thousand tractor-trailer trucks, rafting buses and commuter vehicles travel daily in the summer—also posed a dilemma. In addition, the limited riverside bank space at Dam No. 2 would not accommodate thousands of spectators and the event management infrastructure.

The Upper Ocoee River became the most viable location for Olympic whitewater competitions, but when the TVA tested the flow rates of the 200-foot-wide Upper Ocoee, it learned that it would need to release more than twice as much water from Lake Blue Ridge than it currently released to attain the velocity of 3,000 cfs (cubic feet per second) for Middle Ocoee whitewater competitions. That amount of water would adversely affect power generation revenues and reduce TVA's upstream water storage reserves for Ocoee system operations. "I defer to the professional opinions of the TVA on the impacts of loss of power production as well as its expertise in hydraulic design," voiced Ramey. Starting below the Blue Hole, a popular swimming hole, project planners decided to narrow the width of a 500-meter-long section of the Upper Ocoee to 70 to 100 feet wide, achieving the required water depth and hydraulic features at a 1,200 to 1,400 cfs flow rate to support world-class competitions.

"Nearly two years of planning and design went into the development of a site plan that harmonized with the natural beauty of the Ocoee River landscape," said Wright. After obtaining the results of the Environmental Impact Assessment, permits from the Corps of Engineers and the State of Tennessee, and verification that the Ocoee River was no longer considered a nominee for protection under the Wild and Scenic River Act, the USFS Ocoee River project team initiated the construction project.

In July 1994, the U.S. Army Corps of Engineers (USACE), 41st Bridge Company of Fort Campbell, Kentucky, erected a bridge, donated by the Department of Defense, saving the USFS nearly $400,000. The Bailey Bridge would allow construction traffic to cross to the river's left bank. The bridge was named after British civil engineer Donald Bailey, who in 1941 had designed a bridge that troops could erect, dismantle and relocate quickly with standard tools. USACE staff sergeant and bridge engineer Bill Gibson and the troops unpacked seven tractor-trailer trucks loaded with bridge materials transported from Pueblo Depot, Colorado. In the pouring rain, they bolted together fifty-foot-long, double-truss spans. By the third day, the unified, muscular machine had lined up beside the metal frame, dug toe-deep in the thick mud and heaved the twenty-ton structure in place. The Tennessee Forestry Association donated $10,000 worth of oak decking, processed at three East Tennessee sawmills, to cover the bridge floor's wooden frame and stringers. The open-weave bridge would permit unobstructed TV camera coverage of the slalom races.

Fifty company members, including a sergeant who was the grandson of Tennessee's World War I Medal of Honor recipient Sergeant Alvin York, had planned to stay at the USFS Thunder Rock Campground near Ocoee Powerhouse No. 3 during the mission, but rainstorms threatened the loss of military equipment and access to the campground. Copper Basin High School set up army bunks in its gymnasium and opened its locker rooms for showers.

After completion of the project, men dunked Captain Craig Korcz, the senior commanding officer, in a wading pool. Ocoee River's shallow waters prevented the traditional toss from a bridge pier. Hosted by the Copperhill Chamber of Commerce, the Ocoee River bridge dedication ceremony celebrated the 41st Bridge Company's final mission before its deactivation in September 1994. "The Caissons Go Rolling Along" echoed through the Ocoee River Gorge. Lieutenant Colonel J. David Norwood, the USACE Nashville District commander, spoke at the event. The Bailey Bridge was rare, both in times of peace and in a Tennessee forest, he said, and "will

Bailey Bridge construction. *Paul Wright.*

not only bridge this gap but will also symbolize the teamwork spirit" of the Ocoee River Project. After a picnic, the Ocoee Outfitters Association offered complimentary rafting trips on the Middle Ocoee. "The bridge is now the landmark for the location of the Olympic venue," wrote Wright, "and I fully expect it to be the most photographed Bailey Bridge in the world."

The USFS project team began working seven days a week to meet the required August 1996 deadline. The son of USFS Project Engineer Jerry Barrow, eight-year-old Paul Barrow (later a U.S. Marine Corps captain), wrote in his school essay, "My dad works for the USFS....The USFS is trying to make the river skinnier for the elmeks [Olympics]. My dad thought the job would be fun but that sortove [*sic*] wore off. He does not get to play with us much. I hope the job will end soon."

The USFS contracted the Pickering Firm of Memphis, which subcontracted the architect and whitewater athlete John Anderson of Bethesda, Maryland, to design the whitewater racing course. Keith McLaughlin, who specialized in computer modeling of whitewater channels, assisted with the project. USFS engineering inspectors worked with L-J Incorporated of Columbia, South Carolina, to construct the course. Crews formed levee foundations about twenty to fifty feet from each riverbank to narrow the channel, covered their surfaces with two- to six-ton boulders harvested from Chilhowee Mountain and pressed rocks into grout-filled gaps.

In Tucson, Arizona, USFS Landscape Architect Bill Peach and USFS Engineer Jack Callahan inspected clay models of rocks, sculpted by the Larson Company, for placement in the watercourse. Larson professionals had crafted realistic rock formations for the Chattanooga and Monterey Bay Aquariums and a Japanese polar bear exhibit. In Ocoee's riverbed, the artificial rock features intensified river velocity, diverted water from collected pools and augmented river hydraulics. The rough-surface, concrete boulders textured with cracks and crevices were "indistinguishable from the surrounding bedrock," said Wright.

Crews hauled more than sixty thousand tons of rock to build rock walls, terraces, highway-bank armoring for flood protection, a take-out ramp on river left near the Bailey Bridge, the administration building's rock-fill foundation and other projects. Bell South covered much of the cost to bury six miles of electrical and fiber-optic cables in the shoulder of US-64 from Ducktown to the whitewater center. The USDA Natural Resources Conservation Services donated half of the hundreds of shrubs, trees, flowers and grasses planted in a native garden. Contractors built a secure area for athletes and platforms for judges and the media. Near the administration building, crews erected a 336-foot-long cable-stay bridge built by the Steadfast Bridge Company of Fort Payne, Alabama. This "Legacy Bridge" and the downstream Bailey Bridge bookended the competition channel. Workers sandblasted graffiti that vandals had painted on riverbed rocks, leaving only the "smiley face" to greet international athletes. The removed images inspired the names of the individual hydraulic features in the watercourse.

The American Canoe Association (ACA) helped plan, obtain and install suspended slalom gate systems to meet international competition regulations. Aluminum flagpoles ordered by the USFS from the American Flagpole of Virginia were adapted with nautical hardware and used as gate masts. At the request of the U.S. team, vertical gate poles with flat bottoms arrived from France—the standard rounded bottom poles allegedly cost the American team a medal during the 1992 competition.

In 1995, a Valentine's Day flood blasted away pebbles pressed into levee surfaces and damaged a bridge abutment, rock walls and river access roads. Workers secured six hundred tons of replacement chinking material for the levees from a rock source near North Carolina's Nantahala River. During the flood, the TVA released rising waters from Ocoee Dam No. 3. Fortunately, crews evacuated their equipment before it was lost. The flood incident,

Ocoee River whitewater channel construction. *Paul Wright.*

however, provided an opportunity to study the force of the aquatic flow on the features constructed in the channel. The grouted boulders and steel-reinforced rock walls held firm. In October, the remnants from Hurricane Opal also battered the Ocoee River Project but left only minor damage. During a bitter winter, work continued through eight-inch-deep snows and subzero temperatures but delayed the delivery of laminated beams for the administration building from upstate New York. In 1996, Congress failed to reach an agreement on the Interior Appropriations Bill, closing national forests and grasslands. The CNF furloughed 250 employees, but the shutdown did not affect Ocoee River Project contractors.

"The Forest Service has an opportunity to provide domestic and international visitors with a memorable experience on our national forest lands," a CNF staffer wrote. He requested volunteers to design brochures, interact with the media, provide linguistic services and offer accommodations for global guests. Forty-two families and USFS employees, members of the "Whitewater Zoo Crew," offered in-home arrangements for pre-Olympic events, such as the 1995 Ocoee Slalom Challenge and the 1996 International Qualifier. USFS staffer Lewis Kearney and his wife, Marilyn, hosted the French three-time world champion kayaker Myriam Jerusalmi and her British world champion husband, kayaker Richard Fox, during one competition. For the Olympics, leaders organized a small village at Lee University in Cleveland, Tennessee, to accommodate coaches and competitors.

During the Ocoee Slalom Challenge, thirty countries participated in the inaugural race on the new Ocoee River course. World champion Scott Shipley of Poulsbo, Washington, powered the opening kayak run with a golden paddle. That year, the American Canoe Association awarded the USFS the J. Henry Rushton Award for its excellence in the advancement of paddlesports. By May 1996, the project team had completed most of the Olympic preparations. A helicopter transporting Vice President Al Gore from Chattanooga to the International Qualifier opening ceremonies circled above a dense Ocoee Gorge fog for nearly an hour before landing at Boyd Gap on the Ocoee Scenic Byway. "Without this team effort, the Olympians would not be coming to Tennessee," Gore said at a podium beside the Ocoee River, unaware of the bear foraging behind him. "Long after the Olympic flame is extinguished and the torch goes back to Athens, Greece…kayakers and canoeists will still be coming to enjoy the Ocoee River."

In July 1996, USFS Chief Jack Ward Thomas, who had visited the Ocoee River site three times during its final two years of construction, attended the Olympic whitewater competitions. "As I toured the venue the day before the

An Olympic Ocoee River competitor. *Paul Wright.*

event," he wrote, "I never felt more proud of the Forest Service in my life." The field staff "persevere. They achieve. They inspire me. The struggle is worthwhile, it truly is."

Sometime after midnight on the eve of July 26, 1996, Eric Rudolph planted a pipe bomb at Centennial Olympic Park in Atlanta, killing a mother and injuring more than one hundred. "Given the threat of terrorism," wrote Thomas, "security measures were intense and involved officers of the Forest Service, TVA, FBI, Secret Service, Sheriff's Department, Tennessee State Police, and Tennessee Park Police." The USFS coordinated the security efforts, said retired USFS Law Enforcement Officer Russ Arthur. On the hillsides above the Ocoee River, SWAT teams patrolled the area and snipers stood at key locations. Uniformed and plain-clothed officers moved through the crowds, while TV surveillance cameras panned the scene. During a moment of silence for those injured in the bombing, one newspaper reported, a bus backfired on the Ocoee Scenic Byway, unnerving the crowd.

That day, officers stopped Chris Ammons at a checkpoint along the graveled Kimsey Highway (FSR-68), north of Ocoee River Gorge. Staying for the weekend at Hiwassee Outfitters, he and his Alabama friends had watched the Ocoee's Women's K-1 preliminary event the previous day. "In eerie silence," said Ammons, they watched the morning news about the bombing. They had planned to go mountain biking at the Nantahala National Forest Tsali Recreation Area. When officials closed US-64 near the Olympic venue, they drove the Kimsey Highway. As they rounded a curve, a pickup truck driver warned them, "If you have drugs, guns or any contraband, there's a checkpoint ahead," but with only bikes and gear "a friendly ranger at the checkpoint asked where we were headed and wished us a good day."

The Olympic whitewater competition began as scheduled. About forty-two thousand visitors attended the three-day event. U.S. kayaker Dana Chladek won a silver medal in the Women's K-1 whitewater event. "For the first time in Olympic history," wrote Thomas, "the people who staged the event were honored with Olympic medals—a gold for the USFS, bronzes for its two partners. It was a good feeling to have the Forest Service recognized for excellence in performance." In a post-ceremony USFS celebration, the chief handed the gold medal (provided by the International Canoe Federation) to CNF Forest Supervisor John Ramey, whose "masterly job of leadership" held the coalition of partners together during the project. Chief Thomas flew toward Knoxville to catch a flight to Washington, D.C. "As the pilot twisted the plane through the thunderheads, I could see clouds light up with lightning flashes and hear the rumble of thunder. I fancied that as applause from the heavens as I stared out in reverie."

For more than a quarter of a century, tourists have visited the USFS Ocoee Whitewater Center. They have passed a Jewish memorial provided by the jeweler Larry Epperson to commemorate eleven Israeli athletes killed during the 1972 Olympics in Munich, crossed the USFS Legacy Bridge, walked under flags of many countries waving in an Ocoee breeze, shared picnics where Olympians and media personnel once gathered and found Olympic gate system holes, now rootholds for wildflowers. Byway travelers have stopped at the center before visiting the Boyd Gap Observation area; the Brush Creek Trail System and shooting range; the Little Frog Wilderness; the 220-acre Rock Creek Gorge Scenic Area; and the waterfalls of the bass stream Goforth Creek, a habitat for the rare Archer's toothed land snail (*Fumonelix archeri*). Hikers and bikers have explored the Tanasi Trail System and Old Copper Road Trail that leads upstream to a paddler's launch area near TVA's Ocoee Dam No. 3.

Students from Chilhowee Middle School, Copper Basin High School, North Whitfield Middle School and others have attended "Ocoee Nature Days" at the center. In September 2019, students from Polk County High School guided participants to outdoor stations offered by groups such as

Above: Shelby and Lydia Wallace and Michael Worsham explore wildlife nesting boxes near the former Ocoee Whitewater Center. *Author's photo.*

Below: The Copper Basin's once barren landscape. *Ducktown Basin Museum.*

USFS staff at the Ocoee River Legacy Bridge. *Paul Wright.*

the USFS, TWRA, Tennessee State Parks and Southern Appalachian Wilderness Society to learn about wildlife, forestry, aquatic systems, trail maintenance and other topics.

Ocoee Whitewater Center visitors have witnessed fish and invertebrate populations returning to healthier aquatic habitats. Between the 1840s and 1980s, Copper Basin mining operations left a desert-like environment upstream. Forests stripped for firewood by miners, open pit copper smelting practices and sulfuric acid production caused erosion, sediment runoff, water and air pollution and a nearly eight-thousand-acre barren landscape. During an Upper Ocoee River environmental impact study conducted prior to the construction of the Olympic whitewater course, USFS snorkelers and others found only three fish in three days in a three-mile section of the river, said retired USFS Fisheries Biologist Jim Herrig. In the 1930s and 1940s, the CCC, USFS, TVA, schoolchildren, mining company employees and Copper Basin residents planted more than 2 million trees. Later, helicopters spread acid-tolerant grasses and legumes, crews applied fertilizer and lime and researchers studied ways to improve reforestation efforts. Around 2001, TDEC and Glen Springs Holdings improved water treatment plants, removed PCB-contaminated soils and acid-producing mining wastes and capped lead-contaminated waste in the basin. By 2003, the Environmental Protection Agency (EPA) had declared the Ocoee watershed a "superfund" site, deserving monetary support for the recovery of its natural resources. After spending millions of dollars on cleanup projects, planting an estimated 17 million trees and undertaking other reclamation projects, the Ocoee River region is green again. A short drive on US-64 East from the Ocoee Whitewater Center offers an in-depth history of copper mining at the Ducktown Basin Museum at the former Burra Burra Copper Mine.

The 2022 fire at the Ocoee Whitewater Center destroyed the energy-efficient administration building with exposed beams, walls made from sandstone boulders harvested from Chilhowee Mountain and picture windows that offered supreme southern views of Ocoee River Gorge. The blaze also consumed the gold medal awarded to the USFS, the Olympian Scott Shipley's donated kayak, a handmade quilt, paddlesport exhibits designed by the USFS and American Canoe Association and other irreplaceable items. Polk County officials and the USFS are discussing plans to rebuild.

HIWASSEE RIVER

TN-30 veers north off the Ocoee Scenic Byway and passes the CNF Work Center and USFS Parksville Lake Campground to arrive at former CCC Camp McCroy, now a 4-H camp. A right turn leads to Archville and the Kimsey Mountain Highway, a rugged roadway that follows a former Cherokee route across a ridgeline to TN-68. Named after Dr. L.E. Kimsey, a Ducktown physician for fifty years, it cuts through Jenkins Grave Gap. In an 1854 snowstorm, Thomas Jenkins died while delivering mail from Benton to Ducktown. In 1897, Elizabeth Morgan also died nearby in a fire at her parents' farm. Near the gap, the CNF built a spur road in 1929 to the now-removed Sassafras Knob Lookout Tower on Little Frog Mountain. TN-30 continues north toward Hiwassee River.

The 147-mile-long Hiwassee River leaves its headwaters on Rocky Mountain, Georgia, flows through Chattahoochee and Nantahala National Forests and enters Tennessee. It dips past the former railroad whistle-stop, Apalachia Station, briefly follows TN-68 and heads west toward the community of Reliance. On an 1867 Kentucky-to-Florida excursion, John Muir followed the Hiwassee River section near Reliance. The twenty-mile-long John Muir National Recreation Trail (NRT), built in 1972 by the Youth Conservation Corps and the Senior Community Services Employment Program, traces his route along the north shoreline.

Hiking an average of twenty-five miles per day, Muir entered the Tennessee Valley between the Cumberland and Unaka Mountains. After fording Clinch River, he sent plant collections from Kingston, Tennessee, to his brother in Wisconsin. "A buxom Tennessee 'gal,'" he wrote, directed him on his way. He walked "through many a leafy valley…and cool brooklets" and reached Madisonville, where he saw the "most glorious billowy mountain scenery." He mentioned a visit with a "John Vohn." Perhaps he meant Dr. John Vaughn (1821–1890) and his wife, Fannie Wheeler (1820–1890), who operated an inn and tollgate near the Tennessee/North Carolina line.

"You, who are traveling for curiosity, and wonder, ought to see our gold mines," said a gentleman, speaking, supposedly, about the Coker Creek mines. "Our fathers," Muir's host explained, "skimmed off the cream of the soil. The worn-out ground won't yield no roastin' ears now. But, the Lord… meant for us to bust open these copper mines and gold mines, so that we may have money to buy the corn that we cannot raise."

Muir climbed a peak in the Unicoi Mountain Range possibly, on today's Cherohala Skyway:

Such an ocean of wooded, waving, swelling mountain beauty…forest-clad hills…seemed to be enjoying the rich sunshine.…All united by curves and slopes of inimitable softness and beauty.

On September 19, Muir hiked along the Hiwassee River (spelled "Hiawassee" by Muir, as seen on older maps):

My path all to-day led me along the leafy banks of the Hiawassee, a most impressive mountain river. Its channel is very rough, as it crosses the edges of upturned rock strata, some of them standing at right angles. Thus, a multitude of short, resounding cataracts are produced.

The multitude of falls and rapids in the wilderness finds a voice. Such a river is the Hiawassee, with its surface broken to a thousand sparkling gems, and its forest wall vine-draped and flowery as Eden. And how fine the song it sings!

He followed the river to Murphy, North Carolina; visited the site of Fort Butler, a detainment fort for Cherokees forced to move to western territories; and continued his southbound one-thousand-mile walk.

The John Muir NRT joins the Benton MacKaye Trail near the confluence of Childers Creek and the Hiwassee River. The trails head upstream for about ten miles to the mouth of Coker Creek. The BMT breaks away to follow the Unicoi Mountain Trail, while the John Muir NRT follows the Hiwassee River to the Tennessee border. At Coker Creek, a USFS trail follows the stream to a series of six- to thirty-foot-high cascades and offers

Archville CCC Camp Old Hickory, 1936. *Thurman Parish Jr.*

In early Reliance, Jim Kirkland drove the school bus, a covered wagon drawn by two mules. In the late 1940s, I rode a motorized bus to our two-room schoolhouse. Older boys carried drinking water from Luther Presswood's spring, about a third of a mile away. Model A Fords and horse-drawn wagons hauling supplies traveled the graveled Highway-30, but most people walked. When I was eleven, I began exploring the forest, mostly alone. I became familiar with the forest around Reliance, Springtown and Greasy Creek, but when the USFS hired me in 1962, I began learning about the country south of the Ocoee River. For thirty-two years, I worked in the woods all day. I collected stories from former Forest Service staff and people who once lived in areas that became part of the Cherokee National Forest. I did not want to see it get lost, so as time passed, I tried to record it.

By Thurman Parish Jr., USFS staff, 1960s–1990s.

many swimming holes. The lively little falls vie for the eye along the gorgeous, rocky landscape. A shorter trail to the Coker Creek Scenic Area, protected since 1988, is accessible by county roads off TN-68.

Retired judge Carroll Ross officiated the wedding of James (Jim) and Judy Passmore on the John Muir NRT at the Childers Creek bridge, built by the Youth Conservation Corps in 1974. As a young man, Jim hunted squirrels above the current USFS Quinn Springs Recreation Area south of the Hiwassee River. Once, when he stumbled across a whiskey still and pulled back the edge of a tarp on the mash barrels, he heard a shotgun blast. "I served as an army pilot in Vietnam," he said, "but the first time someone shot at me was when that moonshiner shot through the trees to scare me off."

Jim and Judy descend from generations of Higdon and Haskins families of Polk County. Some of the CNF property along the Hiwassee and Ocoee Rivers belonged to Jim's ancestor D.C. Haskins. Jim's grandfather George Washington Passmore, a miner, preacher and 1928–32 Polk County trustee, lived in the Copper Basin before moving to Benton.

Judy's father, Edward (Ed) Higdon (1909–1986), was the grandson of Amanda Linderman Higdon (1845–1926), a Coker Creek native, and Calvin (Cal) Vincent Higdon (1836–1919), a Civil War veteran. Ed worked with the CCC at Camp McCroy and served as a CNF fire tower watchman. His wife, Opal Tilley Higdon (1911–1991), taught in a one-room schoolhouse in

Left: John Muir (1838–1914). *Wikimedia Commons.*

Below: Judy and Jim Passmore's wedding ceremony on the John Muir NRT. *Judy Passmore.*

the Greasy Creek community. After the CCC, Ed worked as a hydroelectric dam operator at TEPCO's Ocoee Dam No. 1. After 1940, TVA employed Ed to work at its Blue Ridge Dam in Georgia and, later, its Hiwassee and Fontana Dams in North Carolina. In 1948, he threw the switch on TVA's Watauga Dam in today's Watauga Ranger District. Born in Ducktown in 1943, Judy moved with her family to Elizabethton, Tennessee, where her father worked at the Watauga Dam. After retiring from administrative work at East Tennessee State University, Judy returned to Polk County, where she and Jim are members of the Polk County Historical Society.

In the mid-1880s, Cal and Amanda Higdon moved to the north bank of the Hiwassee River. When the railroad company made plans to build a track along the river (the current Old Line Railroad), the couple enlarged their house to become both a home for their seven children and a boardinghouse for railroad dignitaries and travelers. Verandas along both levels of the two-story structure offered splendid views of the river. Cal operated a ferry across the river until crews built the Reliance Bridge in 1912. The Higdons later sold the property.

In July 2022, two-speed "Tin Lizzies" puttered past the deserted Higdon Hotel on Childers Creek Road along the Hiwassee River toward the CNF. Passengers dressed in early 1900s attire used cellphone cameras to photograph the hotel and waved a handkerchief in greeting. A bobtailed calico cat and its black companion scouted the home site for rodents while James Harold Webb Jr. (Harold), the great-grandson of Joseph Dallas Vaughn (1845–1917) and his wife, Sarah Reed (1842–1936), shared stories of local history.

In 1880, Dr. John Vaughn's son, Joseph, purchased Elisha Dodson's grist/lumber mill and more than six hundred acres along the Hiwassee River. Dodson had built his mill near an angled set of rapids and an old Cherokee fishing weir. The fertile river valley produced corn; pumpkins the size of watermelons; and Cushaw squash, a white-striped, bluish-green member of the crookneck squash family. Farmers cut off its tasty, thick neck for cooking and saved its bowl of seeds to plant the next year.

Vaughn dismantled the Dodson house beside today's TN-30 around 1888 but kept some of its window sashes, doors and posts to enhance his new home. Harold's grandmother Alice Rachel Vaughn Webb (1884–1975), widow of Charles Courtland Webb (1879–1950), lived in the Vaughn-Webb House until age ninety, walking a fourth of a mile down the highway every day to work as a clerk at the Webb Brothers Store. Harold moved into the home after her passing.

Near the old mill, the brothers Oliver (1907–1992) and Joseph Harold Webb Sr. (1909–1985) opened the Webb Brothers Store in 1936, where Oliver served as postmaster of the Reliance Post Office. The brothers built a new store in

Vaughn-Webb House. *Bruce A. Roberts, https://www.be-roberts.com.*

1955 and removed the original building in the 1970s. In 1968, the year Harold Jr. began his University of Tennessee–Knoxville (UT) studies in natural science and secondary education, he purchased a four-man raft from an army surplus store to float on the Hiwassee River during school breaks. The next summer, he returned home and found his raft on top of the farm's cattle truck. His dad had started renting it to fishermen and other river runners. Later, Uncle Oliver numbered truck inner tubes from 1 to 10, which "we had played with in the creeks as kids," said Harold, and hauled them on the farm truck to the launch site for customers to float down the river. Two years later, the Webb brothers were providing shuttle service for fifteen rafts and three hundred tubes per season for floaters to travel from the Apalachia powerhouse to Reliance.

During his college years, Harold Jr. ran the livery service during the summer season, transporting UT athletes upriver to the put-in site. After graduation in 1973, he worked at Olin Chemicals in Charleston, Tennessee, by evening and ran the shuttle service by day until he returned to Reliance to run the store and farm full time. In the mid-1970s, the USFS began requiring a Special Use Permit to operate a business within the national forest and restricted the number of permits to four Hiwassee River outfitters. Today, the Webb Brothers Float Service is the only original shuttle service still operating on the river. He and the other outfitters now accommodate around 1,200 floaters per day during the peak season; 95 percent of Webb's service operates within the CNF.

In the 1970s, an architect college friend encouraged Harold to nominate the Reliance community for listing in the National Register of Historic Places. In 1986, officials authorized the listing of the Reliance Historic District, which included the Higdon Hotel, the Vaughn-Webb House, the Hiwassee Union Church/Masonic Hall, the railroad Watchman's House and the Reliance Bridge. Harold and several partners purchased the Higdon Hotel in the 1980s. They began renovating it in the 1990s, planning to house tourists attending the 1996 Olympic competition on the Ocoee River. However, conflicts ensued, and the plans stalled. Later, Harold bought out four members of the group. Today, the building remains vacant.

In the 1980s, the Tennessee Department of Transportation planned to replace the iron Reliance Bridge across the Hiwassee River on TN-315. Preservationists formed the Friends of Reliance, a nonprofit organization, and campaigned for six years to save the five-span Pratt triangular truss bridge. County commissioner Fred Lindner cited the Scenic River Law, requiring the state to preserve its rivers and their historic structures. Harold had a personal interest in preserving this landmark. "My great-grandfather had deeded the bridge and the land along its abutments to Polk County for public use. If removed, it was to revert to his heirs." The stones used to build the piers came from his farm and the current national forest lands. When Harold staged a sit-down protest on the bridge, Polk County deputies arrested him for criminal trespassing at the proposed demolition site. "I went to jail, but they had arrested me on my own bridge." The charges were dropped and the bridge dismantled. Harold salvaged iron, with its hand-hammered rivets, from the old bridge to build a fence near the Watchman's House. He built wooden steps from floor beams discarded by crews rebuilding the L&N Railroad bridge and trestle across the Hiwassee River in 1975.

Harold's 1861 Watchman's House sits a few feet above the railroad tracks. When a train passed, the L&N Railroad agent stood on the balcony of the house and watched for sparks thrown from coal-burning locomotives onto the wooden trestle. Barrels on the trestle held water for watchmen to douse early blazes. Harold manages it as a guesthouse for visitors exploring the CNF and the Hiwassee River area.

In 2001, members of the Czech whitewater team booked the Watchman's House for an Ocoee River paddling competition. They were watching TV when terrorists flew airplanes into the Twin Towers on September 11, which canceled the competition. In 1993, Harold hosted World Cup whitewater competitors at the large Vaughn-Webb House with one bathroom and no air conditioning. "It was one of the greatest experiences of my life, but I wasn't prepared for international guests." When he hosted a Slovenian medalist

The Old Line Railroad passes below the Watchman's House. *Christi Worsham.*

and his coach, "Yugoslavia just broke up. I didn't even know where Slovenia was!" The Italian Pierpaolo Ferrazzi, who won gold in slalom kayaking in Barcelona's 1992 Olympic Games, also stayed with him.

South of Hiwassee River, visitors drive TN-68 to Old Farner Road and turn onto Apalachia Tunnel Road to hike the USFS trail along Turtletown Creek. A rocky escarpment divides Hiwassee's tributary into a twin thirty-foot-high waterfall. An additional 0.7 mile leads to the lower, hourglass-shaped falls. An 8-mile-long pipe that funnels water from the Apalachia Dam near the North Carolina/Tennessee state line to the powerhouse plows through the mountainside near the trail. Cherokees who escaped the 1838 Forced March hid in this area and established the Turtletown community.

Around 1942, the TVA built the Apalachia Dam, tunnel and powerhouse to generate power to produce aluminum during World War II. Construction crews transported supplies to the worksite by railroad. For heavy truck traffic, the TVA upgraded the McFarland–Turtletown Road (now FSR-23) and built Smith Creek Road (FSR-236) from McFarland to its powerhouse construction site near the mouth of Smith Creek. The company established Smith Creek Village south of the powerhouse for TVA supervisors. Tunnel portals at Apalachia Station, Turtletown Creek, McFarland, Smith Creek and a site eight hundred feet below the dam allowed construction workers greater access. A cable car transported TVA officials across the river. Pedestrians cross the river now near the powerhouse on a 1948 suspension bridge.

Filmed on Coon Denton Island in the lower Hiwassee River near Calhoun, Tennessee, the 1960 movie *Wild River* dramatized the conflicts between residents and TVA agents. In the movie, set in 1933, TVA's land purchasing agent, Chuck Glover (played by actor Montgomery Clift), clashes with eighty-nine-year-old Ella Garth (Jo Van Fleet), living on a family-owned island.

"Mr. Roosevelt," said Ella, "says this country is going to the dogs. The only way he can figure to stop it is to put my island under water." She believed

Movie scene from *Wild River. Tennessee State Library and Archives.*

he didn't have the right to make her leave. She pointed to her farmhand's hound dog: "I want to buy Ole' Blue, Sam. How much you want for him?"

"Oh, I wouldn't sell him."

"I didn't ask you if you want to sell him. I said I'm buying him for $15."

"Oh, no, ma'am. He ain't worth nuttin' but I ain't gonna sell him....He's mine! You ain't got no right to make me."

"Come to think of it, Sam, I don't, do I?" She turned toward the TVA agent. "Sam and me, we don't sell. Sam, the dog, and I don't sell my land that I poured my heart's blood in."

"It's called progress," explained Glover. "We aren't taking away people's souls. We aim to tame the river, dam after dam after dam."

"Well, I like things running wild."

Director Elia Kazan casted about one hundred local residents and filmed the battle of wills on the Hiwassee River and Chickamauga Lake. The historic district of Charleston, Tennessee, became "Garthville," and the Cleveland Armory became a studio for indoor settings. After Ella's eviction in the film, a Beechcraft Staggerwing flew over a full reservoir behind a dam, but it was not a TVA dam on the Hiwassee River. The producer filmed TVA's highest dam, Fontana Dam on the Little Tennessee, backward, said David Swafford, a tour guide of *Wild River* filming locations.

AROUND 1890, CREWS CONSTRUCTED a railroad along the Hiwassee River providing rail service from Marietta, Georgia, to Knoxville, Tennessee. The track climbed the 3.5 percent grade over Bald Mountain by switchbacks. By 1898, the two-mile "Hiwassee Loop" coiled around Bald Mountain on a trestle at a 1.5 to 2 percent grade and replaced the inefficient original design. By 1902, the Louisville and Nashville (L&N) Railroad had purchased the line, providing freight and passenger service. Two years later, the company bypassed the Hiwassee River route by building a flatland route from the current Etowah, Tennessee, to Cartersville, Georgia, to connect to the old Western and Atlantic Railroad that ran south from Chattanooga. The mountain route is called the "Old Line" and the 1904 route the "New Line." Around 1941, the TVA upgraded the Old Line tracks at Farner to support the transport of construction materials for its dam project.

After the Old Line ended its passenger service in 1951, its copper ore freight service in the 1960s and the transport of the copper byproduct sulfuric

McFarland's concrete mixing station. *Michael Worsham.*

acid in 2001, organizations and government leaders campaigned to save the abandoned railroad. Tasked with the responsibility of improving the region's socioeconomic opportunities and reversing the copper industry's environmental damages, Glenn Springs Holdings Incorporated offered a loan to the Tennessee Overhill Heritage Association (TOHA) to purchase the rail line. TOHA purchased the line through the Rails-to-Trail program to ensure that the corridor would remain intact if the excursion service failed. In that event, the organization would sell the railroad materials and offer the corridor to the CNF as a trail system.

After the TVA upgraded a thirteen-mile rail section along the Hiwassee River in 2002 to transport new transformers to the Apalachia powerhouse, TOHA and the Tennessee Valley Railroad Museum (TVRM) offered eight thousand guests a scenic trip from Gee Creek to the powerhouse. In 2006, a group of Chinese steel companies repaired the line for a six-month iron ore freight service from Copperhill to the main Chessie-Seaboard Railroad (CSX) line at Etowah. With these improvements, TOHA and TVRM could begin operating passenger train excursions, navigating the Hiwassee (or Bald Mountain) Loop, now listed in the National Register of Historic Places. Today, visitors take a full-day trip on the "Copperhill Special" to Copperhill/McCaysville at the state line or a half-day trip on the "Hiwassee Loop" to the siding at Farner.

About ten river miles downstream from Farner, McFarland—a former railroad community with a store, depot, hotel and post office—grew into a major rail maintenance facility in the late 1800s. Crew members living in repurposed wooden boxcars provided frequent track repairs along this midway section, the original Bald Mountain switchbacks and, later, the upgraded spiral loop.

In the early 1900s, the USFS occupied offices at the McFarland Hotel, called the "Government House," to manage its lands near the Hiwassee River. Occasionally, the railroad delivered USFS firefighting equipment to the rail village. Sparks from train engines occasionally ignited the adjacent woodlands, especially on the loop, requiring a quick USFS and firefighter response. Eventually, the USFS acquired acres of land surrounding McFarland, accessed today by turning west off TN-68 onto FSR-23 at Turtletown. Visitors find the haunting remains of megastructures, such as a tunnel portal built by the TVA in 1941 during the construction of the penstock from its dam to the powerhouse.

In 2017, Cherokee Hiking Club president and retired USFS Engineer Jack Callahan led a group on a hike from the Apalachia Powerhouse on the John Muir NRT/BMT to the "Narrows" on Upper Hiwassee River. After graduating in 1970 from Auburn University with a civil engineering degree, Callahan designed trails and roads for the USFS in Alabama, Arkansas, Texas and Virginia using land gradients, stream crossings, former skid roads, environmental issues and scenic landmarks to design their locations. Retired from the CNF since 2000, the seventy-five-year-old Callahan now helps plan hikes in the CNF and beyond. After passing sheer rock faces as they entered the Narrows, the group found "a favorite lunch spot," wrote Callahan in his trip report, where rocks in the river formed "short-drop waterfalls and deep pools." Beside the trail, the hikers identified fall mushrooms, ginseng, hearts-a-bursting shrubs (*Euonymus americanus*) and paw-paw trees.

The American paw-paw tree (*Asimina triloba*) is the host plant for Tennessee's state butterfly, the large black-and-white striped zebra swallowtail (*Protographium marcellus*), seen in Tennessee from March to August. Its triangular-shaped wings have blue and red spots at the end of its hindwings that taper into long tails. The females lay eggs on paw-paw leaves and trunks individually to prevent the caterpillars from eating each other. The caterpillars may ingest paw-paw plant chemicals that protect it, and the future adult, from predators. The adults feed on milkweeds, redbud trees and blackberry bushes instead of the foul-smelling paw-paw blooms that carrion flies and beetles prefer. With few pollinators and limited seed dispersal, the paw-paw root system extends its range with suckers that sprout across its paw-paw patch.

In the 1970s, the Upper Hiwassee River between the Apalachia Dam and the Hiwassee-Ocoee State Park at US-411 became Tennessee's first state-designated scenic river. The USFS designated the region, bordered by the CNF downriver to the Reliance Bridge, as a hemlock conservation area, a state mussel sanctuary and a habitat management zone for about eight rare plants, including the Ruth's golden aster.

From the late 1800s to early 1900s, botanist Albert Ruth (1844–1932), a University of Tennessee–Knoxville educator and Knoxville city schools superintendent, collected more than eight thousand plants before moving to Texas in 1907. Near McFarland, he collected the aster in the rock crevices in the Hiwassee River Gorge. The rhizomes of Ruth's golden aster find rootholds in the shallow soils in rock crevices. Above its basal leaf cluster, silver-haired leaves grow on hairy, slender, three- to ten-inch-tall stalks that hold branches with florets of sunburst-yellow, daisy-like flower heads from July to September. Botanists rediscovered Ruth's golden aster, lost to science for decades, in the 1970s on boulders in the Hiwassee and Ocoee Rivers. The plant's preference for full sun exposure, some botanists believed, may be why researchers never found it on the phyllite rocks of the Conasauga, Jacks or Tellico Rivers. It was listed as endangered by the USFWS in 1985, and its habitat and limited distribution make it vulnerable to environmental threats, such as water pollution, competitive plant species and human impacts in recreational areas. When an acid spill from a train derailment threatened the aster's habitat, the TVA released water from Apalachia Dam to dilute the chemicals.

Around 2012, organizers met with CNF, TWRA, Tennessee State Parks and tourism officials to establish the Hiwassee River Blueway, which offers

Since I was a Cub Scout, I looked forward to participating in the Great Hiwassee River Raft Race. The rafts were made from bamboo and tied to inner tubes. If you used too much bamboo, it was too heavy and wouldn't go fast; too little, and it wouldn't stay together. You had to make sure that the knots were tied well enough to keep the inner tubes from breaking away. The inspectors checked to make sure you had the correct knot in the correct place and that the raft was safe and stable. The race is judged in design (with crazy costumes), Scout skills and speed. We passed swimmers, fishermen and, of course, other rafts. You look around and it's just you, the water, the trees and the sky. We would chant to keep paddling rhythm and it always echoed, like the trees were talking back to us.

By JACOB WARD, Eagle Scout, Troop 10, Cleveland, Tennessee.

public access areas that connect the paddler's world to the region's natural and cultural resources. Fly-fishing guides lead year-round trips, and the Hiwassee Chapter of Trout Unlimited holds fly-fishing classes. Annually, since 1978, the Cherokee Area Council of the Boy Scouts of America sponsors the Great Hiwassee River Raft Race.

Beyond Reliance, the river parallels TN-30 past the USFS Hiwassee River Picnic Area and the CCC-constructed Quinn Springs Recreation Area south of the riverbed. The USFS Lost Corral Horse Camp and the CNF two-thousand-acre Gee Creek Wilderness, protected by Congress in 1975, at the base of Starr Mountain, lie north of the river. Relics left by miners, producing iron ore for the copper smelting industry in the mid-1880s, remain in the wilderness among the forested cove of boulders, cascades, caves and high rock walls. An irresistible display of spring wildflowers flourishes along the trail. Around 1902, Gee Creek quartzite miners lived at Tennessee Copper Company's village of Austral, now the Hiwassee/Ocoee State Park at Gee Creek. Downstream, the river passes the Hiwassee River Heritage Center (the former site of Fort Cass at Charleston, Tennessee) and the Cherokee Removal Memorial Park at Blythe's Ferry, dedicated to the nearly nine thousand Cherokees and five hundred Creeks held captive here until they crossed the Tennessee River on the Trail of Tears. The Hiwassee and Tennessee Rivers converge at Chickamauga Reservoir Lake near Chattanooga.

STARR MOUNTAIN

Pastor Tazz Reid of Cleveland Community Church grew up in East Tennessee and lives on Starr Mountain. He and his nineteen-year-old Tennessee Walking Horse, Eliazer, have traveled more than three thousand miles on CNF's equestrian trails. In the 1800s, Middle Tennessee farmers began cross-breeding Canadian Pacers with Spanish Gaited Horses, developing the sturdy Tennessee Walking Horse, also known for its regal stance and smooth, four-beat gait. Eliazer, the sure-footed steed on CNF's Sylco, Starr Mountain and Citico Creek Trails, has served as a pack animal for CNF environmental projects.

"Few fishermen know that they owe their day's catch to horses!" said Tazz, former president of the Southern Appalachian Backcountry Horsemen (SABCH). In the 1990s, equestrians partnered with CNF Fisheries Biologist Jim Herrig and the USFWS, TWRA and Trout Unlimited in a brook trout restoration project. In the 1950s, wildlife staff stocked streams with non-native, hatchery-raised rainbow and brown trout that out-competed native brook trout. CNF's Tellico Fish Hatchery began raising endemic Southern Appalachian brook trout, genetically distinct from the northern species, to restock mountain streams and displace, or coexist, with the nonnatives.

"There were CNF restorative projects with a road access," said Herrig, but some ideal aquatic habitats lacked a convenient access and were too distant for hikers to carry the breeding stock or fingerlings. "So, we wondered, would horses work? Could we keep the trout alive?" In 2011, biologists held a trial run. At the hatchery, they loaded 140 rainbow trout into saddlebags.

Tom Speaks, CNF Forest Supervisor from the mid- to late 2000s, joined equestrians on the trout restocking project. In the 1990s, he worked in the land acquisition program. "We put together a fine land acquisition group with some highly capable, motivated individuals," said Speaks. "As Forest Supervisor, I was able to complement them by bringing support for the program and opening a few doors to allow the Forest Service to work successfully on some high-profile acquisitions." "We would not have a completely protected A.T. corridor in the South without his work," said Dave Sherman, former USFS Lands Acquisition Coordinator in Washington, D.C. In 2022, Speaks was inducted into the A.T. Hall of Fame. *Jim Herrig.*

For forty-five minutes, horses, mules, riders and fish traveled two miles to the Green Cove Trout Pond with no loss of life. "We knew then that horses offered a feasible way to transport trout."

In the fall spawning season, before brook trout deposited their eggs in the gravel beds of Sycamore Creek, packhorses carried fish-stunning equipment to a remote watershed. As seventy stunned fish floated to the surface, volunteers netted them and placed them in aerated water containers. Boy Scouts carried the buckets about one hundred feet to load them onto horses. After team members secured the containers to each side of a horse's packsaddle, equestrians transported them two miles up a steep trail to trucks on a nearby road. The fish spawned at the hatchery, grew during the winter into thousands of healthy fingerlings and rode horseback in the spring to restock Tennessee streams.

TWRA official Travis
Scott stocking brook
trout. *Jim Herrig.*

On Starr Mountain, Tazz rides over forty miles of CNF's equestrian trails. When fallen trees blocked many of the bridle paths, volunteers partnered with the USFS to clear them in 2006, which led to the formation of the local chapter of SABCH. The club continues to assist the USFS in maintaining hiking and riding trails. In October 2020, Tazz led a hiking trip on the eastern side of Starr Mountain. Below its western flank, in the late 1700s, Caleb Starr moved from Pennsylvania and established a farm in Conasauga Valley, worked as a trader with the Cherokees and married the granddaughter of Nancy Ward, the beloved Cherokee leader. Caleb and his wife raised twelve children on 640 acres, granted to each Cherokee family in the Treaty of 1817. In 1838, eighty-year-old Caleb and his wife were forced to leave their valley beneath the mountain that bears his name and walk the Trail of Tears.

En route to the trailhead, the hikers drove on TN-315 past Dugan Branch and a meadow with a boulder that had held a CCC camp flagpole and turned on Bullet Creek Road. Morning dew glistened on the pastoral landscape. Freshly cut hay filled old barns. Pygmy and not-so-pygmy goats bounded toward a roadside fence, their bells pealing for a handout. FSR-44, called the "Starr Mountain Motorway" by the CCC boys who built it, led into the CNF. Sunlight streaked through a sylvan palette of golden yellows and bright reds. Falling leaves, retired from service, twirled a dozen pirouettes before settling on the forest floor. Nearby, a mountain bog supported rare plants, like the white fringeless orchid (*Platanthera integrilabia*), in its saturated soils. Faint trails led to Bullet Creek and Yellow Creek Falls near the intersection with FSR-220, where two hunters yielded the roadway at a wide turnout.

To the left, FSR-44 continued along the southern ridge of Starr Mountain, traced the northeast boundary of the Gee Creek Wilderness and looped back to TN-315. The hikers turned right onto FSR-220, past the site of the former White Cliff Mineral Springs and Mountain Health Resort. During the Civil War, Union general William Sherman supposedly destroyed the Tellico Iron Works in Tellico Plains, rode horseback up Starr Mountain to stay at the resort and left it unharmed. After a fire destroyed the resort around 1870, J. Harvey Magill of Niota, Tennessee, rebuilt a lavish inn and managed it for twenty-five years. Surrounding forests provided materials for handcrafted doors, stairways and columns. Guests enjoyed cool mountain air from three-story verandas. Organists welcomed guests to a stately lobby. Bands performed in the ground-floor ballroom. The inn offered natural science and history lectures, an on-site physician and the medicinal benefits of mineral springs. Recreational pleasures included croquet, bowling and horseback riding. Guests hiked to Bullet Creek Falls or to the white cliffs overlooking Tellico River Valley, named for the Cherokees' former town, Great Tellequah. After Magill's death around 1897, the new owner operated the facility as a boardinghouse. In the early 1900s, it became a hunting lodge. Owners razed the weather-worn shell in 1937. It remains a pocket of private property surrounded by the CNF.

The hikers parked at the gated FR-297A (Starr Mountain Extension) to explore Panther Bluff, the boulder-strewn hideout of the hermit Mason Evans (1824–1892). Rejected by his lady love, Evans, a former schoolteacher, shunned society and lived a solitary life in the wilds of Starr Mountain, occasionally venturing into the valley to sleep in barns or raid farms for food. Tazz's grandmother told him that a farmer once found his rooster missing. He approached the hermit, plundering around his farm.

"Mason," he asked, "you got my rooster?"

No reply.

"Have you seen my rooster?" he insisted.

Mason finally mumbled, "Well, it was tough, anyway."

A kindhearted soul noticed Mason's threadbare dungarees and hung a new pair on a line for him to find when he passed by. Later, the farmer saw Mason combing a neighbor's field with the new overalls. He had tied the two legs together and slung it over his shoulder like a knapsack. He was tossing veggies into its open waistband.

After crossing two wildlife grazing fields, the hikers bushwhacked about a quarter of a mile to Panther Bluff on the northwest edge of Starr Mountain.

Tazz Reid leads a Starr Mountain hike. *Tazz Reid.*

Peachy-yellow sassafras saplings offered a rooted handhold down the steep, leaf-littered descent. Greenbrier barbs grabbed a pant leg or two. A brown leaf from a white oak circled off its twig and plunged stem-first to its inevitable fate. Ken Jones, a Starr Mountain resident, has captured bobcats, deer, bear, wild boar and an armadillo on his trail camera, but only energetic squirrels busied themselves about the treetops that day. The buck rubs of a white-tailed deer on red maple trees signaled the upcoming breeding season. Turkeys called from a ridgeline but remained out of sight.

The hikers climbed under rocky overhangs, slid around house-sized boulders and scrambled up a rugged incline to Panther Bluffs. At Mason's cave-like opening, a stone slab stretched into the narrow, dark cavity for at least eight feet, perfectly sized for a hermit's cozy cocoon. Perhaps Mason had ground meal in a smooth rock depression at the cave's entrance and collected water at a spring "down the hillside, about a stone's throw away," said Tazz, who camped at Panther Bluff thirty years ago. On a nearby rock shelf, cliff swallows had nested above a former roosting site for pygmy bats. "They're the size of a fingertip. Tap sleeping pygmies and watch them sway but never wake up."

Did the rejection of his true love or mental illness send Mason into forty years of solitude? Were his mind and soul tormented, as novelist R. Frank McKinney claimed? Did he find peace and fulfillment in his cave-like home far from economic, political and social strife? Did he find comfort among the wild creatures on his Starr Mountain throne overlooking Caleb Starr's Conasauga Valley? "People say he was crazy," said Tazz, "but I say, he just had the guts to do what I always wanted to do."

Lawbreakers, moonshiners and the Cherokees also found hideaways among the rocky caves and bluffs and underground passageways on Starr Mountain. After two USFS employees discovered ancient Native American art in a cave on private property near the mountain in 1980, the CNF archaeologist contacted University of Tennessee–Knoxville anthropology professor Charles H. Faulkner. *National Geographic* funded his research team's Mud Glyph Cave Project to study the Southeast's first discovery of mud figures drawn by an ancient civilization. Mud glyphs are images scratched into the mud-covered walls of a cave. Around AD 1300, Native Americans crawled into the cave's opening to enter a high chamber. With the light of a rivercane torch, they drew hundreds of animals, stick figures and line drawings in the mud on the walls. The team mapped the cave, surveyed and photographed the images and collected soil samples from floor depressions. The Smithsonian Institute evaluated fireplace charcoal to identify plant products and to estimate the age of carbon-based materials. The Mud Glyph Cave is sealed today to protect the sacred drawings from human mischief.

Conasauga Creek tumbles about thirty feet to form Conasauga Falls and then courses beneath the northern end of Starr Mountain, which is "shaped like a ship," said Tazz. The State of Tennessee's Bowers Spring Lookout Tower rests on its narrowed bow section, pointing northeast toward Tellico Lake. Its port and starboard surfaces drop off like the sides of a cruise liner.

PART II

Tellico Ranger District

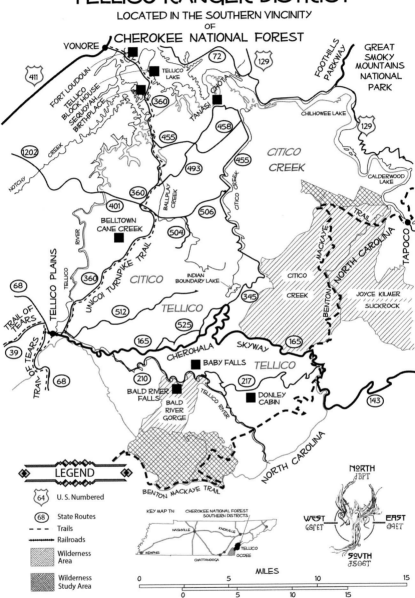

TELLICO RANGER DISTRICT
LOCATED IN THE SOUTHERN VINCINITY
OF
CHEROKEE NATIONAL FOREST

VONORE

GREAT
SMOKY
MOUNTAINS
NATIONAL
PARK

72

129

411

FOOTHILLS PARKWAY

FORT LOUDOUN

TELLICO
LAKE

TELLICO BLOCK HOUSE
SEQUOYAH BIRTHPLACE

360

TANASI

CHOTA

458

CHILHOWEE LAKE

129

455

CREEK

1202

493

455

CITICO
CREEK

CALDERWOOD
LAKE

NOTCHY

360

BALLPLAY CREEK

506

CITICO CREEK

401

BELLTOWN
CANE CREEK

504

BENTON MACKAYE TRAIL

NORTH CAROLINA

TAPOCO

RIVER

TELLICO PLAINS

UNICOI TURNPIKE TRAIL

CITICO

INDIAN
BOUNDARY LAKE

345

CITICO
CREEK

JOYCE KILMER
SLICKROCK

68

360

512

TELLICO

525

165

BENTON

39

TRAIL OF TEARS

TRAIL OF TEARS

165

CHEROHALA   SKYWAY

TELLICO

68

210

BABY FALLS

217

143

BALD RIVER
FALLS

BALD
RIVER
GORGE

TELLICO RIVER

DONLEY
CABIN

NORTH CAROLINA

LEGEND

64   U. S. Numbered

68   State Routes

- - -   Trails

+++   Railroads

▨   Wilderness
Area

▩   Wilderness
Study Area

STARR   General Recreational
MNT.   Districts

BENTON MACKAYE TRAIL

KEY MAP TN   CHEROKEE NATIONAL FOREST
SOUTHERN DISTRICTS

NASHVILLE   KNOXVILLE

MEMPHIS   TELLICO
OCOEE

CHATTANOOGA

MILES

0   5   10   15

0   5   10   15

KILOMETERS

NORTH
�112ꓤ0И

WEST
ꓕƧƎꟽ

EAST
ꓕƧⱯƎ

SOUTH
ꓕⱤꓕ Ɑ0Ƨ

Ken Czarnomski, Phoenix2Reach@gmail.com.

COKER CREEK

In 2021, near the Coker Creek Visitor Center, Joseph Kenneth (Ken) Dalton and his wife, Kathleen (Kat), lived on Hot Water Road, named in years past by moonshiners warning outsiders that they would be "in hot water" if they proceeded farther. Ken (1931–2021) grew up in the Coker Creek community, cradled between the Conasauga and Coker Creeks, on land his ancestors had settled in the 1800s. His widowed mother had raised seven children on their forty-acre farm. As a schoolboy, Ken worked in the evenings for farmers, raising crops for the Stokely Brothers Cannery in Tellico Plains (later Stokely-Van Camp Incorporated).

In 1898, four Stokely brothers grew up farming their family's large fields. A neighbor jokingly asked their father what he could grow in such rocky ground. "It'll grow boys!" he replied. As adults, the brothers and A.R. Swann opened a food processing plant on the French Broad River near Newport, Tennessee. They worked "without disruptive discord or struggle for power," wrote Wilma Dykeman, Tennessee state historian and wife of James R. Stokely Jr., son of the cannery's president. The Newport business "multiplied into other little plants up scattered rivers and streams." Between 1926 and 1982, Stokely employed locals to work at its Tellico Plains plant and in its crop fields during the canning season. Farmers, like those who hired young Ken, harvested beans, peas, tomatoes and corn to sell to the canning company.

Ken's brother Thomas joined the CCC at F-2 Camp Rolling Stone, Company 1454 at Coker Creek, built by the enrollees in 1933. Camp

Ben Ellis plows corn near Coker Creek, 1946. *Tennessee State Library and Archives.*

activities, like tennis, baseball and schoolwork, balanced their labor in the field, managing CNF's roads, trails, forests and wildfires. On Thanksgiving Day 1935, four camp cooks prepared a feast of ham, roast turkey, mashed potatoes, giblet gravy, Georgia-style candied yams, buttered peas, creamed corn, Queen olives and rolls with fresh creamery butter, as well as mincemeat pie, chocolate cake, pumpkin pie and doughnuts for dessert. Like many enrollees, Thomas fought in World War II after his discharge from the CCC.

By age seventeen, Ken left Coker Creek to work with polo horses at Bendabout Farms near McDonald, Tennessee. He became a champion rider, carving his own mallets for polo matches. When he moved back to Coker Creek, he worked for logging companies. In the 1960s and 1970s, he became a blacksmith for the Tellico Mountain Camp (later called Coker Creek Village). The Christian summer camp, established in 1963 by Sanford and Esther Gray, offered hiking and horseback riding trips into the adjoining CNF. At the camp, Ken also provided farrier services for the annual wagon train that promoted the construction of a highway between the CNF and North Carolina's Nantahala National Forest, now called the Cherohala Skyway. Later, he helped the CNF fight wildfires.

Ken's hobbies of carving toys and making furniture as a boy became skilled trades in metalwork, basket weaving and woodcarving. Kat excelled in painting, jewelry making and other arts. In the 1970s, they bought the Waucheesi Weavers business, started around 1949 by Maggie Parton Murphy. Maggie reportedly wove a cloth on hand looms at the Arrowmont School of Arts and Crafts in Gatlinburg, Tennessee, to present to Eleanor Roosevelt. The Daltons renamed the weaving center Coker Creek Gallery. They led workshops in six states, taught classes at John C. Campbell Folk School for twenty years, demonstrated their craftsmanship to international guests at the Cultural Olympiad Festival ahead of the Ocoee River Olympic games and helped organize the Coker Creek Artisans. In France, they exhibited Southern Appalachian traditional arts at Euro-Disney (now Disneyland Resort–Paris). Museums around the world, including the Smithsonian Institute, have displayed their handiwork.

"Remember the falls, Kat?" asked the quiet, soft-spoken ninety-year-old as he leaned back in his chair with a nostalgic grin. "That's where I first kissed you, on that rock at the base of the falls. Remember?"

A cabbage field and Stokely's cannery, Tellico Plains, 1950. *Tennessee State Library and Archives.*

"Over forty-five years ago," eighty-three-year-old Kathleen whispered. "Of course I remember." The couple met at the Tellico Youth Camp, where he was a blacksmith, and she managed the Coker Creek Artisans. As a child, Kathleen traveled to Coker Creek with her parents on Sunday afternoons. After she graduated from high school, she moved to her five acres purchased in the Coker Creek area. CNF forests and local history inspired her artistic talents.

As a Coker Creek Ruritan Club member and cofounder of the Tennessee Overhill Heritage Association (TOHA) in 1990, Ken helped preserve his hometown's natural and cultural history. When the USFS planned to close the washed-out Coker Creek Falls access road in 1978, Ken and Harold Witt

Ken and Kat Dalton, 2021. *Author's photo.*

suggested that the Ruritan Club adopt a reconstruction project. As youngsters, Witt and Dalton had camped often at Bears Den, a rock outcrop near the falls. After raising $8,000 for the restoration of the parking lot and the one-mile-long roadway, the club worked with the Forest Service to complete the seven-year-long project. "I wanted older, less agile folks to be able to visit the falls area that I'd been exploring since I was a boy," said Dalton. In 1986, the USFS opened the restored access road. On the White House lawn in 1988, President Ronald Reagan presented the Pride in America Award to Witt, Dalton and the Tellico District Ranger Guy Thurmond. "The Forest Service said that a civic group building a road on public land had never been done," added Dalton. CNF's Coker Creek Falls is about eight miles south of the Coker Creek Welcome Center on FSR-2138. The trail enters a narrow gorge with bank-to-bank rock ledges forming a cascading creek.

At the Coker Creek Welcome Center, Mary Jane Reece pulled resources off the shelves to support her mental recall of local history. "We love people to express an interest in the history of our little community," she said. For thirty years, Mary Jane, the treasurer for the Coker Creek Economic Development Group Incorporated (also called Coker Creek Heritage Group), has lived in the area. Her husband, Millard Brown Reece Jr. (1935–2021), was the nephew of Congressman B. Carroll Reece (1889–1961), who delivered the farewell commencement speech at his alma mater, Watauga Academy in Butler, Tennessee, before the TVA's reservoir submerged the institution. The post office is located next door to the museum. From the 1940s to 1990s, Mamie Murphy served as the Coker Creek postmaster. After mailing letters to the governor for sixteen years suggesting that the state motto, "Volunteer State," be added to Tennessee license plates, the state added the slogan in 1977.

In 1819, the Calhoun Treaty, known as the Hiwassee Purchase, removed Cherokee families from the region between today's Hiwassee, Little Tennessee and Tennessee Rivers, leaving a southeastern section under Cherokee ownership. Some families, like Old Roman Nose and his children, Betsy, George, Ginnesa and Winny, living in Cades Cove (now in Great Smoky Mountains National Park), moved to the Cherokee lands, known as "Eunnaika" and later called Coker or Coqua Creek. Betsy Coker became a revered leader of the Coker Creek Cherokee community but died in 1838 in Illinois on the Forced March to the western Indian Territory and was buried in an unmarked grave.

In the 1820s and 1830s, gold was discovered in Coker Creek and its tributaries, like Dalton Branch, Peels Branch and Hot Water Branch. The Six Mile, Whippoorwill and Conasauga Creeks and the White Oak Flats between the headwaters of Ballplay and Citico Creeks also revealed their golden secrets. Brazen prospectors with no respect for the Cherokee landowners flooded into the region. Even Fort Armistead, constructed in 1832 and manned by the U.S. Army to deter the unlawful entry of miners, failed to cease the relentless rush to strike it rich. After the federal government forced the Cherokees to move west of the Mississippi, Coker Creek mining operations expanded. By 1864, an estimated one thousand workers had extracted gold in the Coker Creek region, transporting most of it to the Dahlonega, Georgia U.S. Mint office. When mining companies resumed operations after the Civil War, miners searched unsuccessfully for the main vein until the 1970s.

Around 1970, the Coker Creek Ruritan Club organized the Autumn Gold Festival at the Tellico Mountain Camp, celebrating its gold fever history during CNF's fall-color splendor. Each October, the festival held handicraft, syrup making and musket rifle demonstrations; panning for gold, wood chopping and crosscut sawing contests; and feasts of wild boar, barbecued chicken and roast beef. "Old mining prospectors," announced a festival's program, "will have their long toms, sluice troughs, and gold pans in full operation." In the CNF, today, the hand-panning method of recreational gold collecting is only permitted in designated streams. As natural resource managers, the USFS and the Tennessee Department of Environment and Conservation (TDEC) monitor the effects of human-caused disturbances in aquatic habitats. Contact the Tellico Ranger Station for up-to-date gold panning information.

The Coker Creek Welcome Center is located beside an ancient pathway that connected Tugaloo, the capital of the Cherokee Lower Villages, near today's Toccoa, Georgia, with the present-day cities of Hiawassee, Georgia, and Hayesville and Murphy, North Carolina. From Murphy, travelers cut through Unicoi Gap in the Southern Appalachians and entered today's Tennessee. This 1700s Cherokee/English settlers' trading path continued past Coker Creek and the Cherokee town of Great Tellequo to the Cherokee Overhill Towns of Chota and Tanasi. Before the TVA filled its Tellico Reservoir, archaeologists uncovered Cherokee burial sites in the Overhill region; 191 bodies were reinterred in a burial mound near the Sequoyah Birthplace Museum. At today's Chota memorial site, raised eight feet to remain above the reservoir's flood level, the Eastern Band of the Cherokee Indians placed a gravestone at the reinterred remains of War Chief Oconostota. In 1989, the TVA and Tennessee Historical Commission Foundation erected a monument for the submerged site of Tanasi. The state and a river now bear the name of this Cherokee village, first recorded as "Tennessee" on Lieutenant Henry Timberlake's 1762 map. Signs near the Sequoyah Birthplace Museum direct visitors to these memorial sites.

When the British sought the Cherokees' allegiance during the French and Indian War (1754–63), the Cherokee leader Attakullakulla agreed to send warriors if the British built a fort near the Overhill Villages to protect their families during the conflict. Led by Captain Paul Demere, British soldiers and sixty packhorses carrying equipment departed Fort Prince George (near present-day Clemson, South Carolina) and entered the region via the Unicoi (or Unicoy/Overhill) Trading Path. Ten days and one hundred miles later, the Cherokee leader Old Hop welcomed them into the Overhill country. The troops passed the Cherokee towns of Great Tellequo, Chota, Tanasi, Toqua and Tommatley to build the first British fort west of the Appalachians on the current Little Tennessee River. The diamond-shaped Fort Loudoun was named for John Campbell, the 4th Earl of Loudoun and the British commander of its North American forces.

After Demere's interpreter, William Shorey Sr. (1720–1762), fluent in the Cherokee language, left Fort Loudoun, poor communication caused splintered relationships between the British and the Cherokees. By 1760, broken promises and cultural misunderstandings by both parties had led

SE-QUO-YAH

Sequoyah (George Gist, circa 1775–1843) created the Cherokee alphabet around 1820. *Tennessee State Library and Archives.*

to a Cherokee attack on Fort Loudoun. After the British surrendered, Oconostota and a group of Cherokees escorted about two hundred troops and fifty civilians from Fort Loudoun to camp at the mouth of Cane Creek on the Tellico River. The next morning, the Cherokee escorts were gone, but nearly one thousand Cherokee warriors surrounded the camp. After they killed Captain Demere and about twenty men, the rest of the British became Cherokee prisoners. However, Attakullakulla saved his friend Captain John Stuart from his captors. Historians believe that the Cherokee attack was in retaliation for a group of Cherokees killed by the British at Fort Prince George.

In 1813, the Cherokees signed an agreement with Tennessee and Georgia businessmen to widen the Unicoi Trail as a wagon road, which granted use of the "free and public highway" for twenty years, after which the road "with all of its advantages, shall be surrendered up and transferred to the Cherokee Nation." The Unicoi Turnpike Company completed the construction project by 1819. Livestock drovers joined merchants with wagonloads of goods on the busy turnpike. A tollgate operator near Unicoi Gap at the North Carolina/Tennessee border collected fees to help pay for the privately funded roadway. Betsy Coker, George Coker and others constructed stock stations every eight to ten miles to offer food, supplies and overnight accommodations. Cherokee families with farms along the route sold corn to the men herding livestock. From East Tennessee to the Piedmont in South Carolina, packhorses transported deer hides that the Cherokees traded for blankets, tools, guns and other items. The deer hides shipped from Charleston to England became leather gloves, knee britches and book covers, especially for Bibles.

On the Unicoi Turnpike near Coker Creek, Phillip Merony and James Milligan established a prominent waystation with a store, an inn, a spring, livestock pens and home-cooked meals. Colonel Gideon Morgan Jr. (1778–1851), a commander of a Cherokee regiment in the War of 1812, and his wife, Mary Margaret (Sevier), of Cherokee descent, discovered gold on Hot Water Branch. Prospectors began crowding the turnpike in the 1820s and 1830s. They stopped at Merony's for supplies. Morgan, however, wrote a letter to Andrew Jackson, requesting that the U.S. government build a fort to prevent miners from trespassing on Cherokee-owned lands. In 1832, General W.K. Armistead and troops arrived, removed Merony's Stand and established Camp Armistead. In 1835, the encampment—now fortified with defensive walls, barracks and other structures—became Fort Armistead.

By 1838, the U.S. military had removed about three thousand Georgia and North Carolina Cherokees from their homes, holding them at Fort Butler near today's Murphy, North Carolina. From Fort Butler, the soldiers marched them nineteen miles along the Unicoi Turnpike to Fort Armistead—the year that both parties had agreed to return the route to full Cherokee ownership. The turnpike instead became a portion of the Trail of Tears, an estimated one-thousand-mile journey to the Indian Territory (now Oklahoma). In East Tennessee, the army held men, women and children at Fort Armistead and marched them in divided groups past Coker Creek on two different routes toward Tellico Plains. The routes then passed the current cities of Etowah and Englewood on their way to present-day Athens. The contingent walked south to Calhoun and crossed the Hiwassee River by ferry to Fort Cass, the removal headquarters near present-day Charleston, Tennessee. After the Forced Removal, Robert Tunnel, Coker Creek's postmaster from 1831 to 1839, acquired the Fort Armistead and surrounding property but presumably moved from the area after 1842.

During the Civil War, Union and Confederate forces traveled along the Unicoi Turnpike. In 1862, the Confederate troops of William C. Walker's Battalion of Thomas' Legion of Cherokee Indians and Mountaineers (69th North Carolina Regiment) occupied the site near Fort Armistead as Camp Coker Creek. Army deserters and other renegades hid in the forests along the turnpike to attack or rob travelers. Bushwhackers and Civil War veterans are buried at the Coker Creek and Ironsburg Cemeteries.

For decades, the former stock stand, Cherokee removal fort and Confederate encampment remained deserted. Better roads left the turnpike abandoned. Leaf litter covered foundations, trees rooted in old fire rings and voices of the past faded, except for stories told by the locals. When Ken and Kat Dalton bought the twenty-seven Fort Armistead acres, "old-timers told us that Indians were held at a stockade here," said Kat, "until soldiers moved them west." The Daltons kept the property undisturbed by farming activities or development. After Ken found artifacts, such as buttons from an 1830s U.S. Army uniform, and a friend showed him depressions left from the old fort and turnpike, the couple contacted research archaeologist Brett H. Riggs in 1990. The CNF archaeologist also became interested in the property. USFS Lands Acquisition Officer Lewis Kearney began a long process of talking with the Daltons about selling it to the Forest Service. "I remember the exact spot where I was standing when they agreed to sell," he said. The CNF later awarded the Daltons a plaque in recognition of their interest in preserving this significant heritage site.

After the CNF purchased the property in 2006, the national forest entered into an agreement with the Research Laboratories of Archaeology at the University of North Carolina–Chapel Hill to inventory the tract's archaeological resources. From 2008 to 2012, Dr. Brett Riggs, a research archaeologist specializing in Cherokee studies, led the efforts to map and evaluate the area, identifying sites such as a powder magazine, barracks, stone-lined pits, rock bases of clay-and-stick chimneys and structural foundations.

In the 1990s, the Blue Ridge Heritage Initiative and its partners began designating cultural trails in North Carolina, Georgia and Tennessee, including Cherokee Heritage Trails. As part of this program, the TOHA collaborated with the CNF and others to launch Tennessee's Unicoi Turnpike Project. In 1999, after the White House Council named the Unicoi Turnpike portion between Murphy and Vonore as one of the nation's sixteen National Millennium Flagship Trails, TOHA and its partners—including the CNF, Partners of the Cherokee National Forest,

Benton MacKaye Trail Association, Coker Creek Economic Development Group, Hiwassee Hiking Club, National Trail of Tears Association, Eastern Band of the Cherokee Indians and Tribal Historic Preservation Offices—helped fund the turnpike project; mark an auto/hiking trail; improve the Unicoi Gap parking area; and create exhibits, trail guides and maps.

At Vonore, the Unicoi Turnpike National Millennium Trail auto route travels south on TN-360 past Fort Loudoun, the Tellico Blockhouse, the Sequoyah Birthplace Museum and the Chota and Tanasi memorials. At Tellico Plains, it follows TN-68 toward Coker Creek. Beside the welcome center, it turns onto the paved and graveled Joe Brown Highway, named in 1923 after a North Carolina politician and sawmill owner who lived near the state line. At Unicoi Gap, the roadway descends to Murphy.

About 0.3 mile south of the welcome center on the Joe Brown Highway, a graveled road leads to the Doc Rogers Fields. A CNF trail passes through former farm fields near the juncture of Long Branch and Coker Creek, restored by the USFS with native grasses—an ideal habitat for Bobwhite Quail (*Colinus virginianus*). Habitat loss, pesticide use and coyotes have led to the decline in the East's only native quail species. As an indicator of success, Tazz Reid reported a covey of bobwhite quails there in 2020. The Unicoi Mountain Horse Loop Trail passes the fields, turns southeast to cross Long Branch and climbs to Peels Top. Joining the Benton MacKaye Trail across the ridge at the state line, the horse trail circles west toward Unicoi Gap on Joe Brown Highway, passing a spur trail to the skeletal remains of Doc Rogers's grand home on Unicoi Mountain.

After William (Doc) Alfred Rogers (1883–1967), a native of Violet, North Carolina, earned his medical degree, he opened a Tellico Plains medical office in 1908. Around 1949, he and his wife, Arminda, built a grand, three-story rock home on Unicoi Mountain and lived there for six years. In the mid-1950s, Doc moved from his mountain home, purchased the quarry site of the Tennessee Rock Products Company in Tellico Plains and converted its silo into an apartment building. When fire safety regulations halted his plans, Doc practiced medicine in his house built beside the "Roundhouse" while Floyd Davis managed the home on Unicoi Mountain. In the 1960s, the CNF purchased the mountain home, later consumed by fire in the 1980s. A tall chimney and three rock walls with large window openings remain at the site. Water seeps through the rock base of the fireplace and flows downhill through the center of the home where low-lying vegetation claims the old floor space. A moss-covered springhead lies fifty feet uphill. A rusted ambulance, marked with a faded red cross, rests on its side.

Dr. W.A. Rogers's "Roundhouse," 1954. *Coker Creek Welcome Center.*

Around 2004, volunteers and the USFS completed the Unicoi Turnpike Hiking Trail in the CNF between Doc Rogers Fields and Unicoi Gap. From the trailhead on Joe Brown Highway, hikers can walk to the former CCC Camp Rolling Stone. The encampment included a headquarters, barracks, cabins, school, mess hall, garage and other structures. The workers diverted

Dalton Branch into a rock-lined swimming hole. A regenerated forest now covers much of the site, but explorers can locate foundations, chimney piles, stonework and rock steps. The CCC built bridges and widened roads, such as the Old Furnace Road and Joe Brown Highway. In 1986, the journalist Fred Brown interviewed Frank Hawk, a former Camp Rolling Stone supervisor, a Coker Creek resident and the grandson of a Cherokee. "Our main project was truck trail building so the Forest Service could get timber out." He also organized crews to help the CNF fight wildfires. Coker Creek native Myrtle Tilley told Brown that she married a man from Mississippi stationed at the CCC camp. During the Great Depression, "everybody was destitute," she said. She needed a job. The men at the camp hired her to wash their clothes. With a washboard in a black pot and a bar of soap made from lye and pork fat, she scrubbed a shirt for ten cents and a pair of pants for fifteen cents. After the CCC departed the camp in 1937, the Chattanooga/Cherokee Area Boy Scout Council leased the 15.2 acres from the USFS in 1938 for a summer camp for advanced Scouts. They hiked in the CNF, worked fifty hours on camp improvement projects to earn "beaver" status and completed services to earn a "Rolling Stone" insignia.

The Unicoi Turnpike Hiking Trail passes the CCC swimming hole and reaches the gravestone of a Union soldier that reads, "Amaziah (Hamp) Dotson. Killed by Rebels Here July 3, 1864. The Old Toll Gate Stood Nearby." The trail crosses the auto route a few times before ending at the juncture with the Benton MacKaye Trail at Unicoi Gap.

In 2009, the federal government designated the Trail of Tears between Hayesville, North Carolina, and Athens, Tennessee, as a national historic trail. In a joint venture with the USFS in 2012, The Conservation Fund purchased a 461-acre tract containing a portion of the trail east of the Joe Brown Highway from the River Valley AgCredit. In 2014, a year before the Forest Service was set to acquire the tract, it used the proven method of building "tank traps" and earthen berms to prevent erosion and block a road to illegal off-road vehicles. This long-accepted practice, however, was not the best option for this sensitive historic section of the woods road. The agency also failed to obtain permission from the partnering land conservation organization that owned the land at that time or conduct required environmental and cultural analyses, including tribal consultation.

From 2015 to 2019, the USFS negotiated a legal agreement that included a remediation plan for the trail in consultation with tribal government officials from the Cherokee Nation, the Eastern Band of the Cherokee Indians, the United Keetoowah Band of the Cherokee Indians, the Muscogee (Creek) Nation and other federally recognized tribes of the Creek Confederacy; the Tennessee State Historic Preservation Office; the National Park Service's National Trails Office; the National Trail of Tears Association; the Coker Creek Heritage Group; the Advisory Council on Historic Preservation; and other stakeholders. After the legal agreement was signed in December 2019, Cherokee representatives joined a team of Western Carolina University archaeologists, led by Brett Riggs, who has studied the Trail of Tears for thirty years, to conduct the archaeological work to support the trail remediation efforts.

In late January, USFS staff, personnel from the Eastern Band of Cherokee Indians and the United Keetoowah Band of Cherokee Indians and community volunteers began repairing the trail. An excavator flattened down the berms as an archaeologist from the Eastern Band of Cherokee Indians observed. During the four-day operations, the crews rolled out jute netting to control erosion, staked down bales of straw, built a split-rail fence and planted grass seed. Near Peels Branch, volunteers planted native Cherokee wildflowers, such as Sochan, bee balm and turtlehead. After the completion of the repair work, the USFS closed the area to visitors for at least three years to allow the site to heal. To monitor the trail's recovery, volunteers took turns each month walking the trail, sending photos and a short report to the project coordinator. The tribal archaeologist from the Eastern Band of the Cherokee Indians also periodically visited to monitor the trail recovery.

"People had a passion for the restoration project and kept going to the point of exhaustion," said the USFS Southern Regional Office Trail of Tears Coordinator Melissa Twaroski at a debriefing dinner at the Coker Creek Ruritan Club building.

Like the Trail of Tears, Fort Armistead is a sacred site to the Cherokees. "The USFS considers it too fragile to open to the public," said Mary Jane. The Coker Creek Heritage Group, the USFS, local leaders and tribal officials plan to discuss future interpretive public options for the fort, "possibly a trail with signage or guided tours. The Coker Creek Heritage Group has an empty room beside the welcome center that could hold a Fort Armistead educational exhibit." For now, high-tech security cameras and motion sensors monitor the protected heritage resource. In May 2022, the National Historic Landmarks Review Committee approved Fort Armistead as a National Historic Landmark, and the National Park Service's National Trails Office approved the Coker Creek Welcome Center and the Charles Hall Museum and Heritage Center in Tellico Plains as official interpretive facilities on the Trail of Tears National Historic Trail.

TELLICO PLAINS

Before the 1817 and 1819 U.S. treaties, Cherokees inhabited the Tellico Plains area. In the 1880s, a Smithsonian researcher recorded about fifteen ancient Indian burial mounds, now lost to the ages. In June 2019, the Tennessee Trail of Tears Association and the Charles Hall Museum hosted the "Great Tellico History Day" to honor their heritage. Special guests included members of the Cherokee Nation, the United Keetoowah Band of the Cherokee Indians, the Muscogee (Creek) Nation and the Eastern Band of the Cherokee Indians. The CNF archaeologist presented the history of the Unicoi Turnpike Trail, and Brett Riggs spoke about the removal routes of the Trail of Tears. Organizer Pam Hall Mathews, a museum board member and daughter of Tellico Plains' former mayor Charles Hall, concluded the Monroe County bicentennial event with a Trail of Tears Remembrance Walk and ceremony.

Throughout Charles Hall's adult life and thirty-plus years as a mayor and civic leader, he collected regional stories, photographs and artifacts. In 2003, Hall (1924–2014) and his wife, Billie (1925–2015), opened the museum, which preserves more than ten thousand items. The displays include a molar of an extinct horse species found on the North River in 1977; pig iron spikes from the Tellico Iron Works found in the Tellico River in 1986; firearm, military and tool collections; Cherokee heritage items; America's largest display of telephone equipment; and a fire finder from a Starr Mountain Fire Tower. As a boy growing up in Tellico Plains, Charles sat "around the old pot-bellied stove at my father's country store," he wrote, "listening to elderly men tell of their exploits in the late 1800s and early 1900s."

Tellico Plains country store, 1941. *Tennessee State Library and Archives.*

Perhaps young Charles listened to tales about millers, tanners, ginseng farmers, iron and slate miners and railroad workers with the 1880s Nashville and Tellico Railroad (later the 1910 Athens and Tellico Railway, purchased by the L&N Railroad in 1911). Surely, loggers spun a yarn or two in Hall's country store about their work with the 1891–1905 Heyser Lumber Company, the 1890s–1924 C.A. Scott and Company and the 1906–24 Tellico River/Babcock Lumber Company.

Above: Cold Spring Tower. *Tennessee State Library and Archives.*

Opposite: CNF's Assistant Forest Supervisor E.W. Renshaw, with SX Radio, 1939. *B.W. Chumney Collection/Thurman Parish Jr.*

In 1925, the CNF acquired Babcock's forty-four thousand acres in the Tellico region and, in the 1930s, forty-seven thousand acres in the Citico/ Slickrock region. Gottfred Wilhelm (Pop) Munz purchased Babcock's former hotel, a popular lodge during the annual CNF boar and bear hunting season. When Charles was ten years old, the USFS established CCC camps nearby. When Charles was in his twenties, the U.S. government opened a Tellico Plains internment camp for two hundred World War II German prisoners. The prisoner Gunter Espich painted "his view of the camp," wrote Pam, "as seen through the woven wire fence" surrounding the camp. The oil painting is now displayed in the museum.

After the CNF formed the Tellico Ranger District around 1925, District Ranger R.L. Foute operated the ranger station in downtown Tellico Plains. The staff built lookout towers on Hemlock Knob and Buck, Beaverdam and Waucheesi Balds. The USFS also built the Cold Spring Lookout on Salt Springs Mountain in the northern section of the Citico region. Crews strung telephone wires for hundreds of miles from the lookout towers to the ranger station.

In the 1920s and 1930s, the USFS began experimenting with a safer, less costly and more reliable means of communication for fire detection and wildfire management. "Cranking the phone or picking up the receiver to talk to the ranger during an electrical storm was about as hazardous as reaching for a rattlesnake in a gunny sack," wrote one USFS historian. After abandoning the idea to release homing pigeons at firelines to carry messages back to headquarters and to signal Morse code messages by deflecting sunlight with shuttered mirrors, the Forest Service pursued research in wireless electronic communication systems at its Forest Service Radio Laboratory in the Northwest.

Gael Simson, a World War I radio operator and electronics scientist, studied lightning storm patterns for the USFS to help predict which ones started wildfires. At the lab, he built a fifty-pound transmitter-receiver system and traveled with it across the country to test frequencies. By 1934, USFS Electrical Engineer Harold Lawson had headed to the Southeast from the lab with his new portable, lightweight, low-powered radio equipment to demonstrate its use to Forest Service personnel. In August, he arrived at the CNF supervisor's office in Athens, Tennessee. A church member and hardware store owner suggested that Lawson recruit his electronics-minded son, Gaylord Knight, to help him string a wire from the church steeple to an antenna across the street. After the father had purchased one of the first home radios in Athens, Gaylord had studied the model and built his own set. He had operated a radio repair shop since grammar school. Lawson, impressed with the young man, encouraged the CNF to hire Gaylord to repair and maintain their telephone and radio systems. In 1936, Gaylord, CNF's communication technician, moved his office from Athens to the new CNF administrative office in Cleveland. By 1941, Gaylord became Region 8's first USFS communications officer in Atlanta and helped the USFS transition from phones to radios. In 1934, the region reported seven thousand miles of telephone lines and fifteen radios. Forty years later, at Gaylord's retirement, the Southern region maintained four thousand radios and no telephone lines.

In 1937, the year that the Tellico Ranger District moved its headquarters from Tellico Plains to abandoned CCC Camp Chickasaw, the CNF began improving firefighting communications by placing radios in its fire trucks and lookout towers. Officials noted, however, an increase in small but frequent wildfires and hired W.R. Murphy, a Texas psychologist, to investigate the issue. For months, Murphy interviewed the locals. One Sunday, he joined a preacher, blessing the town from a fire tower, who shared the town's secret with him. The townspeople needed firewood to heat homes and cooking stoves, but the USFS only allowed people to collect fallen, dead timber. So, residents started a small fire, cut down trees for a firebreak, helped extinguish the flames and then later gathered the charred wood. When the CNF began marking trees for public use, the frequent fires ceased.

A notorious CNF arsonist, Coker Creek resident John Wesley Irons, evaded law enforcement for eighteen years. After a Forest Service agent arrested him in August 2007 at a Walmart parking lot, he waived his rights for an attorney and consented to an interview. An agent read his Miranda rights on the grounds of the 1794–1807 Tellico Blockhouse, a military outpost near Fort Loudoun, before questioning him. The sixty-year-old told officials that he began setting fires as a teenager and had started hundreds of CNF fires, including one on Starr Mountain. He admitted that he had burned fifty buildings, including the Coker Creek Village. He also admitted that he had set fire to a USFS employee's home with him and his family inside and later called the man to apologize. Irons was indicted on seven counts of setting fire to timber and seven counts of maliciously damaging government property with a significant risk of injury.

In 2011, after Irons pleaded guilty in a Knoxville federal court to one count of arson in 2002 and another in 2007, the government dropped the other charges. The court sentenced him to five years in prison, and he was banned from the CNF for life. Homeland Security officers at Glynco, the Federal Law Enforcement Training Center in Georgia, interviewed Irons for a training video about his incendiary techniques and means of eluding law enforcement. "Irons walked into a wooded area," said retired USFS agent Russ Arthur, "to place twelve-inch-long candles in the ground along a trail. He used time-delay devices to ignite them" so he could flee unharmed. His wife dropped him off at the scene and returned later to pick him up.

USFS employee Beecher Colvin (1928–2015) could "quickly pinpoint a fire and the cause of it," said the retired Tellico District Ranger Wallace Graham. After earning a forestry degree at Mississippi State University, Graham worked for the USFS in Louisiana, Arkansas and Alabama before accepting the district ranger position in 1977. "When I arrived, the Tellico reported 150 fires a year, and Beecher was a forestry technician," he said. Graham met Beecher about three years earlier fighting wildfires in California when he was working with the USFS Alabama firefighters and Beecher was the leader of the Tellico crew. As district ranger, Graham promoted Beecher to law enforcement. "He knew more people in Monroe County than a politician, always smiling, a wonderful person. He would solve problems that others would make into bigger ones."

"He was a legend," said Mary Ann Akins-McMillan, Beecher's daughter-in-law. "I've never met anyone with greater principles, and he was remarkable

at finding the source of a wildfire." Once, he drove Mary Ann to a fire scene in his "cruiser" and showed her how an arsonist had built a fire-starter by pushing the head of a wooden kitchen match into the tobacco end of a cigarette. He then created a little stand of crisscrossed matches to hold it, tucked dried leaves underneath it and lit the cigarette. The cigarette ignited the kitchen match that inflamed the leaves. Beecher had found the apparatus fallen on its side.

Opposite: V.F. Colvin uses an alidade in the Hemlock Knob Tower, 1938. *Tennessee State Library and Archives.*

Above: Tennessee firefighting efforts, 1941. *Tennessee State Library and Archives.*

Beecher had learned to spot fires at an early age. When he was sixteen, he assumed his father's role as the Hemlock Knob Tower warden when his father, the Graham County, North Carolina native Ferd Colvin (1879–1945), became ill. Later, Beecher served at the Cold Spring Fire Tower. So did his first wife, Beulah.

"Long the exclusive dream of menfolk, the rugged Forest Service has succumbed to femininity," reported the *Knoxville Journal* in 1954. After two women successfully performed temporary lookout duties while their husbands worked a fireline, the CNF offered permanent positions to Beulah Colvin and Mildred Jean, the wife of USFS Hemlock Knob lookout warden Onus Thompson. Beulah served in the Cold Spring Tower; Mildred scanned the landscape from the Hemlock Knob Tower.

"The women have an important job," USFS Fire Dispatcher B.W. Chumney told reporters. In the 1930s and 1940s, Chumney worked at the CCC Tumbling Creek Camp and other side camps before working for the

CNF in timber management and, later, as CNF's fire dispatcher until his retirement in 1977. At the Cold Spring Tower, he said, "Beulah receives important messages on her radio and then relays them to the men on a fireline equipped with mobile receivers." She also relayed weather reports and other information from the Cleveland office to radio-receiving sets in CNF's northern zone. At Hemlock Knob Tower, Mildred used a telephone for communications.

When the women worked at the tower for several weeks during a fire season, the mothers moved in with their young children. The USFS placed woven wire along the steps and around the tower to keep the youngsters from falling off. A 1950s photo shows one woman cooking over a stove in the lookout in her skirt and apron. A baby doll is perched in the window. "Once," said Mary Ann, "Beulah had her toddler, Jerry, with her [later Mary Ann's husband]. She had radioed the coordinates of a wildfire, keyed off her microphone, turned around and saw a second fire coming up the ridge in the opposite direction." Beulah moistened her son and the cab with wet cloths and yelled "Mayday! Mayday!" into the microphone, but the radio was dead. Through the smoky haze, she thought she heard an engine. "Beecher said he had a bad feeling," left the fireline, borrowed a USFS bulldozer and cut a trail for his wife and son to escape.

In August 1986, the TVA reported a sixteen-inch rainfall deficit. One USFS official feared that the fall season would become a "tinderbox, with topsoil so dry that even the soil will burn." In preparation, the CNF bought new fire equipment, placed volunteer fire departments on alert and trained prison inmates and University of Tennessee forestry students in fire control methods. Fire managers believed that arsonists were responsible for two-thirds of Tennessee's wildfires that year, so the Tennessee Division of Forestry hired the retired USFS Arson Investigator Beecher Colvin. "The state hired Beecher as a fire investigator after he retired from the USFS," said Graham, "but he got his training working for the CNF! When I left Tellico in 1989, the fire numbers were down to thirty to forty a year, mostly due to Beecher's efforts."

TELLICO AND BALD RIVERS

From its headwaters in North Carolina's Snowbird Mountains, the sixty-mile-long Tellico River flows past CNF's Big Oak Cove, Stateline, Holder Cove, Davis Branch and Birch Branch Campgrounds. Beyond the USFS Pheasant Fields Recreation Area, Tellico Trout Hatchery and Green Cove fishing village, it picks up Bald River, North River and other tributaries. After it passes Tellico Plains, the river heads toward TVA's Tellico Reservoir, where, in 1973, the endangered snail darter (*Percina tanasi*) postponed, but did not prevent, TVA's 1979 construction of the Tellico Dam.

From Tellico Plains, TN-165 passes Quarry Creek Road, Lyons Creek/Old Furnace Road (FSR-76) and the Oosterneck boating take-out area on Tellico River. Visitors turn right onto Tellico River Road (FSR-210) for a journey along the river through the CNF. Straight ahead, at a three-way intersection, the road roughly follows the former railbed of Babcock's Tellico Lumber Company. A right turn onto Wildcat Creek Road (FSR-384) takes motorists toward Coker Creek or to Bald River Road (FSR-126). A left turn onto FSR-126A leads to the Tellico Ranger Station, the site of the 1930s CCC Camp Chickasaw, now listed in the National Register of Historic Places. The Forest Service occupies former CCC-constructed buildings. In the ranger station, a CCC exhibit pays tribute to its forest management contributions. The ranger station's fire finder supposedly served the Hemlock Knob Lookout Tower. Caney Branch leaves its headwaters north of the Cherohala Skyway and flows beside the former encampment in a wide valley.

In April 1996, after a visit to the USFS Region 8 Headquarters in Atlanta, "completing my pledge to visit every regional headquarters," wrote

A Tellico Plains CCC camp hiking club. *Tennessee State Library and Archives.*

USFS Chief Jack Ward Thomas, he visited CNF's Ocoee River Olympic whitewater project. He then headed to the CCC reunion and dedication ceremony at the reconstructed Tellico Ranger Station. Boy Scouts presented the colors at a flag ceremony. District Ranger Larry Fleming, Tennessee congressman John J. Duncan Jr., the CNF archaeologist and the National Association of Civilian Conservation Corps Alumni president spoke to the group before a barbecue dinner. In 2008, at the seventy-fifth CCC anniversary at Tellico, a former CCC camp cook who owned a Knoxville restaurant, a CCC worker who had planted the sycamore tree in front of the ranger station and a recruit who had built the stone wall in front of the old ranger's house attended the event. One former CCC worker told the celebrants the story of a thief in the night who stole a roll of copper tubing from the camp, presumably for his moonshine still.

The Tellico Ranger Station offers maps and information about trails, road conditions, hunting and fishing opportunities and more. After leaving the ranger station, visitors can follow Tellico River Road and take adventurous drives north of the road, such as the North River Loop (FSR-

Tellico Ranger Station, 1941. *Tennessee State Library and Archives.*

217) by CNF's McNabb Creek Group Campground. The forty-three-mile-long North River Road–Stratton Gap/Cherohala Skyway Loop passes the USFS Donley Cabin. A Mr. Hughes reportedly occupied the secluded cabin during the Civil War to evade military service. After the war, Jack Donley (1845–1941) returned to East Tennessee from Montana with an Indian wife and lived in the cabin. The growing Donley family added a second hand-hewn, half-dovetailed log room to the original structure. Upgrades over the years combined Swiss chalet, German and English architectural styles. After the CNF bought the home site and surrounding acreage from Babcock around 1925, Donley's descendants used it as a summer cabin and managed beehives for honey production under a USFS Special Use Permit until 1994. The USFS currently rents Donley Cabin for three-night stays and recommends that visitors bring foam pads to sleep on the plywood bed surfaces. A ten-mile, one-way North River Road drive past Donley Cabin climbs about two thousand feet in elevation to Stratton Gap. Blooming beauties in spring, like Dutchman's breeches (*Dicentra cucullaria*), squirrel corn (*Dicentra canadensis*) and several species of trilliums, highlight the trip.

Above: Hiker Brian Solomon visits Donley Cabin. *Bruce A. Roberts, https://www.be-roberts.com.*

Opposite: Bald River. *Tennessee State Library and Archives.*

The Tellico River Road cuts through a gorge with jagged rocks, bus-sized boulders and wide-angle, riverside views. Passengers can soak in the scene while drivers navigate tight curves along the narrow route. The road crosses to the south bank before CNF's showstopper, Bald River Falls, highlights the journey. Beside a roadway bridge, Bald River showers down the mountainside for one hundred feet with magnificent power and beauty and flows under the bridge to join Tellico River's wild, freewheeling spirit.

Around 1928, after USFS crews widened Babcock's logging route and covered its railroad trestles with wooden planks, motorists began visiting the falls. One of Beecher Colvin's first USFS duties was to greet visitors signing a CNF logbook beside the bridge. In the 1930s, the Forest Service replaced the Bald River trestle bridge with a concrete structure. In the 1970s, increased recreational traffic caused "pothole after pothole," said Wallace Graham. "I received more complaints about that road than any other during my tenure." After frequent road repairs, crews resurfaced the Tellico River Road around 1989. By 2024, officials were planning to complete a $9.5 million project replacing the bridge with a two-lane vehicle structure and a separate pedestrian walkway and observation deck.

Forest growth conceals scars left by Babcock's logging railroad that crossed the top of Bald River Falls. West of the falls, the USFS hung logging chains between railroad posts to define the entrance to the Bald River Trail. In 2021, maintenance workers repaired rock walls and about 120 feet of trail-tread. They also built stone steps along three steep switchbacks to improve safety and reduce erosion. The trail, at times, traces the old rail bed beside Bald River to Bald River Road (FSR-126). It passes through CNF's 3,721-acre Bald River Gorge Wilderness, federally protected since 1984.

Farther along Tellico River Road, a woodland path from a USFS picnic area leads downstream for a bluff-side, grandstand view of the stunning fifteen-foot drop of Baby Falls. Kayakers turn flips off the falls and navigate the swift-water action of Tellico River's Class II–V rapids. In August 2021 at 6:15 a.m., Brian Solomon videotaped five otters playing near the base of the falls, while snow crystals lingered in sheltered forest coves after an early season snowstorm.

Beyond the USFS Walnut Grove Picnic Area and an intersection with North River Road, fishermen enjoy a quiet river section near a pedestrian bridge. Yellow-painted markings on trees beside the river indicate sites that the TWRA Tellico Trout Hatchery staff have stocked with trout. The day following a TWRA restocking project or during the first days of fishing season, "you better bring your own rock if you want to stand on one!" said Graham. In the 1950s, Swainson Drug Store clerks in Tellico Plains began issuing fishing permits at 4:00 a.m. to anglers wanting to reach a favorite flat rock before daylight. At the day's end, fisheries biologist Price Wilkins and assistant Beecher Colvin recorded daily catch totals.

Near a second North River Road intersection, Tellico River Road drivers arrive at the CCC-constructed USFS Dam Creek Recreation Area. At the

Opposite: Bald River Falls, 1972. *Tennessee State Library and Archives.*

Left: Tellico River fisherman, circa 1938. *Tennessee State Library and Archives.*

parking lot, lichen- and moss-covered rock walls open at a set of stone steps, inviting guests to unpack a picnic in the CCC's signature wood beam shelter. Patriot, a Shiba Inu on a leash, strolls with her lady across a bridge to gently ascend a footpath. A hushed peace quells the memories of Heyser Lumber Company's disquieting clamor. In the 1890s, loggers hand-carved Heyser's Road to access timber in this region. The company built one splash dam on the North River and built one of its two Tellico River splash dams at the mouth of Dam Creek. Loggers removed riverbed boulders, placed cut logs in the rivers behind each dam, waited for the waters to rise and then coordinated the opening of each dam to create a mighty flood, pushing the logs downstream to the company's sawmill in Tellico Plains.

Continuing upriver on Tellico River Road, the USFS Spivey Cove Campground occupies the former CCC Company 1469, F-9 Camp Bedford Forest encampment. Beyond the Green Cove Lodge and Store fishing village, the TWRA Tellico Trout Hatchery sits at the site of the old Pheasant Fields Babcock logging camp. In the 1930s and 1940s, the CCC built the Pheasant Branch Rearing Pools, diverting water from Pheasant Branch into six circular structures. In the 1940s, Sycamore Creek fed additional linear raceways and earthen pools, and by the 1960s, Tellico River had provided water for more raceways. In the 1990s, upgrades added a hatchery building, and the TWRA raised southern-strain brook trout for brook restoration projects. The facility now receives nine-inch-long rainbow trout from the USFWS Dale Hollow National Fish Hatchery in Clay County, Tennessee, and raises them to a stocking weight of three-fourths of a pound to one pound. Annually, the TWRA releases about seventy-three thousand trout into Tellico River, around thirty-six thousand trout in Citico Creek and lesser amounts in Polk County streams and Green Cove Pond. In 2022–23, staff updated the ADA-accessible, two-acre Green Cove Pond located in the CNF and held fishing events for children under thirteen and adults over sixty-five. Near the hatchery, the TWRA also offers an accessible "Moment of Freedom Dock" on the Tellico River.

The graveled Bald River Road (FSR-126) offers a thirty-one-mile loop drive that rejoins Tellico River Road near the ranger station. It is a great route in the winter for open views or in the fall for landscapes painted in leaf-dropping red, yellow and orange. However, ask at the ranger station for a map and current road conditions before embarking on this remote mountainous adventure. It can be impassable for a Corolla Hatchback!

Seining rainbow trout at Tellico Fish Hatchery for stocking rivers, 1938. *Tennessee State Library and Archives.*

Deep gravel placed on the road after recent logging operations causes tricky navigation on tight curves or steep descents. A slippery mud-climb is also challenging. In season, hunters in orange and dogs in radio collars cruise in pickup trucks on the narrow road.

After turning onto Bald River Road, visitors pass FSR-5023, which leads to Green Cove Pond and the open-air Green Cove Tabernacle built in 1941. About three miles later, Bald River Road travels on a narrow corridor between the Bald River Gorge and the Upper Bald River Wilderness Areas. The Kirkland Creek Trail slices through the nine-thousand-acre Upper Bald River Wilderness, designated by Congress in 2018 to protect the headwaters of Bald River. Beyond the USFS Holly Flats Campground on the banks of Bald River, the road passes the Bald River Trailhead and reaches Basin Gap. Here, a steep 1.7-mile climb on Lookout Road (FSR-1126C) traces along the western boundary of the Upper Bald Wilderness area to reach the panoramic views atop 3,692-foot Waucheesi Mountain. Since 1984, the Fort Loudon Electric Cooperative and others have obtained a USFS Special Use Permit to operate radio communication facilities on the mountain. Near the site of a former lookout tower, the USFS operates a repeater site.

Around 1960, Knoxville Boy Scout leaders, Fort Loudon Association members and the East Tennessee Historical Society adopted a project to restore an ancient Cherokee and white settler trading path that connected to the Unicoi Turnpike Trail known as the "Waucheesi Trail." The committee called the reclaimed trail in the CNF "Warrior's Passage." At a Tellico Ranger Station meeting, CNF officials approved the project. In 1963, Scout leaders and the boys, "who had demonstrated that they could" work harder than what "should be expected of a youngster," began the trail building efforts. The Scouts followed the landmarks of the old route recorded in two-hundred-year-old journals, such as the 1797 notebook penned by Benjamin Hawkins, superintendent of Southern Indian Tribes, and his surveyors. By 1966, thirty-six Scouts had cleared the trail from Old Furnace Road/Lyon Creek Road to Waucheesi Mountain in 823 hours. That year, they hiked fifteen miles from Bald River Falls to join the USFS and other Scouts for a dedication ceremony at Twin Springs Campground, where travelers had rested overnight for hundreds of years. At the event, a bugle call echoed through the forest, reminiscent of military units at the encampment in days gone by. By 1971, two thousand Scouts had hiked the trail, earning a Waucheesi Patch for their achievements. Eight years later, the federal government designated the trail as the Warrior's Passage National Recreation Trail (NRT).

Tellico River
Road. *Tennessee
State Library and
Archives.*

In the 1990s, wildfires destroyed much of the eight-mile trail. Around 2011, Cherokee Hiking Club volunteers helped a new generation of Boy Scouts rehabilitate the footpath. The club continues to sponsor trail maintenance projects on the Warrior's Passage and its extended, six- to seventeen-mile overnight and day-trip routes, with camping available at Waucheesi Mountain or Twin Springs.

Drivers leave Waucheesi Mountain, rejoin the Bald River Road loop and cross the Warrior's Passage NRT twice. After turning onto Wildcat Road, they cross the NRT again before arriving at the Tellico River Road junction near the ranger station. A left turn leads to TN-165 to head east on the Cherohala Skyway or west toward Tellico Plains. With almost two hundred miles of nearby trails, Tellico Plains, the "Little Town with a Big Back Yard" in the CNF, was designated a "Trail Town" in 2014.

Left: TVA Watauga Dam Visitor Center. *Ryan Rice, www. abovegroundmedia.com.*

Below: Turkeys. *Bill Lea, BillLea.com.*

Left: Cherohala Skyway. *Bill Lea, BillLea.com.*

Below: White-tailed deer fawn. *Bill Lea, BillLea.com.*

ET&WNC railroad trestle, Doe River Gorge. *Ryan Rice, www.abovegroundmedia.com.*

Brian Solomon visits a popular CNF waterfall. *Brian Solomon.*

Above: Roan Mountain. *Ryan Rice, www. abovegroundmedia.com.*

Left: Tennessee's state flower, the passionflower (*Passiflora incarnata*). Cherokees called it the "Ocoee." *John Forbes.*

At the CNF/PNF border, a path leads to the A.T. Max Patch Mountain, with stunning views of the CNF and GSMNP. After campers trashed the area in 2021, the USFS banned camping. "This is the last legal overnight tent photographed on the summit," said Thomas Mabry. *Thomas Mabry, Instagram.com/honeybadgerimages.*

Ocoee River and Ocoee Scenic Byway. *Blue Ridge Drones.*

Left: One forty-degree Saturday in December, kayakers flipped off Baby Falls, landing with a glide on a deep pool. *Christi Worsham.*

Below: The 1996 Olympics on the Ocoee River. *Paul Wright.*

Left: Bald Eagles, Watauga River. *Ryan Rice, www. abovegroundmedia.com.*

Below: Ruth's golden aster. *Bruce Roberts, https://www. be-roberts.com.*

Roan Mountain. *Thomas Mabry, Instagram.com/honeybadgerimages.*

Sequoyah Birthplace Museum. *Author's photo.*

Ken Jones and Tazz Reid remove a tree blocking a trail with a crosscut saw. *Ken Jones.*

Holston Mountain. South Holston Lake is in the background. *Ryan Rice, www. abovegroundmedia.com.*

Butler Bridge crosses Watauga Lake. *Ryan Rice, www.abovegroundmedia.com.*

Casper Cox introduces snorkelers to Conasauga River. *Freshwaters Illustrated.*

Above: Sam Feehrer, Parksville Lake. *Sam Feehrer.*

Left: Reenactors cross Watauga River during a commemorative walk on the Overmountain Victory National Historic Trail. *Sycamore Shoals State Historic Park.*

Nolichucky River Gorge. *Thomas Mabry, Instagram.com/honeybadgerimages.*

Snorkeling in Conasauga River. *Freshwaters Illustrated.*

Above: Roan Mountain. *John Forbes.*

Left: Red-cockaded Woodpecker. *Simon Thompson.*

Left: Black bears. *Bill Lea, BillLea.com.*

Below: Shelby Wallace completes a scavenger hunt at the former Ocoee Whitewater Center. *Author's photo.*

Opposite, top: Laurel Creek Bridge. *Jeff Fritts.*

Opposite, bottom: Bald River Falls. *Thomas Mabry, Instagram.com/ honeybadgerimages.*

Gentry Creek Falls. *Chris Berrier.*

Southern Highlands Reverse's executive director Kelly Holdbrooks participates in a spruce restoration project. *Southern Highlands Reserve.*

CHEROHALA SKYWAY

After traveling to Waucheesi Mountain in October 2020, a jeep parade filed into the Charles Hall Museum parking lot before climbing 3,500 feet along the Cherohala Skyway (TN-165/NC-143) to cross 4,490-foot-elevation Beech Gap at the Tennessee/North Carolina border and head toward Robbinsville, North Carolina. Beside the museum, Mini Coopers had returned from their fifty-mile-long skyway journey and parked at the Cherohala Skyway Visitor Center. Two Lamborghinis cruised between the two leaf-looking fleets and stole the show.

Since 1996, the Cherohala Skyway has attracted a variety of motorists. The nearly forty-year-long construction project involved USFS negotiations, political support and fundraising strategies. It included promotional efforts by the media and an annual wagon train event, suggested in 1958 by Sam Williams, a Tellico Plains Kiwanis Club member. That year, the pioneer-style caravan traveled from Fort Loudoun, down Tellico River Road and on to Murphy, North Carolina. It included Tellico Plains town leaders, former World War I cavalry officers, East Tennessee and Western North Carolina residents, sixty-seven covered wagons and 325 horseback riders. Over its thirty-year tradition, the number of participants increased, and the routes changed.

Some residents opposed the project, however. One Tennessee letter to the editor urged the community to protect the mountains "as a source of clear water, fish, game, and a quality almost gone from the Smokies, solitude." In North Carolina, wilderness activist groups campaigned for the protection of the grandeur of Joyce Kilmer Memorial Forest and the Little Santeetlah and Slickrock watersheds. Their passions stalled the plans for thirteen years and altered its final route. After Congress created the combined Joyce Kilmer-Slickrock Wilderness Area in 1975, North Carolina's skyway route skirted the wilderness. By opening day in October 1996, Cherohala Skyway, a federally designated national scenic byway, combined the names of the Cherokee and Nantahala National Forests through which it passed. The name replaced other suggestions, like the "Tellico-Robbinsville Highway" and the "Overhill Skyway," proposed by some USFS officials to honor the Cherokee people.

The Eastern Federal Lands Highway Division (EFLHD) of the Federal Highway Administration (FHA) managed the construction project and held meetings in consultation with USFS engineers at the Tellico Ranger Station. Since the early 1900s, the FHA has assisted with highway and bridge projects on federal lands, like constructing roads for Alaskan Natives and restoring Washington, D.C.'s Pennsylvania Avenue. Based in Sevierville, Tennessee, the EFLHD's construction engineer Lloyd Middleton had worked with the National Park Service to build GSMNP highways and the Foothill and Blue Ridge Parkways. Like his former projects, Middleton designed the Cherohala Skyway to blend into the mountainous topography and provide inspirational vistas for the motoring public.

After surveying and mapping the area, he used his measurements to design the best route over the steep-sloped, high-elevation terrain. USFS engineers and Middleton's team discussed tunneling through a ridgeline versus curving the skyway around it, moving the road away from the Tellico River, protecting natural and cultural resources and other factors. In 1977, the construction work exposed underlying pyritic materials in Anakeesta rock formations to water and air, producing increased acidity levels and releasing sulfides and toxic metals. Aquatic life perished when the leached elements contaminated Grassy Branch in the Citico Creek basin and McNabb and Hemlock Creeks in the Tellico watershed. Project leaders spent nearly $4 million to minimize the acid/toxic drainage concerns. They neutralized acid leachates by treating headwater streams with gravity-metered mixtures of sodium hydroxide and sprayed a lime slurry over roadside embankments. Crews reduced acid runoff on banks and road-fill areas by sealing exposed Anakeesta material with temporary soil blankets. Later, they seeded a layer of lime and topsoil with grass. Silt barriers, drains and asphalt curbing also helped reduce toxic drainage and erosion. In 1979, Middleton coauthored his agency's first manual for erosion and sediment control and incorporated some of those stabilization practices to revegetate Cherohala's roadside shoulders, provide environmental sustainability and enhance natural aesthetics.

The Cherohala Skyway offers overlooks, picnic tables and hiking trails. Near the Grassy Branch Trailhead, the CCC established Co. 3460, F-16 Camp Sequoyah at a former logging camp. At a Rattlesnake Rock parking area, two spring wildflower trails follow a portion of a former skyway-construction equipment roadbed and descend steeply, at times, on a rocky pathway. The Falls Branch Falls Trail leads into the Citico Creek Wilderness past a 180-acre virgin forest of beech, buckeye and other forest giants to a seventy-foot-tall waterfall. The Jeffrey Hell Trail branches off the Falls Branch Falls Trail to tunnel through dense stands of rhododendron and doghobble. In the 1920s, Babcock's lumber company established a camp at Jeffrey Hell near the confluence of the North and South Forks of Citico Creek. A 5,000-acre wildfire torched the area around 1925.

A local tale claims that Ebeneezer Jeffrey lost a hunting dog that had trailed a bear into the tangled understory. Jeffrey chased the dog, telling friends that if he didn't come back, he had followed her to hell. Neither returned. Over the years, Jeffrey Hell has disoriented and subdued other outdoorsmen. In the early 1900s, loggers found human skeletons in rattlesnake dens and bear traps in the area. Retired USFS Marshall McClung reported that search teams in Jeffrey Hell had rescued a dehydrated nineteen-year-old lost for four days in 1994, a lost group of injured hikers in 2010 near a large rattlesnake and two spooked men lost for three days in 2022.

At a dagger-head turn on the Cherohala Skyway, FSR-35 leads to the Miller Ridge Horse Trails. FSR-345 passes the Citico Creek Road (FSR-35-1) to enter the Indian Boundary Recreation Area. At Whiteoak Flats near the base of Flats Mountain, the USFS built a picnic/campground in the 1960s and named it after a U.S./Cherokee boundary line designated in the 1819 Calhoun Treaty. They dammed Flats Creek to create a ninety-six-acre lake with a boat launch, swimming beach and accessible fishing pier. A three-mile-long hiking/biking trail circles the lake.

In the 1970s and '80s, "I worked in the Tellico District during the glory days," said Graham. "We had the budget to undertake good multi-use programs," like improving Indian Boundary's campsites and enlarging the beach area. They also built the bathhouse during the years that "the Forest Service did most of our own work," instead of hiring contract labor. "We also had a great working relationship with the TWRA on wildlife habitat projects." Between 2020 and 2021, USFS-led crews replaced thirteen deteriorated footbridges on the lake trail. Each spring at Indian Boundary,

A picnic area along the Cherohala Skyway. *William Nichols.*

the CNF and the TWRA host "Eco Days" for local students. The educational event fosters an appreciation for the natural world through activities on wildlife, wilderness management, conservation and other topics.

Citico Creek Road roughly follows the route of Babcock's former rail line. From Jeffrey Hell, Ike Branch, Doublecamp, Grassy Flat and other camps in the Citico region, Babcock transported its harvests along the creek and crossed the Little Tennessee River on a trestle built by its crews. From the Slickrock region, the company moved logs over a spur railroad that connected to rail lines at Calderwood until the Aluminum Company of America (Alcoa) constructed Calderwood Dam, flooding the rail bed.

"A significant CNF land acquisition," said retired USFS Type 1 Incident Commander Lewis Kearney, "was the Calderwood tract that connected the national forest to the GSMNP." In the late 1990s, the Federal Energy Regulatory Commission required Alcoa to protect key lands and waters as mitigation for re-licensing four hydropower dams on the Little Tennessee River. After the Brookfield Renewable Energy Group purchased Alcoa's dams, it transferred 4,000 Little Tennessee watershed acres to The Nature Conservancy, which was later acquired by the CNF, the GSMNP and the TWRA. At the "Bridging the Smokies" celebration, Senator Lamar Alexander attended the event and officials released a symbolic bear back into the wilds.

Early wildlife warden. *Tennessee State Library and Archives.*

Citico Creek Road borders the sparkling stream where little girls in hot-pink jackets fish beside grandmothers reading a book; three teenage fishermen line a bridge; big trucks back super-long campers into primitive creekside campsites; a male merganser rests on a rock island while his mate bobs in an eddy; and a dozen salamander species, including the rare seepage salamander (*Desmognathus aeneus*), thrive in its watershed. The roadway passes remnants from logging days, a bear reserve and the Citico Creek Wilderness. A turn onto Doublecamp-Jake Best Road (FSR-2659) follows the northern border of the wilderness to Farr Gap near the Joyce Kilmer-Slickrock Wilderness. Around 2010, a West Tennessee camper near Doublecamp Creek told the USFS that his monkey had escaped. Years later, a spazzed-out SAWS worker, maintaining wilderness trails, radioed his encounter with the creature to the ranger station. When the owner arrived to claim his pet, it was the wrong monkey. In 2015, American Rivers partnered with the USFS and the USFWS to remove a seven-foot-high, man-made dam in the Doublecamp area that restricted the natural movement to upstream habitats for fifty species of fish, including the federally endangered Citico darter (*Etheostoma sitikuense*), smokey madtom (*Noturus baileyi*) and yellowfin madtom (*Noturus flavipinnis*). FSR-2659 circles back over Salt Spring Mountain on the Coldspring Lookout Tower Road to rejoin Citico Creek Road, south of the USFS Jake Best Campground. In the 1930s, the CCC Co. 4494, F-15 Camp Wiley Post occupied today's campground and built Doublecamp Road, the lookout tower and a game warden's home.

Farther north, the USFS Young Branch Horse Camp sits across the road from the Little Citico Creek Horse Trail System in the wilderness area. The road heads toward Tellico Lake, a northern border of CNF's Southern region. Each April, thousands of small-mouth buffalofish (*Ictiobus bubalus*) migrate upstream from Tellico Lake to spawn in the shallow waters of Citico Creek. Visitors stand on bridges, like the Mountain Settlement Bridge, to observe bank-to-bank streambed shows, starring thousands of three- to six-pound suckers. Around 2006, at the mouth of Citico Creek, USFS Fisheries Biologist Jim Herrig began monitoring the buffalo run, noting the streamflow rate and the water and air temperatures. He noted that temperatures fifty-five degrees Fahrenheit and higher prompted earlier seasonal migrations. When rainstorms increased the flow rates, the buffaloes entered the stream within thirty-six hours of the rain event and swam farther upstream. Males swim on both sides of a female, he said, and interlock their tubercules down the side of their bodies with hers. When she releases her eggs, the males release milt that contains sperm. Sticky, fertilized eggs cling to the creekbed substrate.

Back on the Cherohala Skyway, motorists pass the state line, the 4,470-foot-elevation Unicoi Crest and the Stratton Ridge picnic area to arrive at Mud Gap. A three-mile hike along the BMT leads to CNF's Whigg Meadow, settled by the Whigg family in the late 1800s. Hunters later used the cabin until the USFS acquired the tract from Babcock and removed it. In 1945, a B-17 bomber crashed into Whigg Meadow, killing ten men.

On August 21, 2017, CNF's Tellico and Ocoee Ranger Districts fell within the seventy-mile-wide solar eclipse path of totality from Oregon to South Carolina. Like Waucheesi Mountain, Doc Rogers Fields, Beaverdam Bald, Chilhowee Mountain and the Ocoee Whitewater Center, Whigg Meadow became a hot spot to view this historic event. The six-acre, nearly five-thousand-foot-high bald is also a prime destination for flame azaleas, avian research and red spruce conservation efforts.

During the Last Glacial Period, ice floes pushed northern plants and animals southward. When the ice melted and receded eighteen thousand years ago, some northern species adapted to new homes in the South. Isolated pockets of red spruce (*Picea rubens*) and Fraser fir (*Abies fraseri*) thrived in the bitter winters, short growing seasons and shallow soils above 4,500 feet in elevation. Northern hardwoods, like yellow birch (*Betula alleghaniensis*), American beech (*Fagus grandifolia*) and pin cherry (*Prunus pensylvanica*), grew at slightly lower elevations.

Human-induced factors, however, led to the decline of spruce-fir forests. Spruce wood became a valuable commodity in the manufacture of aircraft and musical instruments. Spruce twigs flavored beer and pudding. A Maine factory harvested spruce resin to make gum, sold at L.L. Bean until 1984. The paper industry valued its long, thin-walled fibers to produce pulp. Destructive logging practices and subsequent wildfires allowed faster-growing species, like yellow birch, to outcompete the spruce for the clear-cut, open spaces.

Later, climate change and air pollution caused more damage. When fossil fuel–burning industries released sulfur dioxide and nitrogen oxides into the atmosphere, the elements reacted with water and oxygen to create acid rain, which robbed trees of valuable nutrients. Gas-powered engines emitted nitrogen oxides and volatile organic compounds, causing ground-level ozone, which reduced a tree's resistance to disease and environmental stressors. Around 1908, non-native balsam woolly adelgids (*Adelges piceae*) that arrived on imported nursery stock to North America's northeastern fir forests moved south along the Appalachian chain, killing Fraser firs.

In the high-mountain ecosystems, Carolina northern flying squirrels (*Glaucomys sabrinus coloratus*) (CNFS), spruce-fir moss spiders (*Microhexura montivaga*), Red Crossbills (*Loxia curvirostra*), Northern Saw-whet Owls (*Aegolius acadicus*) and several salamanders lost valuable habitats. In 1985, the USFWS listed the CNFS, a subspecies of the northern flying squirrel,

Northern flying squirrel. *Lee James Pantas.*

as an endangered species. The nocturnal, ten-inch-long mammals glide from branch to branch, feeding on nuts, bugs, sap, birds' eggs and lichens. They search the forest floor for truffles, the underground fruiting bodies of mycorrhizal fungi living on spruce tree roots. The CNFSs den in birch tree cavities and build summer nests (dreys) among a conifer's limbs.

Biologists and conservationists recognized an urgent need to restore spruce-fir forest ecosystems. When four environmentally conscious women learned of each other's passion to restore this valuable ecosystem, their collective minds began to move mountains. North Carolina Wildlife Resources Commission (NCWRC) biologist Christine (Chris) Kelly had learned about Central Appalachian spruce restoration efforts at a conference. USFWS biologist Susan (Sue) Cameron had started developing recovery projects for high-elevation endangered species. The Southern Highlands Reserve (SHR) executive director, Kelly Holdbrooks, and her staff had germinated red spruce trees from seeds at the Toxaway Mountain, North Carolina nursery for years. In Tennessee, The Nature Conservancy's Katherine Medlock was working with the CNF to develop and implement spruce restoration objectives for a collaborative planning effort. The women invited federal and state agencies, biologists and others to a meeting to evaluate their interest in spruce restoration. The turnout was staggering, a standing-room-only response.

Formed in 2012, the goal of Southern Appalachian Spruce Restoration Initiative (SASRI) was to increase the number of red spruce trees on

High above the lakes of Western North Carolina lives a woodland garden where a congregation of trees, plants and flowers sings an ancient song. Southern Highlands Reserve is a nationally recognized arboretum and research center at the forefront of red spruce restoration. Located at an elevation of 4,500 feet, Southern Highlands Reserve's 120-acre site—which includes a 22-acre core park filled with rare native plants—emulates the plant communities found in the high-elevation spruce-fir forests of the Southern Appalachians. Established in 2003, the nonprofit is growing thousands of mature trees to be planted on public lands in North Carolina, Tennessee and Virginia. These forests are the second-most endangered ecosystem of the United States and are home to endangered and rare species. Southern Highlands Reserve and partners are committed to preserving the magic of the Blue Ridge Mountains for generations to come.

By KELLY HOLDBROOKS, Executive Director,
www.southernhighlandsreserve.org.

southern mountains where spruce forests had declined. By 2013, the group had developed a project charter and a spruce restoration plan, modeling their efforts after the Central Appalachian Spruce Restoration Initiative's approach. The project included planting healthy seedlings in canopy gap areas, aiding the growth of naturally established spruce by removing competitive vegetation, improving the soil's nutrients and fertility and monitoring the project outcomes.

Annually, from mid-September to early November, SHR staff helped collect one-and-a-half-inch, reddish-brown spruce cones from healthy forests. At the greenhouse, they extracted the seeds between the cones' broad, rounded scales and planted them to raise thousands of three-foot-tall seedlings. In the fall of 2017, Holdbrooks helped load three hundred SHR spruce seedlings onto a USFS trailer bound for Whigg Meadow. Cameron organized a team of USFS, TWRA, USFWS and University of Tennessee students to haul the one-gallon pots to the site and plant the five-year-old trees beneath an open beech and birch canopy. That year, Chris Kelly organized a similar project, planting nine hundred spruce seedlings in North Carolina's Pisgah National Forest (PNF) at Flat Laurel Creek. In 2021, Cameron helped plant two hundred more spruce trees at Whigg Meadow. In

Spruce restoration project. *Southern Highlands Reserve.*

the future, crews will selectively cut hardwoods at the project site to permit greater sunlight to reach the young spruce trees thriving in the understory. The CNF has led another spruce-planting project near the 6,285-foot-high Roan High Knob Shelter, the highest trail shelter on the A.T.

———————•———————

IN 2019, A YOUNG Swainson's Thrush (*Catharus ustulatus*) joined thousands of other songbirds as it departed the North on its maiden, three-thousand-mile journey to Peru. Perhaps the thrush, weighing no more than a slice of bread and often migrating at night, vocalized its "water drip" or "pip" call as it sailed under the stars. On September 26, it dropped into Whigg Meadow's brushy heath thickets to rest and refuel on fruits and insects. There, a delicate black nylon net interrupted its customary habits.

A bird banding technician gently retrieved the olive-brown thrush from the net, lowered it into a cloth bag and carried it to the banding station to collect data. A team member identified the species by its distinctive buffy-colored eyerings and other markings and measured its weight, size and wing chord (the distance between the bend in the wing and its longest feather). A bird bander determined the bird's age by assessing the color, shape and wear of its feathers and its body mass by gauging the concentration of lipids seen through the semi-transparent skin at the top of its chest. After attaching a uniquely numbered aluminum band to its leg, the team released the thrush to continue its flight toward the tropics. An assistant recorded all data in a daily journal and updated the day's totals of banded species on a whiteboard for Whigg Meadow visitors to see.

In 1998, the federally licensed master bird bander David Vogt coordinated with the USFS to start Wigg Meadow's avian data collection station. For nearly ten years, he tallied more than seventy bird species and banded about ten thousand birds. After Vogt retired, the then state ornithologist of Tennessee Scott Somershoe operated the site. Today, Charlie Muise of Georgia, Eric Soehren of Alabama, Scott Rush of Mississippi and Jay Dedeker of Tennessee manage the station.

Introduced to ornithology in college, Dedeker organizes the seasonal calendar, scheduling at least one federally permitted bander on each shift. He and other volunteers trim brush and remove debris from the net lanes, stake up fourteen twelve-meter-long nets, pitch a canopy for the data collection station and erect educational signs for visitors. Dedeker's family joins him, including his eighty-three-year-old mother, who travels from Minnesota for his assigned banding week and sleeps in the back of his truck. A predawn, daily drive to the meadow on the graveled FSR-217 can be foggy and dangerous, so the USFS permits the banding crew to camp in the parking area adjacent to the meadow.

By 6:00 a.m., the staff had begun unfurling the nets, closed overnight. Licensed master bird banders, sub-permitted banders and skilled volunteer assistants captured, banded and collected data on warblers, vireos, thrushes and other species. Each day, staff set up the scales, leg gauges and rulers and record the wind speed/direction, cloud cover and temperature. Every thirty minutes, technicians checked the nets, removed the captured birds, processed them and released them as quickly as possible.

The most frequently caught bird species at the meadow was the dainty, greenish-colored Tennessee Warbler (*Leiothlypis peregrina*), a breeding bird of northern boreal forests that migrates through the Volunteer State. Alexander Wilson named it for the state where he first identified the species. The Swainson's Thrush is the second-most frequently captured bird each year. "I'll never forget the day Swainson's Thrushes (and a few Veery and Gray-cheeked Thrushes) woke me up with their flight calls," said Somershoe. "We set what I think is a state record of 640 or so Swainson's Thrushes moving over the bald." In 2009, the crew began netting Northern Saw-whet Owls, running nets at night with a playback call of this species. Whigg Meadow and the surrounding forest systems are the southern extent of the breeding range for this owl and other species most often associated with the northern Appalachian Mountains. One September morning in 2022, Muise began unfurling the nets and photographed a Saw-whet Owl perched on the rope securing a net pole. The predator held a long-tailed rodent in its beak. Muise slowly approached within a yard of it, holding a steady gaze with its yellow eyes before it departed with its prey.

Each year, Scott Rush, a Mississippi State University professor, brings students to Whigg Meadow to participate in the project. He obtains the leg bands from the U.S. Geological Survey (USGS) Banding Laboratory in Laurel, Maryland. At the season's end, Rush compiles the laboratory's annual report of Whigg Meadow's newly banded birds and the previously banded/recaptured birds.

After the Migratory Bird Treaty Act passed in 1920, the U.S. Department of Agriculture (USDA) began compiling data to protect and study North American birds. The USGS assumed that role in 1996, coordinating its avian conservation work with the Canadian Wildlife Service. The lab stores more than 77 million banding records, issues bird banding permits to approved stations, provides bird banding licenses to scientists and qualified volunteers and distributes about 1 million individually numbered leg bands each year. Researchers, scientists and land managers study the data to assess migration patterns, population numbers, demographic parameters and changes affecting threatened and endangered species. Like canaries in the coal mines, birds act as sentinels for changes in the environment.

The lab asks individuals to report banded birds encountered away from its banding station. In 2019, a South American resident notified the lab about the recovery of a Swainson's Thrush banded at Whigg Meadow on September 26. Unfortunately, the migrant would not feed on army ants that winter like its cousins or return to its breeding grounds up north to sing its spiraling, flute-like song. It would not repeat seasonal migrations for twelve years like the oldest recorded Swainson's Thrush, banded and recaptured in Montana in 2006. A cat in Peru had killed Whigg's little traveler, less than five months after its likely hatch date.

Two years earlier, Allegheny College professor Ronald L. Mumme had recaptured Hooded Warbler no. 2720-72284 (*Setophaga citrina*) at the Hemlock Hill Field Banding Station in northwest Pennsylvania. The USGS laboratory's database revealed that Whigg Meadow volunteers had banded the juvenile's right leg on September 11, 2014. At Hemlock Hill, Mumme had color-banded about three hundred adults and five hundred nestlings over seven years, but this was his first capture of a previously banded bird. He placed colored bands on each leg and released it at his study area. In May, he observed a one-half-ounce, healthy Whigg male courting a non-banded female. After a predator destroyed the couple's nest in early June, the male's constant, territorial singing, thought Mumme, hinted that his mate might be incubating a second clutch on a new nest.

"We enjoy providing education and interpretation to visitors," said Muise, a Georgia firefighter/emergency medical technician and former naturalist who banded birds in GSMNP. From September to early October, the Whigg Meadow Banding Station managers invite the public to observe their banding process, learn about avian conservation science and, possibly, release a bird from an extended hand. Birding club newsletters and social media sites begin announcing the season's schedule by late summer.

PART III

Watauga Ranger District

Ken Czarnomski, Phoenix2Reach@gmail.com.

DOE RIVER GORGE

On the Tennessee/North Carolina border, a northbound A.T. hiker crosses 4,930-foot Little Rock Knob on the west side of Roan Mountain. Nearby, the Doe River tumbles into its thirty-five-mile journey toward its confluence with the Watauga River at Elizabethton, Tennessee. At TN-143, Five Poplar Branch, Middle Branch and Toms Branch surrender to the Doe River as it turns north.

Two springs feed Toms Branch near the USFS Twin Springs Recreation Area. In 2013, the CNF closed its overgrown pathways in the cove hardwood forest until the Friends of Roan Mountain (FORM), a nonprofit environmental organization, volunteered in 2017 to maintain its lush wildflower gardens. By 2018, FORM had provided the funds and volunteer labor to reroof the 1962 picnic pavilion. In August 2020, the Friends used $3,000 in grant monies to replace its concrete pad and paint the shelter. The CNF provided a new signboard.

FORM assists the USFS and the Tennessee State Parks System with restoration and conservation projects and holds annual Roan Mountain Naturalists Rallies at the Roan Mountain State Park. Each July, it also sponsors the youth-oriented Xtreme Roan Adventures. In 1958, Fred W. Behrend, a local stenographer and later editor of the *Elizabethton Star*, started the events. After his ten-year-old daughter died, the grieving avid birder "couldn't hold my head up to look at the birds and discovered wildflowers." He invited botanists, professors and naturalists to his Roan Mountain outdoor home to give lectures and lead wildflower and bird identification hikes. Today, researchers, scientists and historians educate Roan Mountain rally participants about the area's natural history.

The Doe River drops down a forested mountainside, curves through the CNF along the TN-143, courses through the Roan Mountain State Park and swings by the 1800s Dave Miller Homestead. In the farm fields, milkweeds attract breeding and migrating monarch butterflies (*Danaus plexippus*) to the registered Monarch Watch waystation, protected from herbicides and real estate development.

In Roan Mountain State Park, the Tom Gray Trail follows a portion of the Doe River, a home of North America's largest native salamander, the eastern hellbender (*Cryptobranchus alleganiensis*). Living up to twenty-five to thirty years in cold waters, hellbenders walk along the riverbed at night, foraging for food. To avoid predators, it will swim short distances and duck under flat rocks. Impoundments, water pollution and habitat destruction have threatened its survival.

Beyond the state park, the Doe River takes an oblique turn, follows the border of CNF's Watauga and Unaka Ranger Districts along US-19E/TN-37 and collects waters draining the southern slope of 4,280-foot White Rocks Mountain. Streams draining White Rocks Mountain's northern flank feed the Laurel Fork of the Doe River, which joins the Doe River at Hampton, Tennessee. Southeast of Hampton, the Doe River gushes through a shortcut squeeze in a gorge between Fork and Cedar Mountains, where tributaries coursing down the steep CNF hillsides join the barreling surge. This rugged gorge challenged the construction of the East Tennessee and Western North Carolina (ET&WNC) Railroad.

In the early 1800s, Waightstill Avery, Joshua Perkins and others acquired property in an area now known as North Carolina's Cranberry Iron Ore Belt to extract the high-grade, metallic iron ore. Perkins hauled iron by wagons to his forge on Cranberry Creek and later sold his operations to Abel and William Dugger, natives of Butler, Tennessee.

By the 1870s, Ariovistus (Ario) Pardee, a northern coal industry engineer of canals and railroads, had joined his partners to invest in the Cranberry Iron and Coal Company (CI&CC) and revitalize the failed 1866 ET&WNC Railroad project. Engineer and surveyor Thomas Matson designed the narrow-gauge rail line, completed in 1882, to haul the Cranberry iron ore from Avery County, North Carolina, to the mainline rail connections at Johnson City. The freight rail line also provided passenger and mail service. Passengers boarded at rail stops—like Milligan College, Watauga Point and Sycamore Shoals—near today's Sycamore Shoals State Historic Park.

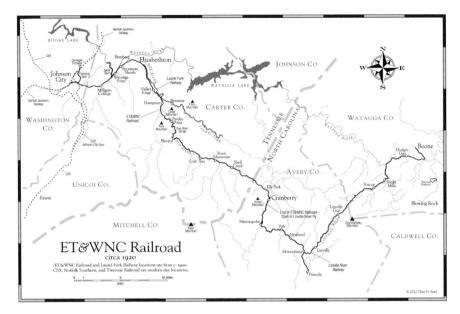

ET&WNC Railroad. *Chris Ford.*

From Elizabethton, the ET&WNC Railroad headed south along the Doe River, passed the Coal Chute and crossed a two-span steel deck bridge (the Valley Forge Bridge) to the north side of the Doe River. East of the Valley Forge platform, near Hampton, it returned south of the Doe over a covered, three-span wooden deck bridge. To avoid the Doe River's hairpin turn at a 1,700-foot-high ridge on Jenkins Mountain, it ducked through 298-foot-long Tunnel 1 and rolled into Doe River Cove, now known as Hampton.

Beyond Hampton, the ET&WNC Railroad passed the sawmill of the W.M. Ritter Lumber Company. The railroad then crossed the Little Doe River on a wooden covered bridge and entered Doe River Gorge to pass through five tunnels and cross multiple railroad bridges. Workers had carved a thirty-six-inch-wide rail bed with hand tools and dynamite along the granite walls of Fork Mountain. "Gandy dancers" sang morale-boosting chants to ease the labor. Ropes and pulleys hoisted mules and equipment from the riverbed to the high, confined worksite. At Pardee Point, named for Ario Pardee and his son, Ario Jr., CI&CC's management leaders, the train often paused for visitors to enjoy the dramatic view.

One mile east of Pardee Point, the track crossed the river, entered a tunnel and crossed the river again. It departed the gorge, followed the Doe River into a broad valley and passed flag stops/stations at Blevins, White

ET&WNC Railroad foreman J.F. Palmer and crew, 1940. *Tennessee State Library and Archives.*

Rock, Crabtree and the town of Roan Mountain. In Roan Mountain, John T. Wilder (1830–1917), a former Union army colonel and Johnson City businessman, built his home (now in the National Register of Historic Places) and the Roan Mountain Inn. From his inn, horse and carriage drivers escorted railroad travelers up a rugged road to Wilder's Cloudland Hotel, straddling the North Carolina/Tennessee state line on the Roan Mountain Highlands. Beyond the Roan Mountain station, ET&WNC trains climbed State Line Hill (now crossed by the A.T.), passed Elk Park, North Carolina, and arrived at Cranberry's iron ore mines.

In 1898, the W.M. Ritter Lumber Company purchased the aborted Linville River Railway and extended the rail line from ET&WNC Railroad's terminus at Cranberry to its logging operations near Pineola, North Carolina. By 1913, Ritter had sold it to the CI&CC, which extended the line to William Scott Whiting's (1871–1952) band sawmill at Shulls Mills and, eventually, to Boone, North Carolina, completing nearly sixty-seven miles of rail service.

During the 1901–22 golden age years of ET&WNC Railroad management, led by Milligan College graduate George W. Hardin (1864–1922), hopper cars

ET&WNC Railroad, Pardee Point, circa 1882. Dr. Abraham Jobe stands beside Engine No. 1, named "Watauga." *Cy Crumley Scrapbook/ET&WNC Railroad Historical Photo Collection.*

carried iron ore from the mines to the Cranberry Iron Furnace in Johnson City six days a week. In 1901, a flood, known as the "May Tide," unleashed a thunderous fury through Doe River Gorge and challenged Hardin in his new role. Rail beds slid down slippery slopes. Stone-filled trestles, like the one built at Pardee Point, caved under pressure, forcing stranded passengers to hike out of the gorge to safety. Hardin directed crews to build retaining walls and replace wooden bridges with steel structures to reduce future flood damage and interrupted rail service.

In 1904, the company added a standard-gauge line to its narrow-gauge tracks from Johnson City to Elizabethton. The dual-gauge line provided rail service for the standard-gauge trains of the Virginia and Southwestern Railway (later Southern Railway) connecting at Elizabethton and the South and Western Railroad (later Clinchfield Railroad) connecting at Johnson City. Engine-mounted swivel couplers allowed the narrow-gauge steam engines to move both narrow- and standard-gauge cars on their respective tracks.

The train whistled its warning at trestles and tunnels, crossings and creatures. Once, a lady walking a trestle failed to hear its cautionary cue.

ET&WNC Railroad manager George W. Hardin inspects the line. *Cy Crumley Scrapbook/ ET&WNC Railroad Historical Photo Collection.*

When she caught sight of the locomotive looming behind her, she held herself flat between the rails as it roared over her. Conductor Charles (Cy) Grover Crumley (1886–1978) invited rural residents to "Hop on!" the slow-moving train and ride into town for supplies. Crumley, as the story goes, watched one sure-footed fellow trekking trackside for some distance.

"Hey, farmer!" Crumley called. "Swing on up here! We'll give you a ride!"

"No thanks," the man said. "I'm in a hurry."

Born in Elizabethton, young Crumley earned $0.20 per day at a textile plant to help his widowed mother provide for seven children. After a 1900 fire closed the factory and the 1901 May flood destroyed the family's home, he earned $0.50 per day as a lumberyard water boy. In 1906, Cy married the daughter of a Southern Railway conductor and left his $0.75-per-day job making buttons at a local plant to work for the ET&WNC Railroad. The company paid the twenty-year-old $1.25 for a seventeen-hour-workday. By 1908, he had begun his fifty-plus-year career as a conductor, punching passenger tickets with his specially designed, heart-shaped railroad nippers. On a 1938 New York City radio show, *We the People*, Crumley promoted four-hour-long excursions, climbing 2,400 feet along forty-five miles on the "railroad with a heart," also known as "Tweetsie." He also starred in "Tennessee Tweetsie," a segment in Universal Studios' travel film series *Going Places*.

Along the rail route through today's Watauga Ranger District, Cy ran a delivery service for backcountry residents, collecting lists of supplies to purchase in Johnson City. He delivered farm tools; cloth for a wedding dress; shoes, sized by a cut-out foot pattern; a corset, size "wide"; spools of thread; food products; and other items. Once, the fireman and brakeman helped Cy deliver a forty-dollar, four-hundred-pound Burnside woodstove. The next day, an elderly woman flagged down the train to hand the fellows chicken, prepared on her new stove.

In the 1940s, the rail line provided employee transportation to the Elizabethton plants producing rayon for military parachutes. By 1950, the lumber industry had dwindled, the Cranberry mines had closed in 1929 and the 1940 flood had damaged the railroad. Travelers preferred the advance of automobiles and better roads. Crews burned some of ET&WNC Railroad's boxcars to harvest the scrap iron. An engineer took a few gondola cars to use as chicken coops. During World War II, two locomotives moved to the Yukon Territory to help build a highway. A few passenger coaches served in Central America. Three Virginia-based railroad hobbyists purchased locomotive no. 12, a combine and an excursion car to join their small tourist railway in the

Left: ET&WNC Railroad's conductor Cy Crumley. *Cy Crumley Scrapbook/ET&WNC Railroad Historical Photo Collection.*

Opposite: ET&WNC Railroad's Caboose 505 being transported to its new home. *Jerry Turbyfill.*

Shenandoah region. When a storm destroyed its tracks, a Blowing Rock businessman brought Tweetsie back to the Boone area, now owned by the Tweetsie Railroad Amusement Park, opened in 1957.

In 1953, Crumley acquired its 1926 Caboose 505 and turned it into a fishing cabin on Watauga Lake. After his death, it became a playhouse beside a home above South Holston Lake. Thirty-five years later, the Avery County Historical Museum in Newland, North Carolina, acquired it to place beside the 1917 Linville Depot, donated to the museum in 2007. Jerry Turbyfill, a museum board member, organized the transport project. In 2014, after a boom crane at each end of the caboose lifted it off its foundation and set it on a flatbed truck, the truck backed up the steep, quarter-mile graveled driveway. In the Roan Mountain community, the team paused for a nostalgic photo op where ET&WNC Railroad's tail-end treasure stopped for passengers sixty years earlier. Jerry and volunteers restored Caboose 505 to its original splendor.

The Archives of Appalachia at East Tennessee State University (ETSU) preserves Crumley's scrapbooks and memorabilia. In 2007, a Cincinnati jeweler posted a conductor's hat on eBay with "ET&WNC CONDUCTOR" etched onto its brass plate. Inside, "Capt. C.G. Crumley" was handwritten on a Tweetsie Railroad Company tag. After fierce bidding among rail fans,

Mike Hardin, grandson of ET&WNC Railroad superintendent George Hardin, placed the winning $3,652 bid. On the ETSU campus, the George L. Carter Railroad Museum members created a scale model exhibit of Tweetsie country. In 1988, John Waite formed the ET&WNC Railroad Historical Society to preserve the railroad's history.

The Doe River Gorge Ministries Incorporated (DRG) purchased, in 1987, the site of two former amusement parks and restored the area as a youth outdoor adventure camp. On summertime Saturdays, DRG hosts public events at its four-hundred-acre Christian camp. On train rides into the gorge, surrounded by CNF mountains, conductor Mark Milbourne shares stories about the ET&WNC Railroad, known for its catchy phrases to remember its long name, like "Eat Taters and Wear No Clothes." Outside camp season, DRG opens the facilities for retreats and 2.3-mile-long rail bed hikes through two tunnels.

About 4.5 miles of the former rail bed follows Old Railroad Grade Road, a county road paralleling US-19E. The railroad's 1889 steel through-truss Blevins Bridge remains on a county road, but the 210-foot-long Sand Tunnel 5 has collapsed. Much of the railroad's right-of-way is "residential, industrial, privatized, or just inaccessible," said Chris Ford, the historical society's president. A 9.7-mile-long section of the rail line, preserved as a

ET&WNC Railroad. *Cy Crumley Scrapbook/ ET&WNC Railroad Historical Photo Collection.*

Tweetsie hiking trail from Johnson City to Elizabethton, was recognized in October 2020 by the national Rails to Trails Conservancy as its "Trail of the Month." In 2021, recreationists proposed the expansion of the Tweetsie Trail between Valley Forge and Hampton. Eastbound hikers and bikers would depart Valley Forge, enter Doe River Narrows and cross the river on a new or restored bridge. Beyond the bridge, the trail would enter ET&WNC Railroad Tunnel 1 (owned by the county).

"The goal is to connect the Tweetsie Trail extension with a new trailhead at Green Bridge Landing and the Hampton Watershed Bike Trail System," said Wesley R. Bradley, a project advocate and Kingsport commercial designer/contractor. "Possibly, one day, it will connect with the CNF trails in Dennis Cove. We've had a few good meetings with the Forest Service about this possibility." The project leaders hope that the Hampton Watershed Trail System will crest over Cedar Mountain, where DRG's property is surrounded by the CNF, to make this connection.

WATAUGA LAKE

At Hampton, US-321/TN-67 leaves US 19-E to head toward TVA's 1,900-foot-elevation Watauga Reservoir/Lake, one of TVA's highest and most scenic basins in the Tennessee watershed system. The agency built its 900-foot-wide Watauga Dam at Cardens Bluff, impounding Roan Creek and the Elk and Watauga Rivers.

Roan Creek flows from Snake Mountain and cuts through the CNF between Stone and Doe Mountains to join Watauga River. A Daniel Boone legend claims that he hiked through Watauga Valley in 1769 and left his lame horse, called "Roan," beside a beautiful stream. On his walk back home to North Carolina two years later, he recognized his rejuvenated horse, giving the stream the name Roan Creek. But as Boone once wrote, "I would not believe that tale if I had told it myself."

From its headwaters, the Elk River journeys north of the old Cranberry mines, drops into a pool at the base of the fifty-foot-high Elk Falls, collects Jones Branch and crosses into Tennessee to parallel a rerouted section of the A.T. CNF's Jones Falls, a double-tiered delight, entices A.T. hikers to take a short detour. The Elk River continues north, tumbles over Splash Dam Falls and slips by the western base of Big Pine Mountain. (Here, the stream parts company with A.T. hikers, who head east to follow the Laurel Fork of the Doe River into the CNF's Dennis Cove area.) In a difficult-to-access, rocky canyon, the Elk River cascades through six tight turns in a narrow gorge and merges with the Watauga River, near today's CNF Little Milligan Boat Ramp.

Watauga River leaves its headwaters on North Carolina's Grandfather Mountain, enters Tennessee, picks up Roan Creek and Elk River and feeds the Watauga Lake. Beyond the dam, it slices through the Iron Mountains and slides around a horseshoe bend to feed TVA's Wilbur Reservoir. Soon, the Watauga River leaves the CNF, collects Doe River at Elizabethton, ripples past Sycamore Shoals and greets the South Fork of the Holston River at Boone Lake near Johnson City.

From 1867 to 1940, floods affected life in the Watauga River Valley. In the May 1901 flood, seventy-five homes were washed down the Watauga River. In 1924, twelve people drowned in a deluge at Cardens Bluff. In August 1940, an avalanche of foaming rapids damaged more than $1 million worth of property. In the Elizabethton area, "Red Cross workers, officers, and volunteers searched frantically for bodies and cared for nearly one thousand homeless," reported a 1940 *Knoxville Journal* story. "A rescue worker toppled from a railroad trestle….He was fatigued after sleepless hours and swooned. His body fell into the swirling waters of the Watauga River and disappeared."

The 1940 flood destroyed Southern Railway tracks and trestles between Elizabethton and Mountain City, repaired after the 1914 and 1924 floods. On the track to Butler, "rails were twisted and tangled…crossties were washed away," wrote historian Herman Tester. In 1902, Butler had celebrated its new passenger and freight railroad service transporting farm products, lumber, iron ore and manganese. It had alleviated the rough, three- to six-hour, twelve-mile-long wagonload and horse-drawn carriage trips to Hampton's ET&WNC Railroad station. One man loaded the same amount of iron ore in railcars at the Butler station in a day that it had taken his ancestors to transport to Hampton in a week.

Watauga Academy students would arrive by Butler's railroad. In 1871, near the mouth of Roan Creek, L.L. Maples organized Aenon Seminary on land acquired from Joshua Perkins. By 1886, the institution had become Holly Springs College. Sixteen dollars paid for tuition and books. "Pupils who are willing to work hard and do right are earnestly solicited," newspapers announced. Around 1906, B.B. and D.D. Dougherty changed the name of Boone, North Carolina's Watauga Academy to the Appalachian Training School for Teachers to allow Holly Springs College to become the Watauga Academy. By 1940, it had become a Johnson County high school.

On the floor of the U.S. House of Representatives, Congressman B. Carroll Reece—a Watauga Valley native, 1911 academy graduate and World War I veteran—recited his May 1942 Watauga Academy commencement speech (an excerpt follows) for the *Congressional Record*. Reverend Maples, his grandfather, was the founder of the Aenon Seminary. His father, John Isaac Reece, a student at the institution, met and later married Sarah, Maples's eldest daughter. TVA's 1942 dam project (delayed until 1948 by World War II) would submerge Watauga Academy and the town of Butler:

> *This occasion is one of pride and sadness...a hail and a farewell. You are being graduated from this university into a world being torn by war and bloodshed....Watauga Academy is to be physically obliterated. Let me beseech you, that in the years to come, when the sunbeams of the tomorrows are sparkling on the bosom of the great body of water and the blue of God's firmament is being reflected in the depths of the lake behind Watauga Dam, that you will still retain in your hearts your love of liberty and progress.*
>
> *Let us dedicate ourselves anew to the immediate task of helping to win this war for freedom and decency and human progress in order that those who come after us may know something of the peace and happiness which you and I in our time have known here at this quiet, lovely seat of learning.*

The 318-foot-high Watauga Dam was one of the nation's highest earth- and rock-filled dams at the time. Crews bulldozed an old rail bed down to the dam construction site, skirting a ravine crossed by the former Headless Lady's Trestle. They built a 3,700-foot-long tunnel from the reservoir to the powerhouse, located about a half mile downriver from the dam. The TVA purchased more than eleven thousand acres of timberland and processed its lumber at a sawmill at Fish Springs, named for a fishing hole on the Watauga River where fish swam into a rock cavity. In the late 1700s, Bishop Francis Asbury, a Methodist circuit rider, crossed "Wattawba about 20 times," he wrote, and ate "perch that was taken from Smith's fish spring. I judge there to be a subterranean communication from that to the river."

In 1945, the TVA acquired the 375-foot-wide Wilbur Dam (or Horseshoe Dam) and its seventy-two-acre reservoir from the East Tennessee Light and Power Company, about two miles downriver from the Watauga Dam construction site. The Doe River Light and Power Company (later Watauga Power Company) started the project in 1909 and gifted the community with its first electrical power on Christmas Day 1911. Knowing that 1940 floodwaters had gushed over Wilbur Dam and damaged its powerhouse, the TVA raised the dam by 5 feet, added a gate-controlled spillway system and upgraded its generation units.

By 1948, the new Watauga Dam had displaced Butler, the "largest populated community and only incorporated town to be inundated by a

TVA's safety officer H.T. Norman overlooks Watauga Dam, 1952. *Tennessee State Library and Archives.*

TVA project," reported TVA's website. In the 1760s, John Honeycutt and others established the settlement as John's Town, which changed in the early 1800s to Smith's Mill after the Ezekiel Smith gristmill on Roan Creek. After the Civil War, the name became Butler to honor the Union army's Lieutenant Colonel Roderick R. Butler, a Taylorsville (now Mountain City) resident, member of the Tennessee House of Representatives and later U.S. congressman. The TVA paid $35,000 for Butler and its infrastructure. "The next mayor of Butler," a sad citizen said, "will be a catfish."

The TVA relocated three bridges, fifty miles of roads and more than one thousand grave sites. Farmers, miners, loggers, businessmen, blacksmiths and more than six hundred families departed for higher ground. Contractors moved more than one hundred homes and fifty buildings. Reverend M.H. Carder led a project to purchase three farms on Cobb Creek. Organizers divided the acreage into home site lots, auctioned them off to the people of Butler and named the new town Carderview. Around 1953, its name changed to New Butler but was later shortened back to Butler.

In 1949, Anna Dugger Adkins was eighteen years old when the TVA forced her father, Warren "Duff" Dugger (1902–circa 1982), Butler's postal deliveryman, to sell his home on Roan Creek Road. Two years earlier, Anna had graduated from Watauga Academy. On Friday nights, the academy featured country music artists, like Roy Acuff (1903–1992). Anna's aunt, Janie Dugger, an Acuff fan and physically impaired since childhood from polio, planned to attend the concert. Climbing the auditorium steps on crutches was risky, her husband thought, and he refused to pay for it.

"I'm going!" demanded Janie, taking twenty-five cents from her coin collection.

"I won't drive you!" snapped her husband.

Anna offered to take her. She held on to Janie, limping up one auditorium step at a time, until a man tapped Anna on her shoulder. "I'll help her from here." After the ladies settled into their seats, the gentleman slipped away.

"Who was that?" asked Janie.

"Roy Acuff," whispered Anna.

Anna's ancestor Julius Caesar Dugger was an early Indian trader, a Revolutionary War veteran and "one of the first white men to settle here in 1780," said ninety-one-year-old Anna. His son John fought in the War of 1812, became a local physician and operated a forge in the Dry Run community with his brother William. John's sons, Abel and William, were early operators of the iron works at Cranberry.

"I didn't like moving from Old Butler," she said. "Everything's gone: the Whiting Lumber Company, the furniture factory, a whole town, a way of life, and especially our railroad." She admitted, however, that some families had benefited from TVA's employment opportunities and paychecks. The TVA paid Butler residents for their homes and then sold them at public auctions. Some homeowners sued the TVA for a higher rate. Others sold their houses and then, like Duff Dugger, bought them back.

"My father got a raw deal," said Anna. The TVA offered Duff $8,000 for his brick house and fifteen-acre farm. When he contested the price in court, he received $11,000 but later repurchased the house for $800 and hired movers to transport it to a hill across from today's Butler Baptist Church. "We ate breakfast at home in Old Butler and ate supper in the same house at the new location." Anna's father and mother, Etta May Estes Dugger (1898–1959), a Johnson City nurse, lived in the home until their passing. Anna chose not to revisit Old Butler during TVA's 1954 and 1983 reservoir drawdowns. The uncovered foundations provoked treasured homecomings for some and bitter memories for others.

Anna Dugger Adkins, Butler Museum. In the wall-sized photo, Russell Mink crosses Old Butler's Main Street to visit his grandfather's hardware/grocery store. His father hand-built the wagon after seeing a Red Radio Flyer pictured in a Sears catalogue. The photo was published in a local newspaper and became the June 2021 cover of *The Tennessean* magazine. *Dan Stansberry.*

From left to right: Carolyn, Pat, Dee and Juanita Tester, near their home in the Midway community, 1945. *Juanita Wilson.*

TN-67 leaves US-321, crosses Butler Memorial Bridge at Watauga Lake and arrives at Butler, where a museum opened in 2000 to preserve the history of the former town. A gun owned by James Baker Dugger (1821–1861), Anna's great-uncle who died in the Civil War, is on display, as are farming tools, logging equipment, a church window and other artifacts. The old Curtis Store and Pharmacy display reminds Juanita Tester Wilson, a Butler Museum docent, that her fourteen-year-old sister, Charlene, would drive her there for ice cream, biting off the cone's base to lick the ice cream dripping from the bottom.

The Watauga Reservoir flooded the childhood home of Juanita's mother, built around 1835 by Benjamin C. Cable (1789–1850). In the mid-1770s, Benjamin's father, Casper Cable, came to America as a German Hessian soldier to help the British fight the colonists. He later deserted the British to join the Americans and eventually built a home in today's Johnson County. Juanita grew up in the Midway community. As a child, she swam in the Watauga River near the former home site of John and Ordie Potter, her mother's sister. The Potters watched their house float downriver in the Flood of 1940, its curtains waving farewell through open windows. Around 1950, Juanita's parents, Luke (1911–1967) and Dee Cable Tester (1914–2010), owned the Midway Service and Grocery beside their home, where Juanita pumped gas for eighteen cents per gallon. At age ten, she sold bait to fisherman headed to the new Watauga Lake and hunting/fishing licenses to sportsman en route to the CNF.

———•———

THE CNF BORDERS THE 1.8-mile-long Wilbur Lake and the 16-mile-long Watauga Lake. Loons, grebes, scoters and scaups drop in occasionally. Ospreys (*Pandion haliaetus*) return in the spring to raise their young. The TVA manages observation sites, picnic areas, a visitor center and the Watauga Dam Tailwater Campground. The CNF manages boat launch areas at Rat Branch, Little Milligan and Sink Mountain. On a peninsula across from the dam, visitors view beautiful sunsets at the USFS Cardens Bluff Campground. Across US-321/TN-67 near the campground, the CNF manages the Pond Mountain Shooting Range. At Fish Springs, where the Dugger brothers operated a former Watauga River ferry, a commercial marina provides boating services. The USFS Watauga Point Recreation Area has a picnic ground, often visited by turkeys, woodpeckers and butterflies. Male Canada

Geese (*Branta canadensis*) flap in a frenzy, each defending its favored female. Sailboats glide over white-capped ripples beneath the USFS Big Laurel Branch Wilderness on the opposite side of the lake.

CNF mountains rise more than one thousand feet above the northern shoreline. There, in 1990, a CNF employee found skeletal remains, trash and overturned rocks outside a cave. Vandals were excavating an ancient Cherokee burial ground for personal collection and profit. Three arrests, court testimonies and one defendant's consent to wear undercover audio-recording equipment led to nine convictions. The suspects, including a county assistant tax assessor and a known felon, had violated the 1979 Archaeological Resources Protection Act.

The USFS contacted the Tennessee State Historic Preservation Office, the Regional Forest Service Committee for the Treatment of Human Remains and the Cherokee people. Officials received the Cherokees' permission to remove the Lake Hole Cave's contents for a tribal reburial. The Appalachian State University Department of Anthropology received approval to conduct scientific studies at the site. Two hundred volunteers—including archaeologists, students and a Cherokee tribal member who studied anthropology at Western Carolina University—recorded thousands of human, animal and plant remains within the limestone and dolomite cavity. They found bone and marine shell beads, stone and antler tools, arrow points and pottery sherds. Radiocarbon testing of a bone tool estimated that the artifacts dated back to the Late Woodland to Early Mississippian periods. The human bones revealed a minimum of ninety-nine male and female individuals, from babies to adults, with disease histories, primarily, of degenerative arthritis, infection and dental disorders. They recovered the skeletal remains of an extinct horse gone by 8500 BP; a giant armadillo, extinct around 10,000 BP; and a fisher, a member of the musk-scented weasel family, last seen in the Southern Appalachians in the early 1800s. A locked gate now prevents illegal entries.

ON US-321/TN-67, A TURN onto Dennis Cove Road (FSR-50) takes motorists on a five-mile, zig-zagged route to the remote USFS Dennis Cove Recreation Area beside the Laurel Fork of the Doe River. Trails lead to Dennis Cove and Firescald Branch Falls. A longer hike with numerous creek crossings heads toward Upper Laurel Fork Falls.

The A.T. crosses Dennis Cove Road at a small parking area. A.T. hikers may take a spur trail (a former A.T. route) south of the road to CNF's Coon Den Falls near a former logging camp or cross the road to head toward the seven-thousand-acre USFS Pond Mountain Wilderness, federally designated in 1986. Between Black and Pond Mountains, Laurel Fork elbows through a gorge of boulder fields and rock cliffs with rollicking force and spectacular beauty. In the 1990s, the USFS awarded the Appalachian Trail Conservancy's (ATC) Konnarock Volunteer Trail Crew a National Primitive Skills Award for constructing the Coonford Laurel Fork Bridge with hand tools (no hardware) and native woods. The forty-foot-tall, fifty-foot-wide Laurel Fork Falls drops into a deep pool with powerful, potentially deadly hydraulics. (Hikers also take Hampton Blueline/Laurel Falls Trail and a portion of the A.T. from a trailhead on US-321/TN-67 to reach the falls.)

Portions of the A.T. follow the former Pittsburgh Lumber Company's 14.9-mile Laurel Fork Railway (LFRy), incorporated in 1910. Unable to negotiate equitable terms for freight service with the ET&WNC Railroad, the company built a standard-gauge track from Elizabethton's railroad connections and roughly paralleled the ET&WNC Railroad lines to Valley Forge, where they parted ways. The LFRy turned east and passed the company's sawmill at Braemer, named after the owner's Pittsburgh home. It entered Laurel Fork Gorge, passed Waycoster Spring and reached Crows (now Dennis Cove), where a wye turned the locomotives around. Beyond Crows, it continued seven miles upstream, passed the small Frog Level station and terminated at a fork to "Bitter End" and "No Man's Land." About fifteen miles of spur logging rail lines snaked up the coves of the company's twelve thousand acres. About fifty trestles and trusses crossed waterways.

By the mid-1900s, flooding had destroyed many tracks and trestles and loggers had harvested most of Laurel Fork's profitable timber. The company sold the sawmill to the Holston River Company to replace that logging company's mill lost to fire in Clinchburg, Virginia. Today, the Braemer mill's office and commissary building is operated as a hostel for hikers. The USFS acquired nine thousand of its cut-over acres. Isolated old-growth forests remain.

Around 2016, the CNF acquired the twenty-acre Shook Branch tract, purchased by The Conservation Fund in cooperation with the ATC from the owners two years earlier. This acquisition, adjacent to the Pond Mountain Wilderness and TWRA's Laurel Fork Bear Reserve, improved the steep A.T. descent from the wilderness area to the USFS Shook Branch Recreation Area on Watauga Lake. In 2021, Tennessee Eastman Hiking and Canoeing Club (TEHCC) volunteers completed the construction of the rerouted A.T. section.

CNF's Shook Branch picnic grounds and swimming area buzzes in the summer. Kayakers launch boats, double-stacked atop a small car. A motorboat sputters, cranks and sputters again. Jet skis pull youngsters on inner tubes. Slalom skiers cut rooster tails. Grandads bob in floating recliners over frequent waves. A barefoot toddler in a pink-dotted bikini plays in the sand. Portuguese water dogs on leashes walk along the grassy bank. A couple fishes beside a dead snake and their nearby canoe, offering an escape to quieter coves.

The A.T. leaves the recreation area and passes the site of the former Watauga Lake Shelter. During his 2009 A.T. hike from Georgia to West Virginia, Glenn McAllister stopped at the shelter and dipped his one-gallon ice cream container in a stream for a sponge bath. He met "Seeker," a long-distance hiker who took cover at the shelter during a rainstorm. She was seeking "a spiritual connection with nature," Glenn wrote, and asked him what *he* was seeking, but his hiking experiences focused on finding. "I

TVA's reservoirs provide recreational opportunities, 1946. *Tennessee State Library and Archives.*

find something; something finds me. The mystery around the bend—that intersection, that serendipitous moment—excited me and kept me walking."

The USFS constructed the A.T. Watauga Lake Shelter in 1980. After 1997 and 2007 upgrades, a Boy Scout installed a bear-resistant, pole-and-pulley food protection system as a 2011 Eagle Scout project. By 2013, however, several undaunted bears had frequented the shelter, as well as the nearby TVA Watauga Dam Campground. The USFS temporarily closed the shelter to encourage bears to find food elsewhere. The TVA installed bear-resistant garbage cans, halted tent camping and educated the public about conscientious outdoor activities in bear habitats. After the CNF reopened the shelter in 2016, the bears returned, destroying tents, outsmarting the food protection system and tearing into backpacks hung high among the trees. To avoid further human-bear conflicts, officials removed the shelter and campsite around 2019.

Each year, CNF officials report human-bear interactions at recreation areas, forcing them to temporarily close designated sites. Over the decades, American black bear (*Ursus americanus*) populations in East Tennessee have increased. Approximately 1,500 inhabit the CNF, while around 1,900 roam in GSMNP. The number of people recreating in the bear's native habitats has increased also. In 2021, about 2 million people visited the CNF; about 14 million visited the national park. More people and more bears create a greater potential for human-bear interactions and conflicts.

By nature, bears avoid public places. Their keen sense of smell leads these omnivores to several dietary options. Adapting their diet to available food sources, black bears consume nuts, berries, fruits, insects and plants. The opportunistic predators also feed on deer fawns, elk calves and other prey. However, odors from grills, picnic baskets, backpacks, bird feeders, pet foods, garbage cans and human handouts entice bears to overcome their human-wary behavior and accept a readily available meal.

CNF, TWRA and GSMNP biologists have formed a black bear cooperative agreement, renewed every five years, to coordinate bear management. "We have an excellent working relationship with the CNF and the TWRA," said GSMNP supervisory wildlife biologist William H. (Bill) Stiver. Each year, GSMNP and TWRA officials work with the CNF to relocate about ten bears (those with short conflict histories or considered less likely to repeat concerning behaviors) from the national park to backcountry regions in the national forest. In August 2020, wildlife agents relocated two female bears, fed in GSMNP by Cades Cove visitors, to a northern CNF district about forty-five miles away. Before they released the sows, separately but at the same site, the team attached GPS-tracking systems. Each female took a different journey. One female foraged around Cocke County, Tennessee; explored Hot Springs, North Carolina; crossed I-40 near the Foothills Parkway; cruised through Gatlinburg; and returned to Cades Cove.

GPS signals tracked the other female heading south of the CNF to cross Interstate 40 three times. After she passed through Maggie Valley, North Carolina, she ate blackberries for days behind the Walmart in Waynesville. She traveled about forty miles to Cashiers, North Carolina; turned north to Bryson City; and swam across Fontana Lake to GSMNP's southern border. She explored Forney Ridge south of Clingmans Dome; passed the national park headquarters; walked toward Pigeon Forge/Sevierville, Tennessee; and reentered GSMNP near Cosby Campground. On her 215-mile, two-month-long journey, the bear roamed west past the park's Smokemont Campground and Oconaluftee Visitor Center and headed south to Cherokee, North Carolina.

To monitor the activities of relocated bears, wildlife officials immobilize them, record their biological data, place a tattoo inside their lip and attach an identification tag to each ear. Stiver worked with a college graduate student intern to analyze twenty-five years of black bear relocation data and learned that "three in four of the ear-tagged bears were never spotted again."

Around 2017, a bear study across Tennessee, Georgia and the Carolinas revealed that seventy thousand bears live in a region occupied by more than 124 million people. In an area heavily populated by both bears and people, the study demonstrated the importance of "addressing the educational components of bear issues across the region," said TWRA wildlife biologist Dan Gibbs. "We wanted an educational program managed by statewide agencies and trusted as the go-to authority on living responsibly with bears. We wanted consistency." Stiver said that his emphasis was "to educate the public on what measures to take to not allow bears to become food-conditioned." In 2018, the fifteen-state Southeastern Association of Fish and Wildlife Agencies (SEAFWA) introduced the BearWise® Program. The web-based public education program provides science-based, readily available information about black bear biology and behavior. It also explains how to resolve and prevent human-caused conflicts with bears. In 2022, SEAFWA transferred BearWise® to the Association of Fish and Wildlife Agencies (AFWA) to expand the program on a national level. Thirty states have joined the efforts. "The BearWise program helps keeps people safe and bears wild," said Linda Masterson, author of the *Living with Bears Handbook* and the BearWise® Program's communications and marketing director. In the

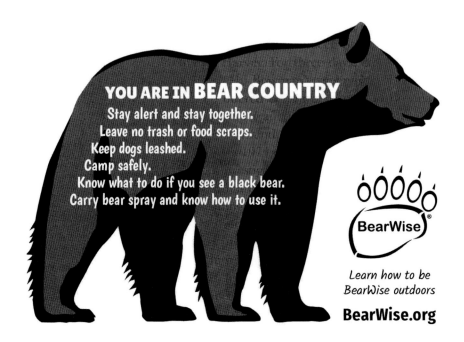

BearWise safety information. *Linda Masterson/ Lavonne Ewing, bearwise.org.*

CNF, the program has partnered with the USFS to provide bear safety tips for kiosks at recreation areas. BearWise® Tennessee also works in association with Appalachian Bear Rescue, a nonprofit organization near Townsend, Tennessee, rehabilitating orphaned and injured bear cubs to return them to native habitats.

———————•———————

AFTER THE A.T. PASSES the Watauga Dam, the trail enters CNF's Big Laurel Branch Wilderness, federally designated in 1986, and the adjacent 4,466-acre Big Laurel Branch Wilderness Study Area (WSA), established around 2004. After organizers formed the Southern Appalachian Wilderness Stewards (SAWS) around 2010, providing volunteer labor to help maintain wilderness trails, Senators Lamar Alexander and Robert Corker Jr. repeatedly introduced the Tennessee Wilderness bill to Congress. In 2018, Congress approved the bill as part of the Agricultural Improvement Act (or farm bill), which upgraded 20,000 WSA acres in the CNF to federally protected wilderness areas, including the Big Laurel Branch WSA. The act increased CNF's total wilderness acreage to 86,000, which also includes the Big Frog, Little Frog, Upper Bald River, Sampson Mountain and Joyce Kilmer–Slickrock areas.

A hiker traces the crest of Iron Mountain through the wilderness with its Big Laurel Branch headed to Wilbur Lake, ancient streams in deep channels, rock cliffs with open views and forested hillsides recovered from wildfires. Seen from a picnic area along Wilbur Dam Road, the fickle, rainfall-dependent falls of Little Laurel Branch tumble down rock bluffs into the lake. Carolina hemlocks (*Tsuga caroliniana*) cling to dry, rocky cliffs. The Carolina hemlock, like the more common eastern hemlock (*Tsuga canadensis*), which prefers shady, moist habitats, has struggled to survive hemlock woolly adelgids, introduced, presumably, on plants imported into Virginia in the 1920s. Discovered in Tennessee in 2005, the adelgids have expanded their range, now syphoning the carbohydrate reserves of hemlocks in twenty states. The USFS and its partners have released predator beetles, applied contact and systemic insecticides and collected hemlock seeds for preservation in gene banks.

The A.T. leaves Big Laurel Branch Wilderness and reaches the grave site of Nicholas "Uncle Nick" Grindstaff (1851–1923). After Nick's parents died, relatives raised the boy until he built a house on his quarter share of the family's inheritance at age twenty-one. Five years later, Nick sold the property and headed west. Some legends say that he became a successful gold miner or sheep herder and that he returned to Tennessee after his wife died and robbers left him penniless.

Nick built a log cabin on Iron Mountain, overlooking Doe Valley to the southeast and the Stoney Creek home of his birth to the north, and lived there with his ox, dog and rattlesnake. For forty-five years, he gathered wild foods, planted vegetable gardens and stored apples in the stump of an old chestnut tree. He earned money working for farmers in the valley to buy goods at a Shady Valley store and transported them by an ox-led sled back to his mountaintop home. The year he died, Nick planted sugarcane to make molasses.

Men found Nick lifeless in his cabin with his devoted canine. Two years later, two hundred family members and friends attended Nick's memorial service on Iron Mountain beside an elaborate monument, embedded with some of Nick's cooking tools. A judge, a preacher, a professor and others presented the eulogies. Since 1936, countless A.T. day-hikers and thousands of thru-hikers (hikers completing the A.T. in one season) have passed the former home of the man seeking social isolation.

"Uncle Nick Grindstaff"

Way up on Iron Mountain
In Northeast Tennessee
On the Appalachian Trail
There's a sight to see...
There's an old, cold gravestone
For a hermit named Nick
Who lived in a shack,
With his dog, all alone.

And, it read...

CHORUS

Lived alone, suffered alone, died alone,
Uncle Nick Grindstaff.

He was orphaned at three,
When he turned 26
Uncle Nick ventured west
To find his fortune in gold.
But they robbed him and beat him,
And knocked him out cold,
And when he woke up,
He heard a sad, mournful sound.
That dog cried so sadly,
Uncle Nick named him Blue
And they went on home to Tennessee
And lived way up on the Iron.

Where they...

CHORUS

On a cold winter eve
Two hunters found the shack
And the old man dead on the floor
And the saddest crying by the dog by his side
Who lay keeping watch over Nick Grindstaff

Who now is...

Living with Angels, and he suffers no more,
Uncle Nick Grindstaff, on God's Holy shore.

By JENNIFER GILLENWATER. The legacy of Nick Grindstaff stirred the heart and mind of this Butler resident, A.T. section-hiker and singer/songwriter. By the time she had hiked off the mountain, she had mentally written these lyrics of her first ballad. "I hike to the monument every year and sing it at his grave site." She has written more than fifty songs preserving Appalachian culture and performs with her group, Nowhere Valley, at Roan Mountain State Park and local festivals.

In the mid-1950s, a fire spread from Iron Mountain to Watauga Lake and burned Nick's old barn, said Granville Taylor, Nick's sixth-generation nephew. For half a century, Taylor has hiked to the monument two to three times a year to squirrel hunt and maintain the site. "My dad took me squirrel hunting at Uncle Nick's place when I was eight," the eighty-year-old said. "I was sixty-two before I found his dog's grave," buried about fourteen inches beside Nick. Around 2016, Taylor collected $900 in donations to rehabilitate the crumbling monument but had to return the money two years later when the plans failed. In May 2022, however, the TEHCC helped the USFS restore the grave site.

In the CNF, the TEHCC is responsible for the maintenance of nearly 134 miles of the A.T. and reports a "strong relationship" with the USFS, Appalachian Trail Conservancy (ATC) and other volunteer trail maintenance crews that trim vegetation, remove downfall, restore bridges and rehabilitate shelters. TEHCC also participates in Nolichucky River cleanup projects, provides A.T. presentations for school and civic groups, offers guided hiking and paddling events and assists the Appalachian Paddling Enthusiasts with beginner's paddling classes and swift water rescue courses.

Frank Oglesby founded the club in 1946 and conducted pre-hike trail reconnaissance trips aboard his private airplane. Early members met with Myron Avery (1899–1952) in Knoxville. Avery—a Harvard Law School graduate, World War II veteran and cofounder of the Potomac Appalachian Trail Club—led the 1927–37 efforts to complete the blazing of the A.T. from Georgia to Maine. He was the first hiker to complete the two-thousand-mile journey, section by section. From 1931 until a month before his death, Avery was the chairman of the Appalachian Trail Conference, now the Appalachian Trail Conservancy. Avery encouraged hiking clubs along the fourteen-state footpath to help maintain it.

The TEHCC became dedicated to the cause. Around 1947, the club adopted the 6.23-mile section from Spivey Gap in Pisgah National Forest (PNF), North Carolina, to the Nolichucky River in the CNF. The Roan Mountain Hiking Club maintained the Holston and Unaka Mountain sections. Jonesborough, Tennessee native Paul Fink (1892–1980), an advocate for a new national park in the Smokies, was instrumental in establishing over 300 A.T. miles in North Carolina and Tennessee. He maintained a 25-mile road-walk section between Limestone (near today's USFS Limestone Cove Recreation Area) and the town of Winner, Tennessee, in Watauga Valley.

In 1952, Stanley A. Murray (1923–1990), a TEHCC member and, later, the 1961–75 ATC chairman, proposed rerouting about fifty-four A.T. miles between the Holston and Unaka Mountains. By 1954, the new route had bypassed Fink's dangerous road-walk and Holston Mountain's communication towers. The improved route takes hikers to Iron Mountain, Laurel Fork Falls, White Rocks Mountain, Little Rock Knob and the Highlands of Roan. Like Myron Avery and Benton MacKaye, Murray wanted a footpath that offered "a new approach to the problem of living," as noted by MacKaye, the author of the "American Greenway" concept.

In 1966, Murray, particularly devoted to the protection of the A.T. section across the Highlands of Roan, formed the Roan Mountain Preservation Committee (RMPC) to assist the ATC in preserving the trail. The Maine native campaigned for its federal protection under the 1968 National Trails System Act. By 1974, the RMPC had broadened its conservation efforts to preserve more valuable ecosystems in the South and formed the nonprofit land trust Southern Appalachian Highlands Conservancy (SAHC). Today,

Benton MacKaye (left) and Myron Avery. *Appalachian Trail Conservancy.*

many thousands of its acquired acres are managed by the USFS. Near the A.T. on Hump Mountain's Houston Ridge in PNF, the USFS and SAHC placed a plaque in honor of Murray's devotion to the protection of the natural world.

LAUREL BLOOMERY

Beyond the Grindstaff monument, the A.T. takes an oblique turn off Iron Mountain and cuts over Cross Mountain, a ridgeline that lies perpendicular between Iron and Holston Mountains. The A.T. follows the northern crest of Holston Mountain, crosses US-421/TN-34 and intersects CNF's Backbone Rock Trail before entering Virginia's George Washington and Jefferson National Forests.

On Cross Mountain, the A.T. crosses TN-91 at a roadside parking area, where the TEHCC and USFS built an accessible A.T. segment for visitors with special needs. The Osborne Farm and bog area provide pleasant views into Shady Valley. TN-91 continues north and junctions with US-421/TN-

34 at the community of Shady Valley. From there, a motorist can travel north over Holston Mountain to the South Holston Lake, drive straight onto TN-133 to the USFS Backbone Rock Recreation Area or head south toward Mountain City.

Mountain City is the seat of government for Johnson County, named for Thomas Johnson, one of its first elected magistrates. He married Fannie Scott of Virginia, a woman who escaped an abduction by Cherokees to bushwhack three hundred miles back home. Taylorsville, named for James P. Taylor (1792–1833), was the county seat until officials changed the name to Mountain City around 1885. About one quarter of Johnson County lies within the CNF.

TN-67 follows Doe Creek and TN-167 follows Roan Creek to encircle Doe Mountain, a prominent feature stretching from Watauga Lake to the edge of Mountain City. In 2012, The Nature Conservancy (TNC) and the State of Tennessee "extracted the mountain from federal bankruptcy proceedings," said TNC's Gabby Lynch, and created the 8,600-acre Doe Mountain Recreation Area. The Tennessee state legislature created the Doe Mountain Recreation Authority (DMRA) to assume management of the multi-use recreation park. The restored 1930s Kettlefoot Lookout Tower offers dramatic views of the CNF region. In 2018, the American Carbon Registry approved DMRA's application to register Doe Mountain as a carbon forest project. Forest-covered sections of the mountain remain intact, absorbing atmospheric carbon dioxide and storing it for decades. Forested lands may help capture atmospheric carbon and mitigate climate change. Scientists will measure the forest's carbon capture and storage capabilities for the next forty years to help formulate future conservation and recreation management decisions.

North of Mountain City, a joyride loop sweeps in and out of the CNF, crosses three mountains, passes rock formations and borders rushing streams. Sports car drivers and motorcyclists on this "Snake-421 Road Trip" ease around four hundred curves as they cross and circumnavigate the northern section of Iron Mountain. The thirty-seven-mile trip leaves US-421/TN-34, passes through Shady Valley on TN-133 and swings through Damascus, Virginia. It returns south via TN-91, slips through the Laurel Bloomery community, angles right onto Cold Springs Road, crosses Laurel Creek and returns to the main thoroughfare near Mountain City.

TN-91/North passes through Mountain City near the circa 1870 home of Colonel Roderick Butler and the Johnson County Welcome Center and Museum. As the highway leaves town, visitors experience the unhurried pace of life in the CNF's region located in the most northeastern corner of Tennessee. The roadway begins to border Laurel Creek as it travels toward the communities of Eureka and Laurel Bloomery. Laurel Creek picks up Shingletown Branch, Gentry Creek and other tributaries as it flows north to join the Holston River in Virginia. Near the Virginia state line, the stream passes by Camp Ahistadi, a Christian retreat in the CNF that operates under a USFS Special Use Permit. A camp trail connects to the Laurel Creek Trail, constructed by the Johnson County Trails Association.

After a strategic planning effort by the county and town governments around 2001, Howard and Linda Moon started the Johnson County Trails Association (JCTA) to provide a county-wide trail system. By 2005–6, the nonprofit organization had received funds through the Federal Appropriations Transportation Bill (later transferred to the Tennessee Department of Environment and Conservation) to construct a trail through the CNF along the banks of Laurel Creek. Inmate labor joined volunteers to construct the 2.5-mile trail from the CNF border near Laurel Bloomery to the Virginia state line.

"We cut back the dense growth of laurel and rhododendron," said Jeff Fritts, a sixty-one-year-old Laurel Bloomery native and JCTA board member, "and discovered the prettiest wagon road along Laurel Creek that crossed the ridge down to Dollarsville." Dollarsville was the site of a former logging camp near the today's intersection of TN-91/North and Taylors Valley Road. Monroe, John and Roby Dollar managed the camp's boardinghouse, office, mess hall and water stop for a railway.

For decades, buffaloes, Native Americans and traders had followed a route through Laurel Creek Gorge, fording the creek several times. Later, settlers built a wagon road beside Laurel Creek, called "Steep Rock Creek" on early maps. The wagon road roughly followed the 1905–19 rail line of T.W. Thayer Lumber Company's Laurel Railway. Known as the "Peavine Railroad," the narrow-gauge rail service transported lumber, iron ore and occasionally passengers from Damascus, Virginia, to the Mountain City Depot. Laurel Creek's wooden bridges are long gone, but TN-91 and the Laurel Creek Trail follow portions of the old rail bed. "A century ago, the former transportation route enhanced the region's economy and quality of life," noted the JCTA website. "Now, we're bringing it back for the same reasons."

Crews discovered old railroad spikes, mule shoes and bridge abutments. They also discovered a forgotten gap through the mountains when a large rock outcropping on Laurel Creek posed a construction challenge. Senior residents suggested building the trail around the bankside geological beauty by veering away from the creek and cutting through Providence Gap, like the early wagon road travelers did.

"We envision trails connecting eighty-seven miles through Johnson County," states the club's website. Long-term goals include building trails from Mountain City to Doe Valley, Doe Valley to Shady Valley and Shady Valley to CNF's Backbone Rock Recreation Area. The group wants to extend the Laurel Creek Trail into Virginia and south to Mountain City. They hope to build a spur trail, connecting the Laurel Creek Trail to the Virginia Creeper Trail, a thirty-four-mile rail-to-trail adventure for hikers, bikers and equestrians.

Sections of the Laurel Creek Trail also follow one of the hunting and exploratory routes that Daniel Boone took during his westward journeys in the 1760s and 1770s and "runs through my front yard in Laurel Bloomery," said Fritts. Early settlers called the Laurel Bloomery community the "Head of the Laurel" or "Wards Forge." In the 1790s, Mayor John Ward, a veteran of the War of 1812, joined Joseph O. Gentry and Lewis Willis to establish a timber and ironworks business on the banks of the creek embraced by mountain laurel. By 1878, residents had named the area Laurel Bloomery after its iron forging operations. Workers transported iron ore from the mines on nearby mountains to the furnace, or bloomery. The forging process changed iron ore into a small lump, or bloom, of wrought iron, about the size of a softball.

Around 1752, seventeen-year-old Boone (1734–1820) moved with his family from Pennsylvania to settle in North Carolina. "It was the first of May, in the year 1769, that I resigned my domestic happiness for a time and left my family and peaceable habitation on the Yadkin River in North Carolina, to wander through the wilderness of America," Boone told the Kentucky land developer and biographer John Filson, who published Boone's first-person account of his adventures in 1794. After exploring the Holston River Valley region, Boone followed that route on later expeditions, crossing the current state line at Trade on an old buffalo trail. From there, Boone traveled near the towns of Shoun (Crossroads) and Mountain City on one favored route and camped along Laurel Creek. Beyond the Laurel Bloomery community, he continued north to the present Virginia state line before crossing north and west through the Holston Valley. Eventually, along this route and others, Boone made his way to the Kentucky region. On one early trip, heading southwest of Trade, Boone visited Johnson County's first recorded white settler, John Honeycutt of Roan Creek, and stopped at Old Butler. This route took him along the

Daniel Boone. *Tennessee State Library and Archives.*

Watauga River toward Sycamore Shoals and onto the Long Island of the Holston in today's Kingsport, Tennessee.

In 1913–15, four state societies of the National Society of the Daughters of the American Revolution (DAR) collaborated in paying tribute to Boone's pioneering spirit. The Tennessee, North Carolina, Virginia and Kentucky societies placed fifty cast-iron markers along a two-hundred-mile commemorative route from a Daniel Boone home site in North Carolina to Fort Boonesborough in Kentucky. In Johnson, Carter, Washington and Sullivan Counties, the Tennessee DAR marked nine sites along Tennessee's "historically best-known portion of the trail" from Sycamore Shoals to Cumberland Gap, wrote Boone historian Randell Jones. Most tablet markers "were placed with attention to ceremony and engagement to the public." An elaborate river rock or a granite base held many of the cast-iron plates.

The organization dedicated a marker at Trade, Shoun and Butler. Today, the Butler Museum displays a Daniel Boone's Trail monument at its entrance. Volunteers moved the marker, discovered at the Pleasant Grove Baptist Church Cemetery near Maymead, Tennessee, to New Butler's Baptist Church in the 1960s. By 2000, history buffs had transferred the marker to the museum. All evidence suggests that this marker was Old Butler's original DAR monument, rescued from immersion under Watauga Lake formed by TVA's dam.

The DAR also placed trail markers at Elizabethton and Watauga. Around 1772, William Bean and James Robertson negotiated a lease agreement with the Cherokees to create the Watauga Association, the first self-governing settlement established west of the Appalachian Mountains and later visited by Boone. In 1775, at Sycamore Shoals near present-day Elizabethton, Richard Henderson and Daniel Boone met nearly 1,200 Cherokees, including their leaders, Attakullakulla and Oconostota, to settle the Transylvania Purchase treaty. The Transylvania Company swapped merchandise and supplies for 20 million acres of wilderness in the current regions of eastern Kentucky and the northern sections of middle Tennessee.

Attakullakulla's son, Dragging Canoe, refused to sign and acknowledge the treaty and eventually led a Cherokee resistance group against white settlers invading the Cherokee homelands south along the Tennessee River. During the four-day Sycamore Shoals meeting, the Watauga Association also paid the Cherokees in trading goods for ownership of their settlement, the Watauga Purchase. Henderson commissioned Boone to proceed west from Sycamore Shoals and blaze a trail for others to follow into the Transylvania lands. This route was called Boone's Trace.

The Tennessee DAR also marked Boone's visit to Austin Springs; Boone's Tree, where he supposedly carved his name into a beech tree after killing a bear; Old Fort, at the former site of Fort Patrick Henry; and present-day Kingsport, where Boone assembled his men at the downstream end of Long Island of the Holston River to begin marking Boone Trace.

Even though Boone visited Laurel Bloomery and chose this route to access the Holston River Valley, the Tennessee DAR did not mark its commemorative route through Laurel Creek Gorge, preferring a route through more of Tennessee. However, a massive Daniel Boone's marker, embedded with an old iron forge hammer, is seen today along TN-91. It is one of 358 historical markers erected across the country by Joseph Hampton Rich of Winston-Salem, North Carolina. It is part of Rich's commemorative efforts between 1913 and 1938 for the Boone Trail Highway and Memorial Association, explained Jones. Rich also placed a marker near a cave where Boone camped in Virginia. After a pack of wolves attacked his hunting dogs, Boone named the site Wolf Hills, now known as Abingdon, Virginia.

In 1981, the National Park Service formed a Daniel Boone Trail study group that included the U.S. Forest Service, the TVA and the States of North Carolina, Tennessee, Virginia and Kentucky. The group evaluated Boone's historic route for protection under the National Trails System Act as either a national scenic or historic trail. After extensive research, eight public meetings, 150 written responses from private citizens and groups and comments received from fifteen state and federal agencies, the park service decided that the Daniel Boone Trail did not qualify for scenic or historic trail preservation. About 95 percent of the 428-mile route followed roadways, and only 25 percent of the route was in public ownership. Today, local organizations have adopted and maintain sections of Boone's route as a Daniel Boone Heritage Trail.

———————•———————

NEAR LAUREL BLOOMERY, IN 1912, Irvin J. Warden and William O. Gentry rebuilt a former sawmill/gristmill on Laurel Creek that had burned two years earlier. By 1920, Warden had built a water-driven electric power station to provide electricity to homes, churches and schools. He delivered ice to Mountain City, Shady Valley and Damascus from his icehouse. In the mid-1960s, a ceramics designer, Nancy Patterson (Lamb), and her business partner, Albert Mock, opened a stoneware factory near Laurel Bloomery.

The unskilled workers of the community had to first learn the craft "by playing with clay," she told a Pennsylvania reporter in 1975. For twenty-seven years, workers molded, glazed and decorated fine dinnerware by hand, sold in stores around the world.

At Laurel Bloomery, Gentry Creek Road (FSR 123) leads about two miles to the USFS Rogers Ridge Scenic Area, named for John Rogers, believed to be the first white settler in the area. Rogers Ridge stretches from the CNF into the George Washington–Jefferson National Forests of Virginia. In the CNF, equestrians, cyclists and hikers access the four-thousand-acre area on the thirteen-mile round-trip Rogers Ridge Trail. The 4,500-feet-high grassy balds offer splendid views of North Carolina's Grandfather Mountain, Virginia's Mount Rogers and the surrounding Tennessee landscape. The borders of North Carolina, Tennessee and Virginia unite on nearby Pond Mountain at Tri-Corner Knob. There, a 1932 USGS Geodetic Survey disc designates the highest-elevation three-state boundary marker in the East. In the 1740s, after President Thomas Jefferson's father, Peter Jefferson, completed his team's survey of the boundary between the colonies of Virginia and North Carolina for the British, the rugged region prompted him to cease further surveying activities. On a place he called "Steep Rock" on Pond Mountain, Jefferson reportedly said, "This is where we stop because this is as far in the wilderness as any white man will go."

In 2018, The Conservation Fund (TCF) acquired more than 100 acres from the Hensley family in the tri-corner area on Divided Mountain, which extended across the Tennessee Valley Divide and the Tennessee/Virginia state line. The USFS developed a Divided Mountain Purchase Unit and added these lands to the CNF. This acquisition created additional access and recreational opportunities in the CNF and North Carolina's Pond Mountain State Game Lands. That year, in collaboration with TNC, TCF also acquired the Wolfe Tract, a 74.22-acre critical inholding adjacent to the Hensley property, and conveyed it to the CNF in April 2021.

The tri-corner acquisitions protect the headwater streams in the South Holston River watershed. Native brook trout thrive in the tributaries of Gentry Creek. Bear, deer and other wildlife inhabit the wild backcountry. The region hosts unique plant communities with uncommon species of orchids, watercress, twayblades, skullcaps and others. CNF's Gentry Creek Falls Trail, named for the early settler and iron ore magnate Joseph O. Gentry, begins near the Rogers Ridge Trailhead. An estimated five-mile round-trip hike climbs 1,200 feet in elevation and fords Gentry Creek fifteen times en route to the falls. The double-drop beauty plunges about 30 feet over a rock face and takes a pooled, aquatic breather before making a second, identical dive over a lower cliff. Dense stands of rhododendron, framing the rush of foam over dark-gray walls, soften the striking scene set in an isolated cove.

Since 1985, TCF has helped protect more than 8 million acres in fifty states, including more than 300,000 acres in the CNF. The TCF and USFS obtained monies for the Divided Mountain project through private donors and the Land and Water Conservation Fund (LWCF). In 1965, Congress established the LWCF, which designated portions of the earnings from offshore oil and gas leases for the funding of state and federal land protection and acquisition. Over the decades, Congress extended the program several times, but the policy expired in September 2018. By March 2019, the efforts of U.S. Tennessee senators Lamar Alexander and Marsha Blackburn and U.S. Tennessee representative Phil Roe led Congress to pass a bill to permanently reauthorize the LCWF program. In 2020, Alexander celebrated the bipartisan support of this Great American Outdoors Act, described by many as the "most important conservation law in half a century." The act guaranteed $9.5 billion over the next five years to help fund public lands projects, such as CNF road and trail maintenance. It also established a permanent $900 million annual budget for the LWCF.

"The LWCF has played a large role in protecting Tennessee's outdoors for over 50 years," Senator Alexander said in a press release. The addition of more than 100 acres to the CNF, between CNF's Rogers Ridge Scenic Recreation Area and North Carolina's 2,900-acre Pond Mountain Game Lands, provided the protection of 127,000 contiguous acres of public land. With LCWF aid, the CNF "will preserve even more of our state's beautiful land, water resources, and recreation areas." At the signing of the Great America Act at the White House, the senator presented President Donald Trump with a walking stick that Alexander had carried on his 1978 hike across Tennessee during his campaign for governor.

SHADY VALLEY

In the valley between the Iron, Holston and Cross Mountains, Beaverdam Creek flows north along TN-133 through the CNF to join the South Fork of the Holston River in Virginia. The highway roughly follows the early 1900s Beaverdam Railroad route that connected with the Virginia-Carolina Railway to serve lumber and mining industries. Railroad builders planned to blast away Backbone Rock, a one-hundred-foot-high spur ridge on Holston Mountain. When the dynamite left a twenty-foot-long tunnel, the first train crew passing through it had to carve the opening higher to accommodate the engine's smokestack. TN-133 now passes through the tunnel at the USFS Backbone Rock Recreation Area. Built by the CCC and upgraded by the USFS over the decades, the site attracts rock climbers scaling cliffs above the creek's horseshoe-bend curve; families enjoying campsites, deep Beaverdam Creek pools and pavilion-covered picnics; and wildflower seekers finding specialties like grass-of-parnassus (*Parnassia asarifolia*). Hikers visit a forty-foot-high waterfall or ascend stairs to the trail across the tunnel. The TEHCC upgraded rock steps, installed cribbing and brushed out a relocated side-trail to the A.T. with the help of Appalachian State University's Watauga Residential College freshmen in 2013 and ATC's Konnarock Crew in 2016 and 2017.

Anglers fish for trout in Beaverdam Creek, stocked, like Laurel and Gentry Creeks, by the TWRA. In September 2021, the USFS, TWRA and the Erwin National Fish Hatchery used electrofishing tools to stun and collect fish on Beaverdam Creek for a wild trout survey. Biologists collected stream

Backbone Rock. *Tennessee State Library and Archives.*

data to determine the size, type and number of species; the health of aquatic habitats; and the need for restoration. A hellbender sighting highlighted the day's work. That month, the CNF also inventoried Carter-Johnson County stream crossings to assess culverts, flood risks and habitats for at-risk species, like the hellbender, brook trout and Tennessee dace (*Chrosomus tennesseensis*). These aquatic habitat assessments were part of the USDA Joint Chiefs' Landscape Restoration Partnership, a $5 million, three-year project addressing the restoration of CNF waterways.

Near Backbone Rock Recreation Area, the Tennessee Lumber and Mining Company operated a mill at the Sutherland community in the 1900s. About a quarter mile southeast of Backbone Rock, the CNF acquired the former site of the 1898–1929 J.A. Neely mine. The national forest also acquired acreage in the Shady Valley Mining District leased by companies like Sutherland Prospect and Hogback Mine from the former U.S. Forest Reserve. Hamilton (Ham) Greer owned one of the area's largest mines on Holston Mountain's Marshall Branch, carting manganese ore washed out of dark-red clay to the rail station at Crandull. Railcars transported the clay to kilns in Shady Valley in an area now known as Brickyard Branch Road to make bricks. Trains then carried the bricks to markets in Damascus, Virginia.

The USFS acquired much of its estimated twenty-two thousand acres of the Shady Valley/Beaverdam Watershed area from lumber companies. Oaks, hickories, pines and poplars grow in coves, on slopes and across ridgetops. Table mountain pines, endemic to the Appalachian Mountains, thrive on exposed, rocky ridges. Sycamores, maples, oaks, beech, basswood and other species rise above dense rhododendron to shade the USFS riparian habitat along the Beaverdam Creek Gorge.

Generations ago, "Shady Valley was home to some of the densest forests in the Eastern U.S.," said Josh Kelly, a field biologist with MountainTrue, a conservation group committed to the protection of the region's forests and waterways. "The stands of white pine (*Pinus strobus*) and hemlock in the valley bottom were noted to be among the highest in timber volume ever recorded in the East." In 2008, Kelly searched for old-growth stands in a Shady Valley chestnut oak forest (*Quercus montana*) on the slopes of Iron Mountain, slated for a CNF logging project. Documentation of a virgin forest could exclude these mature giants from timber contracts. Kelly recorded five chestnut oaks twenty-two to thirty-four inches in diameter measured at breast height (DBH). Core samples revealed 176- to 381-year-old chestnut oaks. "The density of old chestnut oaks is quite notable," he wrote. "In one plot, I found three of the five oldest trees I've ever cored!" He speculated that this area could be "the oldest quarter-acre in Tennessee."

Before channelization projects in the 1930s and 1960s drained Shady Valley's wetlands for agricultural purposes, the ice age–era, high-elevation wetlands supported flora and fauna more common to northern ecosystems. Only a fraction of the original wild cranberry (*Vaccinium macrocarpon*) wetlands remains, however. Mountain peat wetlands of precipitation-fed bogs and groundwater-fed fens are considered some of the rarest ecosystems in the Southern Appalachians, providing habitats

Southern bog lemming. *Lee James Pantas.*

for rare species. Shady Valley specialties—like the glacial-relic four-toed salamander (*Hemidactylium scutatum*) and the star-nosed mole (*Condylura cristata*)—inhabit aquatic areas. Roby B. McQueen and John L. Shumate Jr. discovered the carcass of a least weasel (*Mustela nivalis*), North America's smallest carnivore, in 1966. J. Wallace Coffey later sent the specimen to the Smithsonian Museum. Brushy fields attract meadow jumping mice (*Zapus hudsonius*). Wet meadows are homes to Tennessee's only lemming, the southern bog lemming (*Synaptomys cooperi*), and North America's smallest turtle, the bog turtle (*Glyptemys muhlenbergii*).

In 1986, North Carolina herpetologist Dennis Herman and Connecticut bog turtle researcher Jim Warner discovered this turtle, less than four and a half inches long, in Tennessee. Federally listed as a threatened species in 1997, these semi-aquatic, dark-brown turtles are marked with a signature yellow/orange spot behind each ear (tympanum) and inhabit the muck and mud of shallow Shady Valley wetlands. They nest and bask in the sun on hummocks of sedges and grasses. In 1986, Zoo Knoxville curator of herpetology Bern Tryon (1947–2011) launched a bog turtle research program. The zoo also started a bog turtle captive breeding project for release back in the wild in

1991. Zoo staff and its partners—TNC, TWRA, University of Tennessee–Knoxville (UTK)—as well as private landowners, continue its efforts to better understand this species in the wild.

UTK graduate student Timothy Calhoun lived in Shady Valley from May to September in 2022 and 2023 conducting bog turtle research to estimate its population density. He captured turtles in small, partially submerged wire cages placed in turtle habitats. The oblivious little reptile walked up to a rectangular cage as it foraged and pushed up a flap on either end that dropped behind it, harmlessly trapping it inside. Calhoun also tracked turtles using a device adapted for bog turtle research by a Virginia Tech Conservation Management Institute field biologist. He attached a wildlife game camera to the inside bottom of a large bucket and turned it upside down in the wetland. "Turtles and all sorts of creatures walked under the bucket, and a camera took the picture," he said, "capturing the animal without needing to handle it or stress it out."

Calhoun reported two special captures. One cage held an old turtle with epoxy residue from a previous radio-telemetry study on top of its worn, smooth shell. In 2005, when the turtle was most likely tracked, it "quite possibly was a decade old and had now survived another two decades. The tangible connection to past research was exciting." In another trap, a two-year-old turtle, between the size of a quarter and a half dollar, awaited its release. "From an academic standpoint," Calhoun said, the evidence of recent reproduction gave "hope for the future of this population, but also, something that small is so dang cute!"

TNC bought its first Shady Valley bog in 1978 from Jess Taylor Jenkins (1906–1981), a country store owner with a deep appreciation for the natural world. The Jess Jenkins Bog became "a shrine of major significance," wrote J. Wallace Coffey and John L. Shumate Jr. "It fueled a special mountain pride. The community's respect for a frail bog plant, its pink flowers, and wild cranberries has united us all." At the 1979 deed signing celebration, the ETSU president accepted the property for staff/student research, but the university planned to donate it back to TNC in 2023.

In 1994, TNC purchased the first of several properties that now compose its 150-acre Orchard Bog Preserve and initiated extensive restoration practices. Crossed by a former Beaverdam Railroad extension leading to Shady Flats, divided by Beaverdam Creek and drained by the Army Corps of Engineers and others, these ancient wetlands had lost much of their natural identities. TNC, conservationists, students and volunteers help remove drainage systems, build low-level dams to retain water and remove exotic plants, like multiflora rose (*Rosa multiflora*) that outcompete the natives. At Orchard and Quarry Bog Preserves, CNF staff and Southern Appalachian Bog Learning Network, Zoo Knoxville, MountainTrue and university volunteers have helped with TNC's "Invasive Field Days." Small herds of grazing cows and goats help trim back overgrowth and remove non-native grasses pursuant to USFWS guidelines for so-called conservation grazing.

Purchased in 1998, the 68-acre Quarry Bog Preserve at the site of an early 1900s mining camp for road-building crews became a major TNC restoration project, in 2000, to protect bog turtles. With funding from the USDA/Natural Resources Conservation Service, additional stream restoration work occurred in 2022–23. TNC also purchased its first property at the 29-acre Schoolyard Springs Preserve near Shady Valley School, which offers a boardwalk and pathway along a sandy stream where groundwater bubbles to the surface. Rare plants, like marsh marigold (*Caltha palustris*) and crested woodfern (*Dryopteris cristata*), grow there. Bordered by the CNF, the forested 452-acre John R. Dickey Birch Branch Sanctuary property was donated to TNC in 1996 by Dr. Dickey's granddaughter. The conservancy later acquired 97 acres on an adjoining ridge.

Kenneth McQueen, TNC's Shady Valley preserves manager, coordinates the conservation efforts of the CNF, USFWS and others. Kenneth, a retired Johnson County High School agriculture teacher, is a sixth-generation McQueen in the area, living on his ancestor's property. Around 1835, Rice McQueen left North Carolina and passed through today's McQueen Gap on the A.T. to settle on Holston Mountain. In the CNF and surrounding area, a road, a branch and a knob (the site of a former USFS lookout tower) are also named for him. The family sold several hundred ridgeline acres to the USFS, now protected as an A.T. corridor.

Kenneth's father, Charles, was the Shady Valley Volunteer Fire Department chief and a farm equipment store owner. The Dickey family hired him to oversee their Shady Valley property. After TNC acquired it, the organization retained him to manage its four preserves. For more than thirty years, Charles and later Kenneth have brushed out overgrowth, rotated livestock, built the Schoolyard Springs boardwalk, removed invasive plants, conducted selective logging, managed prescribed burns and tended TNC's cranberry nursery at Orchard Bog. "I also help the USFS and others who come annually to collect cranberry cuttings," said Kenneth, "to transplant to CNF's Osborne Bog and other sites."

The USFWS and the USFS have helped fund TNC's restoration projects to protect Shady Valley's ecologically significant wetlands and the estimated twenty-six rare plants and animals that live there. In the 1990s, the Shady Valley Ruritans Club set up the first cranberry propagation beds in a privately owned bog in the valley. The members harvested donated cuttings, raised them in home gardens and transplanted the seedlings to Shady Valley's wetlands. To help establish TNC's propagation nursery, the USFS provided grant money to the USDA Appalachian Resource, Conservation and Development Council (ARCD) serving six counties in the Watauga Ranger District. "I enjoyed working with the USFS to help preserve our lands, natural resources and history," said Roy Settle, former ARCD coordinator. "The CNF supported many of our projects, addressing environmental, social and cultural interests." The CNF provided a $5,000 grant to expand the Johnson County High School greenhouse program to add a hydroponics project, growing plants without soil, and a tilapia raising activity, turning fecal droppings into fertilizer. USFS funds also helped build a Johnson County Arts Trail and restore a flood-damaged Greene County campground.

TNC has helped the USFS restore hydrologic function at bogs in CNF's Osborne Farm and Barry Farm (Johns Bog). In 2001, the ATC transferred 250 acres purchased from the Osborne family to the USFS, protecting the wetlands and the A.T. corridor and restoring the A.T.'s original route across the fields.

"Sometimes, promoting forest health means removing trees that hinder a desirable and diverse mix of forest canopy and understory species," said TNC's Gabby Lynch. In 2018, TNC enlisted the help of EcoForesters, a North Carolina nonprofit professional forestry organization, to restore oak-hickory communities, improve biodiversity and remove tulip poplars that dominated fields in one preserve "where we wanted to encourage more oaks and mast-producing trees to benefit wildlife." In 2022, the USFS awarded EcoForesters with funding from the Landscape Scale Restoration grant program for its restoration/stewardship projects with private landowners, public land managers and the Eastern Band of the Cherokee Indians.

Successful hydrologic and field management practices have allowed native species to return and flourish. Seeds lying dormant for years found life again. After the first frost, ripened red cranberries provide food for turkeys, grouse, deer and bears. The improved wetlands attract waterfowl, shorebirds and beavers. Hawks, sparrows and warblers inhabit the meadows. Even Golden Eagles (*Aquila chrysaetos*) and Sandhill Cranes (*Grus canadensis*) have visited. Shady Valley is a major food and rest stop along the Appalachian Mountain Migratory route. After the USFS began in 1995 to focus conservation efforts on birds that breed on national forest lands and spend the winter in the tropics, the USFS initiated bird monitoring programs in the area. The Bristol Bird Club has conducted annual Shady Valley bird counts.

J. Wallace Coffey (1940–2016), a *Tennessee Journal of Ornithology* editor and a *Bristol Herald Courier* marketing director, became CNF's first Watauga Ranger District naturalist in 1965, leading hikes at the Backbone Rock Recreation Area and other sites. On a 1961 Mount Rogers, Virginia field trip, he met ornithologist Alexander Wetmore, a member of the U.S. National Museum field team who collected Appalachian bird and animal species in Shady Valley in 1937 for the Smithsonian Museum. For decades, Coffey researched Shady Valley birds and banded birds for the USFWS. In 1991, he promoted an annual Shady Valley Cranberry Festival to celebrate the unique wetland ecosystems. During the first event, the CNF biologist led field trips and TWRA's biologist Bob Hatcher spoke about Bald Eagles (*Haliaeetus leucocephalus*). The tradition continues each October. The watershed "constantly promises new discovery," wrote Shady Valley resident John L. Shumate Jr.

HOLSTON MOUNTAIN/ SOUTH HOLSTON LAKE

Between 1942 and 1950, the TVA created its South Holston Reservoir by building the 1,600-foot-long, 285-foot-high, earth and rock-fill dam on the South Fork of the Holston River near Bristol, Tennessee. About 1,600 of its 7,650 acres lie in southwest Virginia; the rest lie in Tennessee, bordered by the CNF. Visitors drive Denton Valley Road to a peninsula to camp, hike, picnic and swim at the USFS Jacobs Creek Recreation Area. Nearby, the TWRA operates a boat launch, and the CNF manages a shooting range. The 33-acre USFS Jacobs Creek Job Corps Civilian Conservation Center prepares enrollees for careers in carpentry, welding and other trades.

The USFS Little Oak Campground is accessed via Flatwoods Road (FSR-87). From the USFS boundary to the road's junction with Big Creek Road (FSR-87D), the CNF and TWRA approved a 2004–5 study of the small mammal mortality in discarded containers collected along this five-mile, graveled section of Flatwoods Road. Virginia Highlands Community College biology students helped researchers collect about three thousand discarded bottles and cans along the forest edge. The bottling dates indicated that the container debris had remained at the roadside for an average of two years; 107 containers held the remains of 202 shrews, mice, voles and a southern bog lemming (the first collected and reported in a bottle). In one brown glass bottle, researchers found eight shrew skulls. The study's findings suggested that glass bottles inclined at more than fifteen degrees prevented shrews from escaping and collected water that drowned the occupants. After factoring in the miles of roads in the CNF, researchers estimated that 973 small mammals are killed each year in container debris along moderately traveled roads in the national forest.

One and a half miles below South Holston Dam, TVA engineers built an aerating labyrinth weir on each side of Osceola Island as part of its 1991 Lake Improvement Plan. Water pulled from the reservoir for power generation is taken from the bottom of the lake, where it is low in dissolved oxygen. Now, the cold water flowing downstream from the dam tumbles over the weir's running "W" waterfall-like design, creating an oxygen-rich habitat for a wild brown trout fishery. The consistent water flow also prevents a dried-out riverbed during generation-free periods. Rainbow trout, raised in fish hatcheries, are also released below the dam.

A bridge below the weir leads anglers and visitors from a picnic ground to Osceola Island. A 1.8-mile loop trail offers close views of waterfowl. In the winter, perky little Buffleheads (*Bucephala albeola*) drift in the tailwater channel and flash brilliant white feathers when they flip headfirst under the water. As its ripples dissipate into a glassy surface, the little ducks nab beaks full of invertebrates and surface without a sound.

On South Holston Lake in February 2021, thirty-nine degrees Fahrenheit and steady rain did not deter the CNF Keep Rivers Clean volunteers. A Volkswagen company grant funded the environmental cleanup series, administered by The Conservation Fund. Other organizations—like Nobody Trashes Tennessee, Keep America Beautiful, Keep Tennessee Beautiful and a Tennessee Department of Transportation litter prevention program—joined the TVA to sponsor the event. The series also included projects on TVA reservoirs fed by the Watauga, Tellico and Ocoee Rivers. Kathleen Gibi, executive director of the Keep the Tennessee River Beautiful (KTNRB) organization, greeted the lakeside litter volunteers (a board member, Johnson City music director, Jonesborough school educator, former Tennessee state park ranger, retired North Carolina nurse practitioner and others) at the Washington County Recreation Area near Abingdon, Virginia. Organized in 2016, KTNRB was the first Keep America Beautiful partner to focus its conservation efforts entirely on river systems. It hosts volunteer cleanup events, explained Gibi, to help beautify the 652-mile Tennessee River and its tributaries by removing human-generated litter to inspire individuals to become watershed stewards and "to increase public awareness of the environmental impacts of discarded items."

At the recreation area, boaters launched their watercraft. Bundled fishermen drifted in a dense fog. Crows squawked, claiming possession of this human-littered space of fast-food leftovers, while the cleanup crew boarded

Tennessee River cleanup project. *Kathleen Gibi/KTNRB.*

KTNRB's twenty-five-foot, custom-built aluminum boat. In 2019, TVA funds helped purchase the flat-bottomed boat from Iowa marine builders. The Home Depot donated the wood for benches that volunteers constructed beneath the port and starboard gunwales and a toolbox welded at its stern. Yamaha Outboards and the Anderson Marine Family Boating Center near Nashville donated the motor.

Gibi had prioritized the day's shoreline assignments and steered the boat to a red-clay bank. Within an arm's throw of a highway, candy wrappers, straws, balloons, disposable lighters, household rubbish, a toy rabbit and unidentified fragments hung on briars and brambles. The muddy embankment complicated their routine—bend over, pick up, drop in, step forward and repeat. "Eighty percent of the litter in our waterways was littered on land," said Gibi, and was transported to lakes and rivers by wind, rain and drainage systems. "The number one item volunteers collect?" said Gibi. "Plastic bottles. Look in this little backup cove. Maybe a hundred plastic bottles." Discarded years ago, the plastic pollutants, splintered and cracked and buried in mud, will break up but not decompose. The pieces "become a micro-plastic issue. They end up in our water systems where fish eat them. Guess who eats the fish?"

After Labor Day each year, the TVA begins its seasonal drawdown period in the Tennessee River system to prepare for winter floods. Lakeside margins become widely exposed. At the next shoreline pick-up site, a sandy beach trimmed the lake's waterline like a wide belt. Downfallen trees reached across the bank like outstretched limbs ready for a swim. Fishing twine, bobbers, sinkers, hooks, lures and a fishing rod were tangled in the branches. Did a fisherman lose his lot while casting for a walleye seeking cover or a catfish putting up a fight? A string of polystyrene foam particles, like Dippin' Dots ice cream, drew a line about a foot above the water's edge. These bits of foam from packaging material, food containers and flotation devices are 98 percent air. In the slightest water basin breeze, they travel great distances. Fish and other wildlife may ingest the foam pieces. The ribbon of insoluble dots, drawn in the sand by the lapping motion of waves, may remain for years.

By the end of the day, KTNRB volunteers had unearthed 114 muddy tires in sheltered coves. Decades ago, the tires were filled with rocks and submerged for fish attractors or spawning structures. With today's broader understanding of aquatic habitats, the TWRA, TVA and CNF appreciate the team's efforts to remove them. Toy binoculars, flip-flops, water shoes, diapers, oil cans, tennis balls, backpacks, food packaging and other items filled thirty-seven trash bags. The collected garbage weighed more than five thousand pounds. At other Tennessee watershed events, teams removed scrap metal, folding chairs, a portable potty, a couch, a thirteen-inch TV, a mattress, a mini refrigerator and a boat. By the end of the February litter collection campaign on CNF rivers, fifty-one volunteers had removed fifteen thousand pounds of trash.

Gibi throttled up to head back to the ramp. As the bow of the boat made its turn, a Bald Eagle took flight and banked out of sight over the treeline. The fly-by salute, Gibi said, seemed to offer a gesture of appreciation for the volunteers' conservation efforts to preserve its home.

In 1990, the CNF and TWRA erected an eagle hacking platform at South Holston Lake. "The CNF was the first to reintroduce Bald Eagles on national forest lands," said retired USFS Timber, Wildlife and Fisheries Staff Officer Sam Brocato. On the west side of Flatwoods Road (FSR#87), a former settlers' route and logging road near the Josiah Creek Embayment of USFS Little Oak Campground, CNF Forest Technician Larry Street and crew built a twenty-five-foot-wide, fourteen-foot-long platform twenty-five feet high. The lake offered an ideal natural habitat with a large fish population. Officials closed the cove to recreational boating during the six- to eight-week project.

South Holston Lake cleanup. *Kathleen Gibi/KTNRB.*

Three years earlier, Robert (Bob) Hatcher (1938–2014), TWRA's non-game and endangered wildlife coordinator, initiated eagle hacking projects to reintroduce Bald Eagles to Tennessee's waterways. Hacking eagles, a falconer technique, involves feeding and monitoring eight-week-old youngsters at an artificial nesting site for about six weeks until the nestlings are ready to fly. Minimal human contact is emphasized to prevent the eaglets from imprinting on humans as a food source and to help develop independent hunters of fish, rabbits, coots, injured waterfowl and carrion after they fledge.

DDT pesticide use, hunting and habitat loss in the 1950s and 1960s caused Bald Eagle populations in the United States to plummet to an estimated 800 birds. After Congress banned the use of DDT in 1972 and the USFWS placed Bald Eagles on the Endangered Species List in 1978, eagle numbers began to increase. In Tennessee, however, officials recorded no successful Bald Eagle nests from the early 1960s to the early 1980s. In 1980, the TWRA, TVA and Tennessee Wildlife Federation erected Tennessee's first hacking platform at the Land Between the Lakes in the northwest corner of the state and reported an eagle's nest by 1983. From 1980 to 2014, seven hacking sites released 344 eagles in Tennessee, with the most (119) released at the hacking site on Douglas Lake near Dandridge, Tennessee.

At South Holston Lake, Tennessee Tech University biology students fed and monitored nestlings through a one-way window, and the university provided more than $60,000 in grant-funded money for the project. Cookeville residents donated fish and other frozen meat. Community support helped fund the $20,000-per-year restoration project. Federal and state dollars often matched public donations. The Tennessee Eastman Recreation Club (later called TEHCC) contributed to the project. The Dollywood Company in Pigeon Forge, Tennessee, donated $10,000 through the American Eagle Foundation (AEF). An artist donated an eagle portrait for a fundraising auction. Schoolchildren participated in a Bald Eagle drawing contest. J. Wallace Coffey raised donations and public awareness through his work at the *Bristol Herald Courier*. "The USFS found funding for six birds in 1993, and the TWRA and TTU funded the last six birds in 1994 to complete the program," said Sheryl Maddux, retired District Ranger for the Watauga Ranger District.

In 1991, eight-week-old eaglets, bound for South Holston Lake, flew by plane for nearly twenty-four hours from Alaska to Dallas, Dallas to Nashville and Nashville to Tri-Cities Regional Airport in Blountville, Tennessee. (American, Northwest, Alaskan and other airlines provided courtesy delivery service.) "We planned to release 36 birds at a rate of twelve per year for three years," said Maddux, but staff chose to obtain young eagles from Wisconsin after some Alaskan eaglets were injured during the long airline commute. According to Hatcher's records, the CNF hacked twenty-nine Bald Eagles at South Holston Lake during the four-year project. By fall each year, staff had attached radio transmitters and/or colored wing tags to mottled brown juveniles before they took flight over the lake. Within four to five years, mature Bald Eagles, with charcoal-black bodies and majestic white head and tail feathers, usually return to within seventy-five miles of the site of their first flight to mate and raise young.

In 1991, the USFWS downlisted Bald Eagles from "endangered" to "threatened" and, by 2007, had removed the raptor from the federal listing, but the eagles remained protected under the 1940 Bald and Golden Eagle Protection Act. The USFWS reported in 2020 that approximately 316,700 Bald Eagles, including 71,400 nesting pairs, live in the lower forty-eight states, reflecting more than four times the population numbers recorded in 2009. In Tennessee, more than 175 pairs of Bald Eagles reside in the state. Hundreds of northern Bald Eagle residents fly south to overwinter here.

In East Tennessee, Al Cecere founded the American Eagle Foundation (AEF) in the 1980s (formerly the Cumberland Wildlife Foundation), under

Hatcher's tutelage. John Stokes, master falconer and assistant curator at the Memphis Zoo, joined the organization. Today, its eagle conservation mission is to rehabilitate, breed and release Bald Eagles. AEF's non-releasable Bald Eagles are public educational ambassadors.

In the 1980s, "Challenger," the AEF's resident celebrity, was brought to the organization when strong winds blew it off its nest, and the young eagle became imprinted on its rescuers. Challenger learned to fly aloft and return on command to a trainer's gloved hand. During the national anthem, the regal raptor graced the skies over more than three hundred sports events, Native American powwows, presidential inaugurations and other celebrations.

"Excuse me, Senator," U.S. senators' secretaries said in 2004, "but there's a Bald Eagle here to see you!" Cecere and Challenger made unannounced visits to Senate and House offices to campaign for the conservation of Bald Eagles. In a rare unanimous vote, a bill, cosponsored by Tennessee senator Lamar Alexander, became the Bald Eagle Commemorative Coin Act. Senate majority leader Bill Frist from Tennessee said, "No Senate or House member can say 'no' to that beautiful symbol of the United States. Why, it would be tantamount to booing 'The Star Spangled Banner'!" A surcharge on the sale of each $5 gold coin, $1 silver and fifty-cent piece created by the U.S. Mint earned $8 million for Bald Eagle projects across the country. For the first time in history, the U.S. Mint placed the image of a named animal on its coinage. Challenger was pictured on the obverse side of the half-dollar; two nestlings were pictured on the back side.

Since its inception, the AEF has released about 180 Bald Eagles and eleven Golden Eagles in East Tennessee. In September 2016, the *Jefferson County Post* reported that the AEF had released a Bald Eagle at its home on South Holston Lake after the staff had rehabilitated the injured bird. TWRA boating officers had freed the raptor, entangled in a limb at the lake, and taken it to the University of Tennessee–Knoxville Veterinary Hospital for evaluation before staff transported it to AEF for restorative care.

Bald Eagle conservation and education measures continue today. At a celebration of life event for Bob Hatcher in 2014, a special eagle, appropriately named "Hatcher's Legacy," took flight over Bells Bend Park on the Cumberland River. With a strong, seven-foot-long wingspan, it soared over the landscape in its free-spirited tribute, returning to a cleaner, safer environment than its ancestors had endured half a century earlier.

NORTHWEST OF SHADY AND Stony Creek Valleys, the twenty-eight-mile-long Holston Mountain was named for the mid-1700s explorer Stephen Holston (original spelling "Holstein"). North of Cross Mountain, the A.T. roughly follows the Sullivan/Johnson County line across Holston Mountain to the Virginia border. South of Cross Mountain, CNF's Holston Mountain Trail traces the Sullivan/Carter County line along the crest to the 4,170-foot-high Holston High Knob. In the 1940s, crews moved a steel-framed, 100-foot-tall fire tower in Mississippi to Holston High Knob, the mountain's third-highest peak, to replace a wooden, CCC-constructed tower destroyed by fire. The USFS has closed the tower to the public, but visitors can hike a gated road for sweeping views from the site.

From TN-91, motorists turn onto Panhandle Road (FSR-56) and arrive at the USFS Blue Hole Falls parking area on Holston Mountain. Wooden, cliff-hugging steps twist steeply down to a series of waterfalls on Mill Creek. The creek streams through a grotto garden and swimming hole landscaped with stone walls and boulders. In a narrow gorge, it tumbles into four waterfalls, dropping a total of thirty to forty feet. A hemlock trunk stretches toward the water before it turns ninety degrees, rising like a giant flagpole over the Blue Hole. In mid-June, laurel blossoms blanket craggy ledges and gather on creekside slabs, scoured flat by nature's forces. A waterfall swirls the blossoms on the water's surface until its ripples escort them to a resting place to soften the rocky edges. The thorny devil's walking-stick (*Aralia spinosa*), an eastern North American native, shares the scene with delicate ferns and wildflowers.

"Blue Hole Falls sounds like a full-open faucet filling a large tub," said hiking guide John Forbes, hopping with the grace and agility of an antelope across the flat rocks. The Kingsport, Tennessee resident photographed a panoramic scan of the basin to upload a visual teaser to social media, inspiring others to seek nature's solace.

"I don't prep for my hikes, like others do," he said. "I like to feel that lost feeling." With a self-confidence born of years in the forest, John revels in nature's peaks, caves, tunnels, rivers, plants and wildlife. He experiences a self-discovery that defines his life's values when he explores uncharted journeys with an open mind and spirit. "I've learned a valuable lesson while clicking off miles attached to a backpack," said the 2018 *Blue Ridge Outdoors* Adventurer of the Year. "Life itself is a trail. A diminished capacity for success should never temper your love for the pursuit. Never allow limited expectations to get in the way of ultimate success. If you arrive at a dry waterfall after a grueling trek, don't fret. Rejoice in the opportunity to study the form and structure hidden by its flow. Life is a long walk. Make each step deliberately and with a purpose."

Panhandle Road leaves the Blue Hole to parallel Mill Creek upstream to the union of the left and right forks of Mill Creek, which roughly marks the northern boundary of a twenty-nine-acre tract acquired by the Southern Appalachian Highlands Conservancy (SAHC) in November 2023. The SAHC plans to transfer this acquisition, which preserves 1,000 feet of upper Mill Creek's aquatic ecosystems, to the USFS. The roadway briefly follows the left prong before it curves away to weave up to the crest of Holston Mountain. A right turn onto Holston Mountain Road (FSR-202) passes the headwaters of the Right Fork of Mill Creek near the gated road to Holston High Knob tower. A left turn continues along Panhandle Road to travel four miles across the ridgeline. The road passes the antenna farm on Holston Mountain's second-highest point, the nearly 4,260-foot-high Rye Patch Knob. Beyond the primitive CNF Low Gap Campground, the mountain's highest summit, the 4,280-foot-tall Holston High Point, also holds transmission/communication antennas and the 1952 Federal Aviation Administration (FAA) navigational beacon. Portions of Panhandle Road may require astute drivers and four-wheel-drive vehicles.

"Many wildflower varieties grow on Holston," said Forbes, who has photographed intricate details from buds to fading blooms, especially the "eye-pleasing yellows of goldenrods and coneflowers." Flame azaleas (*Rhododendron calendulaceum*) splash orange highlights along the ridgeline in late summer. Orchids grow in wetlands along the Flint Mill Trail. No matter the season, "all days are special," said Forbes. "Recognize it and relish it."

Holston Mountain trails provide access to beautiful woodlands, stream crossings, expansive views, swimming holes and waterfalls. Some trails, however, are overgrown and confusing, with tough climbs or tricky descents. Off Flatwoods Road near South Holston Lake, Flint Mill Trail offers herbaceous beauties and a grand view from Flint Rock, but the steep ascent is an aerobic workout. Hinkle Branch Trail is another challenging climb. Hikers, mountain bikers and equestrians share more than thirty miles of CNF trails on the mountain, like Chestnut Flats, Rye Patch, Morrell and Josiah Trails.

Holston Mountain has been "littered with plane crashes," said Forbes. In 1958, two navy pilots crashed and died after a near-miss collision with a private aircraft. Twelve days later, search teams found the wreckage in the snow near Shady Valley. In 1959, during light snowfall and dense fog, pilots aboard Southeast Airlines Flight 308 failed to properly identify a radio beacon south of Tri-Cities Airport on a nighttime approach. Two miles off course, the plane crashed into Holston Mountain, killing all ten people on board. Rescue teams gathered at the former Boy Scout Camp Tom Howard. "A second staging area was located at a USFS campground, managed between the 1930s to 1960s, on the banks of Sulphur Branch," said Dean Walker of the Holston Mountain Hikers. "The footings for the picnic area still remain." Search teams located the plane's impact zone southwest of today's Double Springs A.T. shelter.

Sixty years later, Walker and hiking club members had an intense desire to find the impact site. "There comes a moment in one's happy, ignorant existence," he wrote, when a person needs to find the answer to a burning question. Besides, after months of extensive research into the accident reports, news articles, online resources, firsthand rescue accounts, as well as exploratory hikes and a fortuitous meeting with Mike Jones (the son of a Southeast Airlines pilot who had located Flight 308's impact site in 2012), "the mountain wanted to speak, and we needed to get busy listening!" In 2019, Walker and others, including the granddaughter of an accountant who had died in the crash, climbed Holston Mountain above Fishdam Basin along a former railroad grade. Years ago, the Andy Smalling Lumber Company had built the steep route in the 1890s. Below the ridgeline, they found a DC-3 wheel assembly, broken glass, burned metal, a radio tube from a navigation radio and other debris providing evidence of the impact site.

In 1961, a fatal army aircraft crash occurred on the northwest side of the mountain below Holston High Point. "It is a steep scramble through dense briers to get to the wreckage," said Walker. "I know from experience!" Beside Panhandle Road on the crest of Holston Mountain, a marker memorializes two German airmen, piloting a U.S. Air Force RF-4C supersonic jet, who crashed near Holston High Point's FAA navigational beacon in 1976. The twin-engine Phantom aircraft joined a second military plane from Shaw Air Force Base in Sumter, South Carolina, on low-level, mountainous terrain training flights. The Phantom, capable of flying 1,600 miles per hour, carried classified photographic detection equipment in the nose section. One plane departed the Tri-Cities Airport area and returned safely to the base. The second crew canceled their IFR (instrument flight rules) status with airport control tower staff and chose to fly by visual references. In deteriorating weather conditions, the Phantom hit a tree and flipped over into hundreds of pieces on impact.

During a 1998 marijuana surveillance flight by helicopter, stormy weather claimed the life of USFS Law Enforcement Officer Stephen Bowman and National Guard pilot Charles Harvey. For three days, crews searched for the wreckage near Hatcher Creek. Bowman's supervisor, USFS Law Enforcement Officer Russ Arthur, offered constant support to Bowman's wife and son. Some family members waited anxiously for word from rescuers at CNF's Little Oak Campground. Bowman, a Unicoi County native, started working for the USFS in 1974. In the 1980s, he began serving in law enforcement and on arson investigations and firefighting missions. "I lost a good friend and coworker that day," said Arthur, in a 2023 e-mail from Uzbekistan, where he was leading ranger training courses. "Steve was the very best at what he did! His woodmanship skills were second to none. He also had a passion for resources protection and never slowed down. The illegal hunters in that area feared him."

In 2007, five East Tennessee Jehovah Witness ministers aboard a Beechcraft Bonanza A-36 left Elizabethton for Abingdon, Virginia, to discuss building a new Kingdom Hall. Reportedly, the overweight plane flying in poor weather crashed soon after takeoff in the CNF about a mile below Holston High Point. In 2014, a Cessna-172 pilot and two passengers left Charleston, South Carolina, to fly home to Ohio and crashed into Holston Mountain after refueling at Elizabethton Municipal Airport but survived. Search teams triangulated a 911 call from the boy on the plane and spotted the crash site from a helicopter. ATV crews climbed the mountain along Bernie Lewis Road off TN-91 to a cell tower and followed an old logging road to Cannon Place Gap. The USFS provided bulldozers to clear a trail about three hundred yards down to the plane. By the light of a full moon, twelve rescuers carried the injured passengers up to the ATVs.

ROAN MOUNTAIN

If words on a page could blend into a drumroll, now would be the time. For now, this tale of CNF history reaches the climactic height of Roan Mountain Massif in the Unaka Mountain Range, where five summits rise five thousand to six thousand feet high for twenty miles along the Tennessee/North Carolina state line. With its natural gardens of rhododendron and flame azaleas, grassy balds, spruce-fir forests, biological diversity and rare species, this majestic landscape has enticed explorers since the 1700s, including André Michaux, John Bartram, John Fraser and Asa Gray. In 1898, John Muir fell ill en route to the Cloudland Hotel on Roan Mountain. He wrote to his wife in California that he had traveled from Cranberry through the most gorgeous deciduous forest he had ever seen. The mountains were "densely forested with so many kinds of trees their mere names would fill this sheet." Muir walked over Roan Mountain's balds, where "the storms of winter prevent trees from growing....I have been quite miserable, but this air has healed me."

On TN-143/NC-261, the A.T. crosses the 5,512-foot-elevation Carvers Gap parking area on the CNF/PNF border. Near the gap, the Roan Mountain Road leads through the PNF to the rhododendron gardens beyond Tollhouse Gap between Roan High Bluff and Roan High Knob, two of the five summits. From Hughes Gap, northbound A.T. hikers climb the Roan Mountain Massif to Tollhouse Gap, the site of the former 1800s Cloudland Hotel built by John Wilder, and reach the 6,285-foot-elevation Roan High Knob. The trail shelter is near its summit. Continuing north, A.T. hikers reach Carvers Gap.

Plank road near Roan Mountain. *Tennessee State Library and Archives.*

East of Carvers Gap, the A.T. crosses Round Bald with its spectacular views. The fragile grassy balds support federally listed plants, such as the Roan Mountain bluet (*Houstonia montana*), spreading avens (*Geum radiatum*) and Blue Ridge goldenrod (*Solidago spithamaea*), or state-listed plants, like Gray's lily (*Lilium grayi*). Beyond Round Bald, the fourth Massif summit, Jane Bald, is named for Jane Cook, whose sister, Harriet, died here in 1870 from milk sickness, caused by drinking milk from a cow that had eaten white snakeroot (*Ageratina altissima*). On the fifth summit, Grassy Ridge Bald, a plaque honors the mountain's former owner, Cornelius Rex Peake. Avid hiker John Forbes has seen snow on Grassy Ridge Bald in July and has watched Fourth of July fireworks from the open meadow. "Several municipalities light up," he said, "like Johnson City, Elizabethton, Mountain City, Bakersville, Burnsville, Spruce Pine and Boone. The views from Jane Bald eliminate Boone's fireworks." The A.T. continues north past the 1977 USFS-constructed Stan Murray Shelter, renamed in 1995 to honor Southern Appalachian Highlands Conservancy's (SAHC) cofounder and his dedication to preserving the A.T. and Roan Highlands.

The CCC constructed the short-lived Roan High Knob Lookout Tower. The fire warden's cabin is now an A.T. shelter. *Tennessee State Library and Archives.*

The A.T. crosses the Overmountain Victory National Historic Trail (OVNHT) in the 4,682-foot-high Yellow Mountain Gap. During the American Revolution, about one thousand frontiersmen passed through the snow-covered gap on September 27, 1780, en route to present-day Kings

Mountain National Military Park, South Carolina, to defeat an army of British Loyalists on October 7, 1780. Two days earlier, the men had mustered in the fields near Fort Watauga at Sycamore Shoals on the Watauga River. There, Colonel William Campbell's men from Virginia gathered with the militiamen of Colonels John Sevier, Isaac Shelby and Charles McDowell.

The assembly left Sycamore Shoals, roughly followed today's Highway 361 and crossed the Little Doe River and then the Doe River to camp in a misty rain at "Shelving Rock," a rock face overhang where they sheltered five hundred pounds of gunpowder manufactured by Mary Patton at her Gap Creek powder mill. On foot and on horseback, the militiamen passed through Sugar Hollow Creek and climbed the Highlands of Roan along a trading route, known as Bright's Trace, named after Samuel Bright, a tradesman from North Toe River, North Carolina. At Yellow Mountain Gap, "the officers gathered their men by company and paraded them, ordering the men to each fire his weapon," wrote historian Randell Jones. "John Sevier discovered that two of his men were missing," suspiciously deserting the ranks to inform the enemy. Near today's Morganton, North Carolina, more men joined the Overmountain men bound for Kings Mountain to pursue British major Patrick Ferguson.

Two hundred years after the battle, in 1980, President Jimmy Carter signed legislation introduced in 1977 by North Carolina's U.S. Congressman James T. Broyhill to designate the route as the OVNHT. In 1975, residents celebrated America's upcoming bicentennial events by organizing a commemorative walk along sections of the route from Sycamore Shoals to Kings Mountain. These citizens also formed the Overmountain Victory Trail Association (OVTA) to campaign for the trail's designation. Today, the USFS, NPS, the U.S. Army Corps of Engineers, the OVTA, three states and others oversee its protection. Each year, Sycamore Shoals State Historic Park re-creates the crossing of the Watauga River by the Virginia militia and the muster of troops at Fort Watauga with living history demonstrations and the "Walking in Frontier Footsteps" tour, sharing stories of Patriots along portions of the 330-mile-long route.

The commemorative hiking trail officially starts at the 693-acre Hampton Creek Cove State Natural Area, passes through the CNF, crosses the Highlands of Roan and connects to Roaring Creek, North Carolina. Highway signs with an OVNHT logo also designate portions of the commemorative route.

Beyond Yellow Gap, the A.T. travels over Little Hump Mountain and crosses bridges built over the bogs in Bradley Gap in a 2022 TEHCC/CNF project. The trail rolls past expansive views from Hump Mountain and passes by Dolls Flats before it courses through Tennessee past the old Wilder mine and remnants of a former railroad bridge. In 2019, the CNF acquired sixty-five acres below Doll Flats from the SAHC to protect A.T. viewsheds; Doll Branch, a tributary of the Doe River; and critical habitats for rare species, like Golden-winged Warblers (*Vermivora chrysoptera*). That year, officials documented twenty-five breeding pairs of this declining species in the Southern Appalachians within a one-and-a-half-mile area.

On the north flank of Hump Mountain, the SAHC purchased 324 acres of land that bordered the CNF and Hampton Cove Creek area from Oscar Julian's descendants and transferred the tract to the USFS in 2018. The acquisition will protect the headwaters of Shell Creek, a tributary of Doll Branch, and the A.T. landscape. "I oversaw the design and construction of the A.T. across the first North Carolina tract purchased from the Julian family and have been waiting since 1983 for the missing piece on the Tennessee side to complete the setting of this Appalachian National Scenic Trail crown jewel," reported ATC regional director Morgan Sommerville.

The A.T. crosses US-19E, dips south near Jones Falls to take its last few yards in North Carolina, turns north through the CNF, courses past a former Buck Mountain Christmas tree farm and heads toward CNF's White Rocks Mountain. In 2011, SAHC assisted with the purchase of 13.2 acres of Buck Mountain located in the Laurel Fork Bear Reserve to protect the A.T. corridor, now part of the CNF.

Fifty years ago, SAHC was founded "by visionary leaders who looked out from the narrow footpath of the A.T. and saw a need to secure undeveloped mountain lands for people, plants, and wildlife to prosper in the future," wrote Carl Silverstein, SAHC's executive director. Beginning in 1974 with its signature conservation efforts to preserve the Roan Mountain Highlands, the land trust organization now expands its land acquisition projects to protect East Tennessee and Western North Carolina mountains, watersheds, farmlands and the A.T. Trailways. SAHC helps piece together USFS fragmented lands to improve species genetic diversity and to provide broader, safer forested areas for wildlife movements. From 7,500-acre parcels of land to tracts of fewer than 100 acres, SAHC "assists our agency partners in securing tracts that they have identified as priority additions to public lands," reported Silverstein. For example, in 2020, SAHC acquired a Tiger Creek tract on Iron Mountain's north slope below the A.T. Clyde Smith Shelter and transferred it to the CNF in 2021. This 54-acre conservation priority, surrounded by the CNF, overlaps a portion of the 608-acre Moffet Laurel Botanical Area, "one of the forest's most diverse habitats," states

Sawing rhododendron burls to make pipe stems near Roan Mountain. *Tennessee State Library and Archives.*

a USFS website. "SAHC provides our partners in the CNF time to move through the requisite process for acquisition."

"These projects can take years to complete," said Angela Shepherd, SAHC's communications director. "Sometimes we are able to act more nimbly to secure a tract when it comes up for sale on the open real estate market and hold it until our partners can complete the process to transfer the land." SAHC manages the property, like the 2022 donation of sixty-seven acres on Dry Creek in Carter County, until the USFS is in a position to acquire it.

In 2021, an ATC, CNF and SAHC forty-year-priority acquisition in the Highlands of Roan, adjoining the CNF, became available at the headwaters of Toms Branch. SAHC purchased the fifty-two acres from the Greer family and plans to transfer it to the USFS. Clayton Lloyd Greer (C.L.) had inherited the property from his father, who assisted with the management of the tollgate on the old Hackline Road, a former route to Cloudland Hotel from the community of Burbank to the top of Roan

Mountain. Telephone communication from Greer's home to the Carvers Gap station coordinated the journeys of hack drivers. As a boy, C.L. stored Coca-Cola in their springhouse to sell to the travelers. After high school, he helped construct today's TN-143, climbing about twelve miles through the CNF to Carvers Gap.

"SAHC's partnership with the CNF includes both land protection and land stewardship aspects," said Shepherd. For forty years, Judy Murray, SAHC's cofounder and director of its first Roan Stewardship program, built collaborative relationships with the USFS, landowners and other parties to help preserve the Roan's fragile ecosystems and scenic beauties. The former chemist for the Tennessee Eastman Company and early TEHCC member studied ecology at the University of Tennessee and organized the stewardship program, led naturalist workshops, recruited volunteers and educated seasonal ecologists. In 2022, the State of Tennessee awarded Murray with the Robert Sparks Walker Lifetime Achievement Award for her environmental service.

In 2020, ATC's Southern Regional Office recognized the leadership of today's SAHC Roan Stewardship director, Marquette Crockett, with the Partner of the Year Award. She leads projects that include management of spruce-fir forests, high-elevation streams and Golden-winged Warbler habitats. Volunteers hand-mow Round Bald to remove blackberry canes and other vegetation competing with the grasses on the sun-drenched meadow and assist with the annual "Grassy Ridge Mow-off." The CNF, ATC, Roan Mountain State Park and volunteers have removed non-native garlic mustard plants. Since 1989, SAHC has presented a Stanley A. Murray Volunteer of the Year Award and, in 2023, recognized a volunteer who plants spruce seedlings to help restore that ecosystem.

SAHC promotes public education by hosting its annual "June Jamboree" with guided hikes and lectures. The stewardship program also supports its partners conducting biological surveys, studying the environmental impacts from feral hogs and recreational activities and researching the Golden Eagle's wintering grounds in the Southern Appalachians. Between 2013 and 2015, biologists set up trail cameras along the mountains on the Tennessee/North Carolina border and other sites to capture photos of eagles during the winter season. The team captured a few eagles and released them with attached GPS transmitters and noted that one male regularly visited Roan Mountain. GPS tracking also revealed that a 13.6-pound female, captured and tagged on Unaka Mountain in 2015 and named "Cherokee," spent her winters around the Nolichucky River and on East Tennessee/Western North

Roan Mountain picnic, 1947. *Tennessee State Library and Archives.*

Carolina mountains, especially in the CNF. Studies like these help the USFS, SAHC and other conservation groups prioritize land protection efforts.

For generations, the Highlands of Roan have drawn admirers from around the world. "Thrill of a lifetime," *The State* magazine boasted in 1966. "There is no other flora display quite like it anywhere." Roan Mountain was a favorite destination for Paul Fink. The adventurer, whose firsthand knowledge and hiking journals helped persuade powerful minds to support the creation of GSMNP, took his first backpacking trip in 1914 to Big Bald Mountain outside Erwin. With "deep ignorance and great self-confidence, we fancied ourselves seasoned explorers," he wrote, and he planned a trip to Roan Mountain the next year. The twenty-three-year-old rode a train from Jonesborough to Unaka Springs, hiked an old roadbed along the Nolichucky River, followed a trail up to the ridgeline, cut through Indian Grave Gap, passed Beauty Spot and climbed Unaka Mountain. There he noted that extensive logging left a "maze of skidways and old railroad beds." The only structure left from the burned-out logging camp was a stable that he and his friend used as an overnight shelter. They followed an old railroad bed to a

THE SINGING INSECTS OF ROAN MOUNTAIN

Summer nights in the Cherokee National Forest would feel lonely without the wilder sounds: the Whippoorwill chorus that dances through folktales; the gurgling of cool, rocky streams; and the banjo-like cluck of green frogs. In 2021, I led a research project with the Friends of Roan Mountain to document a full season of insect songs in the Roan Highlands. We recorded twenty-five species of singing insects during point surveys in the region, with songs archived for perpetuity for a FORM database. More than sixty-five species of singing insects are found in the Cherokee National Forest, and compared to other songs, they receive little recognition. From the froglike grunts of mole crickets (*Neocurtilla hexadactyla*) and the hushing of southeastern true katydids (*Pterophylla camellifolia*) to the tinkling of tiny, colorful crickets known as handsome trigs *(Phyllopalpus pulchellus)*, the woods would not be the same without our invertebrate orchestra.

By CADE CAMPBELL, an ETSU biology graduate, master's degree student and naturalist guide for the Roan Mountain Community, Blue Ridge Discovery Center and Tamandua Expeditions in the Amazon Rainforest.

wagon road at Iron Mountain Gap and continued to the Roan Highlands to camp near the dilapidated Cloudland Hotel with its "glassless windows and sagging floors." The pair climbed over Roan High Knob and received the "peaceful view" of grazing sheep at Carvers Gap. They ventured down the washed-out Hackline Road to catch a ride on the ET&WNC Railroad at Roan Mountain Station. His friend, John Wilder's grandson, took the young men to a "secluded pool in Doe River, safe from view," for a cleansing dip. They rode on the platform of a Pullman observation car through Doe River Gorge and on toward home in Jonesborough by train. By 1938, he had "done a lot of strenuous backpacking in the last 25 years. Now that we are growing older, fatter and lazier, and are inclined to take our outings a little less vigorously," the friends once again chose Roan Mountain for their annual excursion because it was easily "accessible by car."

That year, the TVA, researching sites for Tennessee River projects, wrote that visitors reached Carvers Gap by a former toll road from the Roan

Above: Roan Mountain parking, 1953. *Tennessee State Library and Archives.*

Right: Roan High Bluff and Roan High Knob contain rocky outcrops. *Tennessee State Library and Archives.*

Mountain community in Tennessee and Bakersville, North Carolina, along a "tortuously winding and steeply graded route. Their solid rock bases assure permanence despite the lack of maintenance, so that it is possible, though difficult, to ascend the mountain by car." Today, visitors follow TN-143/NC-261, still curvy but paved, to explore the Highlands.

PART IV

---·---

Unaka Ranger District

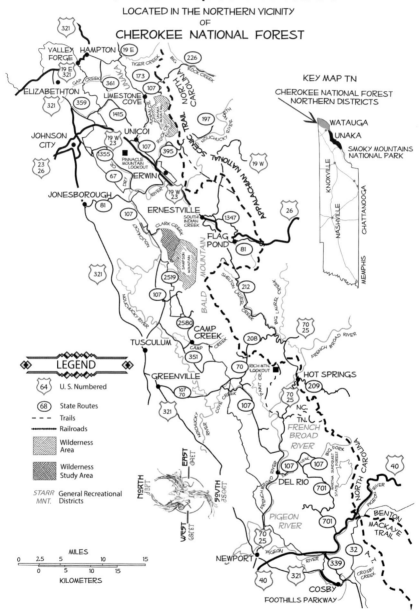

Ken Czarnomski, Phoenix2Reach@gmail.com.

CHEROKEE TYPE I INTERAGENCY HOTSHOT CREW

In 2021, the Cherokee Type I Interagency Hotshot Crew (IHC), one of about 110 elite wildland firefighting crews across the country, celebrated its twentieth anniversary. "After a tough fire season nationwide, the Washington USFS office decided to host two hotshot crews in the D.C. area," said retired USFS Type I Incident Commander Lewis Kearney, but members of the D.C. community seemed to have low interest in forming a hotshot crew at the time. The USFS decided instead to establish a crew in Virginia and, possibly, Kentucky. Kearney called the USFS Regional Office in Atlanta and asked it to consider the CNF, and "we got the crew."

"Over the past twenty years, dedicated people have come through our organization," said Chris Wilson, a seven-year Cherokee IHC veteran and Unicoi County native. The CNF fire management team "has built a professional crew that has sacrificed and grown from experience over the years." During their training as wildland firefighters, men and women learn fire behavior, meteorology, mapping, safety hazards and firefighting methods. They study case studies of previous fire missions, acquire leadership skills and gain experience in the field working with fire crews and equipment. The physical fitness program requires recruits to perform forty sit-ups per minute, twenty-five pushups per minute and pass the "pack test," completing three miles in forty-five minutes shouldering a forty-five-pound pack.

In the early 1900s, catastrophic fires prompted public land agencies to begin training fire crews to combat complex fires in remote areas. In 1910, wildfires in the Northern Rockies converged into the "Big Burn," trapping

Cherokee Type I IHC, Willow Creek Fire, Sierra National Forest, California. 2016.
Brandon Corbitt.

fire crews, engulfing towns and scorching millions of acres. Seventy-eight untrained firefighters, prodded by grit and determination, lost their lives. At a Wallace, Idaho park, the USFS led a 2010 memorial service for those fallen heroes. An air tanker spread red, white and blue fire retardants in a fly-by salute. Before ringing a final, three-strike fire bell salute, a USFS official praised the commitment of the "men who came from lumber camps, mines, and saloons to fight that fire." A ranger, quoted in the 1927 *Journal of Forestry*, told inexperienced men who needed a paycheck to "take horses and ride as far as the Almighty will let you. Get control of the forest fire situation on as much of the mountain country as possible. And as to what you should do first, well, just get up there as soon as possible and put them out."

In East Tennessee, a 1925 drought placed USFS tower watchmen on high alert. On August 27, at Nelson High Point in Unicoi County, Tennessee, D.W. Davis, a Unaka National Forest (UNF) lookout fireman, spotted smoke at 11:00 a.m. near the Tennessee/North Carolina border. (After 1936, when the USFS redrew its national forest boundaries according to state lines, the agency divided the UNF lands between the CNF in Tennessee, the Pisgah National Forest in North Carolina and the Jefferson National Forest in

Virginia. In 1995, Virginia combined its adjacent national forests to form today's George Washington–Jefferson National Forests.)

By 12:45 p.m., District Ranger A.C. Dahl, hired by the USFS fifteen months earlier and untrained in wildfire management, had summoned E.Z. Birchfield and ten local men to hike about five miles from Erwin, Tennessee, to the scene of the fire on Unaka Mountain. Another contingency joined the fire zone battle later that day. More arrived the next morning. Seven men insisted on immediate payment for their work rather than waiting for a USFS payment at the end of the fire mission. City officials of Johnson City agreed to pay their wages of $0.30 per hour, anticipating the $41.40 reimbursement from the Forest Service later. Two sign-on firefighters had no shoes. J.H. Riddles, a Johnson City store owner, bought each man a pair for about $4.00. Four months later, UNF Supervisor W.H. Stoneburner sent a second request to the USFS fiscal agent to repay the merchant.

The firefighters built base camps at the Gouges' farm, Rattlesnake Spring, Rock Creek, Upper Dicks Creek and McInturf Camp. At the Rock Creek

Firefighting in Tennessee, 1939. *Tennessee State Library and Archives.*

Camp (a future CCC encampment and CNF recreation site), the men used a grinding wheel and files to sharpen axes, hazel hoes and brush hooks. Boone's Garage in Erwin, Tennessee, sharpened their mattocks. The crew stamped "F.S." on their USFS-issued tools and painted the wooden handles a recognizable red.

Dahl instructed the men to cut trees, move brush, dig trenches and scrape leaf litter along four firelines to starve advancing flames of forest fuels. On September 6, Stoneburner assigned a unit to construct a firebreak along Dicks Creek to protect a stand of spruce trees on the east slope of Rattlesnake Ridge. By the eighth of September, though, high winds were sending sparks across poorly constructed firelines, igniting new rapidly spreading hot spots. A Johnson City Waterworks crew joined the efforts. Stoneburner also requested help from the workers at the Carolina, Clinchfield and Ohio (CC&O) Railroad machine shops. On September 10, 1925, UNF officials wired an urgent Wells Fargo telegram from Bristol, Tennessee, to the USFS Washington, D.C. office: "Entire force has been on duty two weeks. Fire continues to grow worse. Four fires on Erwin district. Two on Carter district. Repeated incendiarism. Rush help as crews are liable to break any minute."

By October 1, when officials reported the Unaka Mountain/Red Fork wildfire extinguished, the fires had consumed four hundred acres of private property. In addition, the inferno had scorched five thousand acres of USFS-managed land around Red Fork; Stamping Ground Ridge; Keener and Unaka Mountains; and Dicks, Devils and Clear Creeks in the Tennessee region. Along the state line and into North Carolina, the blazes burned the Deep Gap area, now crossed by the A.T. and CNF's Unaka Mountain Scenic Road.

Three USFS supervisors formed a post-wildfire incident review board to investigate the district's suppression efforts. Their damning report cited errors in judgement, poor preparation, ineffective leadership, lack of communication and inappropriate fire control tactics. Firefighters failed to scout ahead to assess changes in the fire's speed or direction, resulting in delayed response times. The inexperienced ranger ("fire boss") had waited too long to request reinforcements and had prematurely discharged half of his forty-nine-member firefighting crew before completing mop-up operations. He had placed incompetent men in charge of fireline construction crews who had failed to thoroughly clear firelines of tree snags, trunks, roots, leaf litter and debris or dig the trenches down to the non-flammable mineral layer. For example, "one scared and useless" fireline construction leader who spotted blazes on a nearby ridge, the review board wrote, "stampeded with some of his crew" to immerse themselves in the security of Dick Creek Falls. After Dahl identified a safe zone and instructed the men to return to the line with ten buckets of water, only four men returned, none carrying buckets.

Even though the fire boss had demonstrated a resolute work ethic and had fought the fires, like his men, for twelve hours a day for two weeks, he lacked the experience needed to supervise a fire suppression crew. The review board recommended an organized approach with a hierarchal leadership structure with a "sub-fire boss," crew leaders, camp directors and messengers for better communication. The final report also suggested better equipment, such as saws, gasoline-powered water pumps and sling psychrometers to measure changes in relative humidity. (Vegetation becomes dry and is more likely to ignite when the moisture in the air is low and the air temperature is high.) In a 1926 letter, the USFS district forester summed up the Unaka Mountain/Red Fork Fire as "the most costly and destructive of our district's history....The usual bad fire is only in part the result of dry weather, high winds, and other acts of God. Man contributes quite liberally." He emphasized two valuable lessons: "1) Jump on every fire by direct attack if feasible, and 2) Once you have a fire under control, mop it up—smash it—and then work on it some more."

In 1939, the USFS organized its first CCC woodland fire crew in Oregon's Siskiyou National Forest with forty of its "enrollees best fitted physically and emotionally for firefighting," explained one article. Most of the men "were accustomed to hard work at relatively low wages." The USFS believed that a fire crew who worked in "unity of thought and action [was] essential for good teamwork and morale." The experimental team wore red badges on their uniforms, marked "CCC-40." Together, they perfected the "one-lick," coordinated method of fireline construction: each swinging a digging tool in one, unified motion; taking one step sideways along the firebreak; and digging again.

In 1940, the success of the original CCC-40 prompted Oregon State College's forestry department to organize wildland suppression crews. Often staffed with former CCC enrollees, these crews set up operations at former CCC camps. By 1947, officials had established the first highly skilled, ready-to-deploy "hotshot" crew in California. After World War I, when the USFS commissioned military aircraft for aerial fire surveillance, the agency began dropping supplies from planes to fire scenes and lookout towers. After a USFS firefighter dropped by parachute from a plane at a wildfire in 1940, the Forest Service initiated smokejumper training. Planes began dousing fires with water. Rugged fire engines and tanker trucks were

An aircraft drops fire retardants. *Tennessee State Library and Archives.*

designed to navigate rough terrain, and helicopters transported hotshots to fire scenes in remote areas.

USFS fire science laboratories advanced the agency's knowledge of fire management techniques, fire behavior, weather patterns and fire retardant chemicals. In the 1960s and 1970s, federal agencies formed the Interregional Fire Suppression Crew (IRFS) program to coordinate the deployment of the nation's wildland firefighting crews, forest fire tactical policies and resources. Today, the National Interagency Fire Center (NIFC) supervises firefighting on federal lands. The NIFC outlines training, certification policies, physical fitness standards and annual preparedness requirements that crews must attain to identify as an elite Type I firefighting crew within the Incident Command System (ICS).

When a wildfire is reported, an experienced fire incident commander (IC) arrives at the fire scene to organize the emergency response operations. Based on topography, weather and other criteria, the IC determines the firefighting strategies and requests the necessary crews and resources. The IC may identify roads, creeks and rivers as natural firebreaks (indirect suppression tactics). Areas inaccessible by bulldozers and without natural firebreaks demand direct efforts by crewmembers who have earned an Incident Qualification Card ("red card") by meeting the interagency certification requirements.

On the CNF, most fires are suppressed with local resources, and initial response personnel are trained firefighters, foresters, forestry technicians or other disciplines. If a fire grows, the IC may order additional resources—such as Type 2, Type 2 Initial Attack (IA) or Type I Hotshot crews—from adjoining administrative units or through the USFS dispatch system. "Type2IA and Type 2 crews are essential to containing a wildfire that has escaped an initial attack or has grown substantially," said Kearney. "And, when ICs get a hotshot crew, they know they're getting a tough and resilient crew."

In 2006, the Cherokee wildland firefighters qualified for national certification as a hotshot crew and managed prescribed burns and wildfires from March to early December. On a fire assignment, a superintendent supervises wildfire operations, and two assistant superintendents direct the work of three squad bosses, two lead firefighters and twelve to fourteen crewmembers. "We hike fast, carrying a forty-pound pack with gear, tools, four quarts of water, and a twenty-four-hour supply of food," said Chris. A chainsaw team cuts down the trees at the site of the designated firebreak. "It's a highly coveted position—the lead sawyer, typically the fittest of the group." A pack carrying a twenty-five- to thirty-pound saw, a saw kit and other equipment can weigh up to eighty pounds. The chainsaw operator with the increased burden receives no extra pay—"just bragging rights." Behind the sawyer, a swamper clears the path of cut logs and brush and cuts the fireline. One or two lead Pulaski members follow next, digging deeply with a traditional firefighter's single-headed axe and hoe. "These high-strung, animal-like people work hard and don't get tired. They really move the earth." Next, diggers dig with shovels, rogue hoes and rakes to create a trench about two to four feet wide down to the mineral soil level. A quality control member assesses the effectiveness of their work. Crews may use drip torches to burn forest and vegetative fuels back toward the advancing fire to widen the firebreak.

On a fire scene, "we may be assigned to staff a helicopter or to serve as an incident squad boss for a Type 2IA or Type 2 crew," said Chris. "We may be instructed to prep a fireline and backburn the area for three days." The crew may divide into two lightning squads, scouting a designated area for early blazes ignited by bolts of lightning. NIHC regulations enforce a work-

Cherokee Hotshots. *Chris Wilson.*

rest schedule. Work two weeks. Take two days off. Work another two weeks and return home for two to four days before rejoining the firefighting efforts.

Wildland firefighting is dangerous work. "You can go into a situation and not see the whole picture," Chris said. "Sometimes, you don't know what the fire is doing on the other side of a ridge." Winds can shift quickly, advancing a raging inferno in a new direction, like the 2013 fire that killed nineteen Granite Mountain Hotshots in Arizona. Safe zones—like a road, water source or previously burned, blackened area—may become inaccessible, "closing the door behind us." Firefighters are killed every year by falling trees. A fire may burn out the bottom of a tree trunk, causing the top to break off, blocking a route or hitting a crewmember. Hiking long distances over rugged terrain in a hot, smoky environment can lead to slips and falls. Crews carry medical trauma kits and train as Wilderness Medical First Responders at SOLO training courses (Stonehearth Open Learning Opportunities) at North Carolina's Nantahala Outdoor Center. "There have been close calls, but no one I directly worked with on the crew was seriously injured or killed. That's something to be proud of considering the hazards of the job."

Type I wildland firefighters receive intense ongoing training, including impromptu proficiency tests and strenuous athletic workouts. In the CNF, the hotshots conduct four- to six-hour practice missions, sometimes at night, simulating medical and physical firefighting operations. On steep Buffalo Mountain, crewmembers bushwhack up through its brushy overgrowth in less than sixty minutes. After the USFS remodeled Pinnacle Mountain Lookout Tower, the hotshots began running up its restored five-mile-long hiking trail in forty to sixty minutes. The crew attends an annual two-week critical training course. In January 2023, at the twentieth anniversary of the Tennessee-Kentucky Wildland Fire Academy in Bell Buckle, Tennessee, the Cherokee Hotshots joined 521 fire incident personnel from forty-four states to participate in fifty fire management course options, said Dale Wine, CNF Fire Training Officer.

Cherokee Hot Shot Base. *Chris Wilson.*

The Cherokee IHC has also deployed on missions in more than ten western states and throughout the Southeast to assist with the emergency response and recovery management of major disasters such as hurricanes, floods and terrorists attacks. In New York City, they helped remove trees in a city park downed by a 2010 tornado and, in 2012, assisted with Hurricane Sandy recovery efforts.

A CNF fire management officer (FMO) supervises its fire programs. The USFS provides firefighting gear, specialized vehicles and fire engines. A contracted helicopter staffed by USFS officials is available. CNF aviation traffic departs Stoney Creek Airport in Elizabethtown and the Copperhill Heli-base. Near the Unicoi Ranger Station, the 2007 state-of-the-art Cherokee IHC base provides quarters for personnel and fitness/exercise equipment.

From 2011 to 2018, Chris traveled eight months a year with the Cherokee IHC, working many overtime hours above a forty-hour week. Today, Chris, a CNF North Zone Fuels Technician, and others teach basic firefighting classes at places like ETSU and the University of Tennessee–Knoxville. Chris also participates in Unicoi County High School's career day, telling students that wildland firefighting is a rewarding career that requires dedication and hard work. "We tell them to think of the hardest day you've ever had and multiply that by fourteen."

BUFFALO MOUNTAIN

In the 1930s, UNF fire wardens gathered on a 3,520-foot-high peak on Buffalo Mountain to hear officials discuss fire management plans for the upcoming fire season. The CCC was constructing the 40-foot-tall Pinnacle Mountain Lookout Tower nearby. Buffalo Mountain, named after buffalo herds that once roamed this area, provided an ideal lookout post on Washington County's highest summit. The tower's 14-by-14-foot cab—equipped with a cooking stove, refrigerator and cot—was surrounded by a catwalk. The USFS added a telephone around 1949.

In 1984, the USFS refurbished the structure, but by the 1990s, aircraft fire surveillance had replaced its service. After weather and vandals damaged the cab, the CNF removed the bottom stairs. Around 2005, "the USFS and community discussed the tower's future," said Sam Brocato, a thirty-one-year USFS official and 2003–12 director/cofounder of the former organization, Partners of the CNF. Ideas ranged from tearing it down to restoring it and renting it to the public for overnight stays. The people of Unicoi County campaigned to restore the historic landmark, their signature identity portrayed on the town's logo. "The project assisted the CNF to develop a close relationship with the mayor and residents," said former CNF Forest Supervisor Tom Speaks. The relationship forged during the tower project helped diminish the opposition to another USFS project and secure the acquisition of ten thousand acres in the Rocky Fork area for the CNF and the state, "vehemently opposed by leaders and residents for thirty years." (Half of the acreage lies in Unicoi County.)

When Pinnacle Mountain Lookout guards spotted smoke, they determined the directional bearing using an Osborne Fire Finder alidade and triangulated its position with bearings recorded at the White Rock and Temple Hill Lookout Towers and, later, Camp Creek Bald Lookout Tower. *Tennessee State Library and Archives.*

Dr. Gary Schneider, a Partners of CNF cofounder/president and a University of Tennessee–Knoxville professor of forestry, led the efforts to raise about $146,000 to rebuild it. The National Forest Foundation, businessmen and others donated funds. Project organizers sold illustrations of the tower, drawn by the mayor, and held a silent auction at a "Tower Raising" banquet. "The preservation of the tower only occurred as a result of the community effort to see the restoration of the tower," said Speaks. Crews replaced the wooden cab with a covered steel observation platform that matched the original size and design.

In October 2011, the USFS hosted a ribbon cutting ceremony. Brocato arranged for Ed Oliver and Jim Foster, two sixty-two-year-old TEHCC members/A.T. maintainers, to design and flag the trail's five-mile-long route up the mountainside. The USFS contracted a heavy equipment company to cut the trail with a small backhoe. TEHCC volunteers and the CNF shaped the pathway with waterbars and slopes to promote water runoff. Unicoi

Pinnacle Mountain Fire Tower. *Jimmy Rumple.*

County leaders expressed gratitude for TEHCC's assistance with the work on "one of the most popular CNF trails in the northeast Tennessee region."

Motorists on Interstate 26 between Erwin and Johnson City can spot the tower atop Buffalo Mountain on the Unicoi/Washington County line. At Exit 32, the Pinnacle Mountain Tower Trail leaves the trailhead at the Town of Unicoi's Jack Snider Park, crosses Unicoi town property for about a quarter of a mile and enters the national forest. As it climbs 1,400 feet in elevation to the top, it crosses Buffalo Creek, passes the headwaters of several streams and reaches Fire Tower Road (FSR-188) before reaching the top. (Drivers can take Greene County's Dry Creek Road and climb Fire Tower Road with four-wheel-drive vehicles to within a half mile of the tower.)

On the mountain's north slope, Johnson City swapped land with the USFS to create the city's 725-acre Buffalo Mountain Park in 1994. In 2018, about four miles from the park, the USFS acquired nearly 500 acres from TNC and The Conservation Fund that protected the headwaters of Ramsey Creek and at-risk aquatic species and helped consolidate national forest lands on Buffalo Mountain. The conservation groups had purchased the property two years earlier from the Holston Conference of the United Methodist Church. Since 1947, the church operated the Buffalo Mountain Camp and Retreat there until a 2012 flood damaged it.

UNAKA MOUNTAIN

Motorists leave Erwin on TN-395 to take a scenic drive over Unaka Mountain. In three miles, they arrive at the USFS Rock Creek Recreation Area, where CCC Camp Cordell Hull men built rock walls, picnic areas, the current bathhouse and a creek-fed swimming area in the 1930s. The USFS added the campground in the 1960s. In August 2021, the voices of children singing "Happy Birthday" floated from the group picnic area to the parking lot. A vireo and flycatcher sang overhead. A six-year-old blonde, wearing a paper crown, slammed a car door and yelled, "Hurry! They'll eat the cake without us!" In her haste, she failed to see a royal beauty. Long brown wings with golden borders lifted a male Diana fritillary butterfly (*Speyeria diana*) from the vegetation beside the asphalt.

Visitors explore pathways and a bike trail at the recreation site. The challenging, two-mile-long, round-trip Rock Creek Falls Trail leads into the 4,472-acre USFS Unaka Mountain Wilderness. Protected by Congress in 1986, it lies on the western flank of the 5,180-foot-high Unaka Mountain. This birding hot spot during spring migration crosses the creek several times en route to a small waterfall cascading over a set of rock ledges. Farther along the trail, the creek drops 60 feet over a steep cliff. Later, Rock Creek falls into a shaded pool, providing a cool dip in warm weather. Rattlesnake Ridge Trail leaves the recreation area and climbs 2,000 feet in three and a half miles to the Unaka Mountain Overlook on the Forest Service road across Unaka Mountain's ridgeline.

View from Unaka Mountain, 1953. *Tennessee State Library and Archives.*

Beyond the recreation area, TN-395 takes an oblique turn south to follow the right prong of Rock Creek. At the state line crest, the highway becomes NC-197, descending into PNF to Poplar, North Carolina. The A.T. crosses the road here at Indian Grave Gap. A left turn onto FSR-230, a graveled road built by the CCC, traces the crest of the Unaka Mountain.

Deciduous fall color displays tempt drivers with high-clearance vehicles to navigate FSR-230 toward Beauty Spot, a grassy bald on the A.T. Roadside gardens of lilies, jewelweeds, asters, goldenrods and other beauties splash a parade of textures and colors. Morning glories intertwine along an old wooden fence, perhaps left from a deserted home site. Bumblebees buzz among milkweeds and other nectar-rich wildflowers. Nature's bounty seems abundant, but still, hummingbirds spar for the sweetest spot. Swallowtail butterflies flit above purple blooms, while a CNF visitor, Brooke Lyda, twirls in shoulder-high wildflowers trying to capture photos of monarchs with her cellphone. Creatures juicing up before the season's end are oblivious to the Cessna-172 airplane circling over the bald. Rumbles of thunder predict an afternoon storm.

Less than three miles from Beauty Spot, the roadway begins to border the southern boundary of the Unaka Mountain Wilderness. It passes the headwaters of Rock Creek, takes a sharp twist or two and arrives at a short, sometimes rough, spur road to the heath bald at Unaka Mountain Overlook or Pleasant Gardens, the site of the former interpretive Raven Lore Trail and picnic ground. Southern views from the overlook can be magnificent. The Rattlesnake Ridge Trail leaves the parking lot and descends through the wilderness area to Rock Creek Recreation Area.

FSR-230 continues east and circles around the northern flank of Unaka Mountain, but the A.T. leaves its parallel route along the roadway, bypasses the overlook and climbs about one thousand feet to Unaka's summit. During the ascent, switchbacks lead hikers through an ecotonal community, transitioning from cove hardwood forests to stands of northern hardwoods. On the summit, often encased in clouds, hikers tread on a spongy bed of evergreen needles beneath red spruce trees.

The spruce, once a dominant high-elevation species in the Southern Appalachians, fell victim to loggers, invasive pests, acid rain and habitat loss. "About 50 percent of its range remains today," said Matt Drury, the ATC associate director of science and stewardship, "and a substantial portion of the remaining forest is not in a healthy and vigorous state." After a major disturbance in a stand of spruce trees, such as logging or blowdowns caused by severe storms, the trees spread dense layers of seeds in their limited mountaintop habitats. This seed dispersal creates compact, unhealthy spruce, competing for resources and restricting genetic biodiversity. Even-aged stands, now with trees forty to eighty years old, are unable to reach their full growth potential.

The ATC, USFS, Southern Appalachian Spruce Restoration Initiative, researchers at Western Carolina and Appalachian State Universities, U.S. Geological Survey's Virginia Cooperative Fish and Wildlife Research Unit at Virginia Tech and others initiated long-term efforts to help restore and preserve red spruce communities. ATC focuses much of its restoration work in the Southern Appalachians on Whitetop Mountain in Virginia and the Roan and Unaka Mountains in the CNF/PNF. On Roan Mountain, Western Carolina University researchers are conducting canopy gap studies. Six plots with canopy gaps ten feet in diameter are compared to six plots with gaps thirty feet in diameter to determine the differences in tree health and growth patterns between the two settings.

On Unaka Mountain, ATC, Virginia Tech and CNF staff, said Drury, are studying the different effects that one-hundred-foot and sixty-foot canopy gaps have on spruce tree growth. Team members thinned out ninety-year-old spruce trees and other vegetation on a twenty-four-acre stand on the north side of the mountain that had endured a wildfire and logging in the 1920s. Reducing the competition provided the space, light, water and nutrients needed for healthy seed production and vigorous growth of younger spruce trees. The goal is to create resilient, multi-aged, multi-sized spruce tree ecosystems that can withstand environmental disturbances and changes in the climate. The successful growth of new spruce in this stratified forest could provide the scientifically based information that helps shape future management practices.

Drury also works with the CNF to treat white ash trees (*Fraxinus americana*) for infestations of the emerald ash borer (*Agrilus planipennis*). The iridescent-green, half-inch-long Asian insect was discovered in Michigan in 2002 and near Knoxville in 2010 and now has been spotted in nearly eighteen states. Drury first discovered affected ash trees (with canopy dieback, D-shaped holes in the bark from emerging adults and sprouted branches clustered around the trunk) on Bluff Mountain along the A.T. near Hot Springs and treated the trees with an insecticide. In the Southern Appalachians, he has treated more than 900 ash trees. About 290 of those were in the CNF in areas along the A.T., like Osborne Farm to Cooper Gap, the Grindstaff monument on Iron Mountain to the highway parking lot, between Brown Gap and Max Patch Mountain and a tract west of Roan Mountain. The USFS asks campers to not bring firewood from outside the campground to prevent the possibility of introducing infected wood.

Beyond Unaka Mountain, the scenic drive passes the trailhead for the three- to four-mile, wickedly steep Stamping Ground Ridge Trail through Unaka Mountain Wilderness. It skirts a white pine plantation planted by the CCC and a man-made fish barrier that creates a brook trout habitat on Clear Fork Creek. A slippery trail along Red Fork leads to waterfalls, including a cascading corkscrew twisting downstream. A hubcap hanging in a tree beside the road is a testament to the washboard, bumpy route that the eroded Forest Service road can become. FSR-230 ends at its junction with TN-107.

A left turn circles back to Erwin past Limestone Cove. Here, in 1863, Confederate soldiers entered the home of Dr. David Bell and killed eight men headed to Kentucky to enlist in the Union army. Farther east on TN-107, visitors picnic, fish and stroll on an interpretive trail at the USFS Limestone Cove Day Use Area located along North Indian Creek. Years ago, trains chugged toward Unicoi, Tennessee, on tracks that crossed through here.

Red Fork Falls. *Tennessee State Library and Archives.*

Recently, the CNF improved its parking lot and worked with Wild South to improve the equestrian/hiking Limestone Cove Trail. The trail begins near a former campground and ascends steeply to connect with the Stamping Ground Ridge Trail along an old logging road.

"Limestone Cove Trail is the premier wilderness equestrian trail in the north zone of the CNF," said Kevin Massey, executive director of Wild

South, "but it had fallen into disrepair. It was overgrown, had trailbed issues and was blocked by fallen trees. Wild South has taken on the challenge of putting it back in service." In cooperation with the USFS, the environmental organization coordinates its "boots on the ground" efforts with community volunteers, the 423 Trail Riders equestrian group and others.

A few miles beyond the recreation area on TN-107, motorists pass the former site of CCC Camp Cordell Hull, named after a Tennessee congressman who became the nation's longest-serving secretary of state during Franklin Roosevelt's presidency. Company 1455 began constructing the camp soon after Roosevelt established the CCC in 1933. Later, Company 1472 occupied the site and became engaged in local USFS projects.

A right turn at the FSR-230/TN-107 juncture leads to Iron Mountain Gap on the state line, where the A.T. crosses the highway en route to the Highlands of Roan. In 1799, John Strother crossed the Roan Mountains when he surveyed the Tennessee/North Carolina state line from the Virginia border to Paint Rock on the French Broad River. In 1966, a journalist with *The State* magazine unearthed and published a field journal that Strother had written about the adventures of his surveying party of chain-bearers, markers and guides. On Stone Mountain, they tried to kill "a very large rattlebug [rattlesnake] but it was too souple in the heel for us." After one blustery night, their horses "were much scattered and troublesome to find." At a campsite near Roan Creek, one crewmember

A Wild South graffiti cleanup project. *Kevin Massey.*

severely cut his foot, and General Joseph McDowell became sick and returned home to North Carolina.

From a high knob, the "mountains appear in every direction high and craggy. The view is wild and romantic…rich with herbage." In June, the high-elevation trees were "just a-creeping out of there [*sic*] winter garb." The men crossed a rocky section of the Watauga River and camped near a spring, where a crewmember killed a bear, stewed it with bacon and served it with tea and Johnny cakes—"a Sabbath breakfast fit for a European Lord."

At a camp near Elk Creek, the horses only had honeysuckle and laurels to eat. The swarms of gnats were horrendous. Near Yellow Mountain, a fellow walked to a Doe River settlement for supplies. The men continued across a road leading from Morganton to Jonesborough and headed to the Highlands of Roan. "The wind has such power on top of this mountain that the ground is blowed in deep holes all over the northwest sides," Strother wrote. Miles of terrain across Roan Mountain were "devoid of shrubbage," where they could view "the wonderful scenes this conspicuous situation affords." Other mountaintop areas required the surveyors to detour the horses around acres of twenty-five-foot-high "laurelly thickets," while the rest of the party hacked through them to mark the state line. The men gathered "fir oil from ye Balsam pine" and collected the roots of a plant that, supposedly, prevented the serious effects of a rattlesnake bite.

Near a camp in a gap at the headwaters of Rock Creek and Doe River, Strother carved his initials "on a sugar tree." Two men left Iron Mountain to walk to a Limestone Cove settlement for a new guide and two gallons of whiskey. After a rough climb up a spur of "Unaker" Mountain, they bushwhacked across the crest of the range for three days. They camped in a dense stand of laurels, but "the whiskey had such miraculous powers that it made the place tolerably comfortable." The surveyors then crossed the river where the "Nolichucky breaks through Unaker Mountain." They crossed the Bald Mountains to mark the state line to the 107-foot-high Paint Rock. Strother wrote that many of the painted illustrations of humans, wild beasts and fish on the cliff were blackened from the smoke of pine knots and campfires burned by travelers on this route along the French Broad River. About one month after the survey project had begun, the company dispersed for home. Strother, however, remained at an inn in today's Hot Springs to "get clear of the fatigue of the tour."

NOLICHUCKY RIVER

In North Carolina, the Cane and North Toe Rivers merge to form the Nolichucky River. It flows past the community of Poplar, named for a poplar tree where Confederate soldiers supposedly found shelter in its giant hollow shell. Today, Poplar is a whitewater paddler's river access area. About five miles downriver from Poplar, the waters churn past the abandoned Lost Cove settlement (1860s to 1950s). No roads penetrated the isolated area. Built in the early 1900s, the Clinchfield Railroad (previously known as the South and Western Railway; later the Carolina, Clinchfield and Ohio Railway; and most recently the CSX Railroad Company) swept by Lost Cove to haul coal from Virginia and Kentucky to southeastern markets. The railroad, located about one and a half miles from the self-sufficient community, provided a connection to the outside world. Beneath Flattop Mountain, the nearly four-hundred-acre agricultural and logging community had a sawmill, a schoolhouse/church and several homes. Ginseng harvesting and moonshining provided extra income.

In 1986, John and Peggy Buckner hiked to Lost Cove, North Carolina, from Unaka Springs, Tennessee, the site of a 1900s luxury hotel near mineral springs. They walked beside the Nolichucky River through the CNF along the railroad tracks to cross into the PNF. "We found rock chimneys, foundations, and a few structures among the open fields," said John. "I picked an apple from an old orchard near one of the home sites." Bullet holes riddled the rusted skeleton of a 1930s Chevrolet flatbed truck that transported lumber and supplies to and from the railroad on a rugged

"LOST COVE"

My name is Tipton. I've come to your town
Looking for a job with pay.
My wife and children will follow me down
When I find a place to stay.

My mother and father lie cold in the ground
There beneath that Nolichucky soil.
After years, here on earth, they finally have found
Rest from all their labor and toil.

CHORUS

Lost Cove, Lost Cove
Where we used to kiss the girls in the ole apple
   grove
Lost Cove, Lost Cove
I leave behind my shack, and my pot-bellied
   stove.

The railroad won't carry us to Erwin no more
Just up that old railroad line
Can't haul in our goods for the company store
So, leaving's just a matter of time.

CHORUS

I've spent my whole life in the cool mountain air
But soon I'll have to leave it behind
When I die, bring me back and bury me there
In Lost Cove, my final rest I'll find.

*By SAM DALTON, singer/songwriter and retired
junior high school history teacher.*

Peggy Buckner, Lost Cove, 1986. *John Buckner.*

pathway. A hillside cemetery honored the hardy souls who once lived there. Friends had warned John about a cantankerous, one-armed caretaker who had grown angry at disrespectful vandals. With his pistol and big dog, he always spoke two words—"Get out!"—but the Buckners never saw him. Three years ago, John returned and found Lost Cove heavily forested with only one structure remaining.

The Nolichucky River leaves the PNF to enter the CNF and shoots through a spectacularly beautiful, two-thousand-foot-deep gorge. Tributaries cascade down high cliffs to join the Nolichucky's 115-mile journey to meet the French Broad River in TVA's Douglas Reservoir. In the narrow ravine—where river, rail and trail vie for passage between the Bald and Unaka Mountains—producers found the ideal backdrop for the dramatic river-running scene in the 1992 movie *The Last of the Mohicans.* Years ago, the CNF considered purchasing the Lost Cove property, explained retired CNF Lands Acquisition Officer Lewis Kearney. He hiked with the CNF Forest Supervisor, John Ramey, and the USFS Washington, D.C. Lands Acquisition Director, Dave Sherman, down the railroad tracks through the narrow canyon for about two and a half miles to scout out the Lost Cove area. When a southbound train quickly approached them from behind, two of the startled men jumped toward the river and the other held himself flat against the rock wall.

In the past, national forest firefighters have hitched a ride upstream from the Erwin railyard aboard a Clinchfield engine to manage wildfires in the region. In the 1970s and '80s, the railroad also offered passenger excursion trips from Marion, North Carolina, twisting through mountainous terrain, crossing over bridges and cutting through tunnels to rumble through Nolichucky Gorge before pulling into the railroad headquarters and shops at Erwin.

After the Nolichucky River's seven-mile bash through the gorge, generating twenty-five named Class II–IV rapids, it drops whitewater riders at the USFS Chestoa Recreation Area south of Erwin. Outfitter vans and buses transport patrons of guided tours from the day-use, take-out ramp back to their headquarters. At Chestoa, canoeists, paddle boaters and tubers, seeking a milder experience, launch watercraft to float downstream or to fish for bass and trout along the Nolichucky's broader, less extroverted personality. South of the river, northbound A.T. hikers reach the Nolichucky Gorge Overlook on CNF's Cliff Ridge, cross the river on the Chestoa Pike bridge two miles later and then pass the recreation area to parallel the Nolichucky River, Jones Branch Road and the CSX railroad tracks. At the mouth of Jones Branch, they depart the riverside area to trek about ten miles through the CNF toward Beauty Spot on Unaka Mountain.

Outfitters lead guided paddling trips down the Nolichucky River. Discussions to achieve federal designation and protection as a National Wild and Scenic River through the national forests began decades ago. In 1980, the NPS reported that the proposed segment was too short and that the railroad cut-and-fill construction along the south bank had diminished its scenic value. However, a 1994 USFS study and environmental impact assessment found that the gorge met the criteria for protection of its scenic, geologic and recreational qualities, as well as for its unique species, like the Appalachian elktoe mussel (*Alasmidonta raveneliana*) and the Virginia spiraea plant (*Spiraea virginiana*). American Whitewater, a nonprofit organization protecting the nation's rivers since 1954, submitted a proposal to have the gorge corridor federally designated. By 2020, local governments, seventy businesses/organizations and twenty-three thousand petitioners had endorsed the endeavor. At an Erwin Town Hall meeting, farmers, residents and insurance agents, however, voiced concerns that the federal designation could affect their livelihoods and private property ownership. State and federal officials have tabled the proposal for now.

Visits to CNF sites in Unicoi County often begin at Erwin. The Watauga Ranger Station is in nearby Unicoi. In the 1780s, a humiliated Andrew

Jackson lost a horse race against the Revolutionary War colonel Robert Love at the Greasy Cove racetrack near Erwin. In the mid-1900s, Southern Potteries established its business to hand-paint and glaze its famous dinnerware. The Unicoi County Heritage Museum preserves pottery pieces and local history in a 1903 building owned by the Erwin National Fish Hatchery that served as the home of the superintendent of Erwin's USFWS spring-fed fish hatchery for nearly eighty years.

In 1897, the hatchery began raising trout to restock streams, transporting them in specially designed railcars. Fishery staff aerated and added ice to the receptacles along the journey. In the past, the hatchery raised a variety of species—including largemouth bass, bluegill and goldfish— but today, the facility is now a primary member of the USFWS National Broodstock Program. It annually produces more than 18 million trout eggs for hatcheries across the country. The educational center encourages the public to learn about their aquatic conservation projects, such as the recovery of pollinator species, habitats and imperiled bat and mussel populations.

West of Erwin, the Nolichucky River continues its north-northwest course through the CNF, slipping between Buffalo and Rich Mountains and beneath the sheer rock cliffs of the Devils Looking Glass. Local lore claims that unsettled spirits cry out from the rocks. On moonlit nights, the cliffs resemble the face of the devil.

Near Shinbone Rock, the Nolichucky River loops into a horseshoe bend and picks up Bumpus Cove Creek (or "Bumpass" and other spellings) at the base of Embreeville Mountain. In the 1770s, mining in the Bumpus Cove region reportedly provided the lead for bullets used during the Battle at Kings Mountain. Around 1800, John Sevier Jr.—the son of the Tennessee pioneer, soldier and politician—bought a mine and about three thousand surrounding acres there. By 1820, the brothers Elijah and Elihu Embree had purchased the Bumpus Cove acreage and named the area Embreeville. Elihu soon passed away, but Elijah formed other partnerships in the mining business and built forges, furnaces and the Embreeville Ironworks manufacturing plant. Around 1833, the partners acquired four hundred acres on the opposite (west) side of Embreeville Mountain on Clarks Creek. There, crews constructed the Clarksville Iron Furnace to smelt the iron ore mined in Bumpus Cove. According to Washington County historian Paul Fink (1892–1980), the Clarksville Iron Furnace plant included "a bellow house, pot house, bridge, coal houses, and dwellings for the workers. The ore was mined near the head of Bumpass Cove, some two-and-a-half miles

A country road in the CNF area. *Tennessee State Library and Archives.*

from the furnace." One account reports that pack animals lugged the ore to the top of the ridge, where crews dumped it down the mountainside and hauled it to the plant. The business sold some of the product locally as castings. Embreeville Ironworks manufactured part of it into wrought iron and nails and shipped the rest aboard flatboats on the Nolichucky River to markets, sometimes as far south as Alabama.

Men built a millrace to divert water from the creek into a waterwheel to power the bellows in the furnace. After a flood damaged the millrace, the company abandoned the Clarks Creek operation in 1844. A two-story-high remnant of the furnace stack, however, still stands about 1.5 miles south of TN-107 on a country road in the CNF. In 1973, the Department of the Interior's Office of Archaeology and Historic Preservation approved the CNF's nomination for its listing in the National Register of Historic Places.

Eventually, Elijah and others acquired thirty thousand acres of land and formed the Washington Iron Manufacturing Company. In the 1860s, Bumpus Cove mining operations provided iron to the Confederates. Crews transported the iron ore on tram railcars to the mouth of Bumpus Cove

Creek and floated them on barges for about a mile to a furnace built on the south bank of the Nolichucky River. In 1889, British investors bought more than forty thousand acres in the area for mining operations and built one hundred homes for their employees. The economic Panic of 1893 thwarted their plans to build a power plant on the Nolichucky River and a one-thousand-acre town for thirty thousand people near the river's horseshoe bend.

By 1909, Bumpus Cove iron production had ended. Zinc mining began by 1913. Later, the cove became one of the nation's largest producers of manganese. After fifty years of mining, all operations ended around 1960. In the early 1980s, authorities closed the sanitary landfill created at the mining site at the head of Bumpus Cove after a public outcry over environmental hazards caused by its illegal and improper management practices.

The Nolichucky River continues beyond Embreeville to depart the CNF. It curves almost ninety degrees and sweeps south of the former Brown Settlement established by Jacob Brown (1736–1785) near today's Mayday, Tennessee. Brown, who served under Colonel John Sevier at the Battle of Kings Mountain, leased and later purchased acres of land on both sides of the Nolichucky River from the Cherokees.

The river continues west along the Governor John Sevier Highway (TN-107) until it briefly reenters the CNF at the Jackson Islands. South of the highway, the USFS operates the Katy Branch day-use area at the site of a former Youth Conservation Corps camp. At the junction of Jackson Bridge and TN-107, a lone chimney in the CNF marks John Sevier's former plantation home, Mount Pleasant, located on a knoll about 1,500 feet from the river. Sevier, known as "Nolichucky Jack" (1745–1815), received the 640 acres in a land grant in the late 1700s. During the Revolutionary War, Sevier was a military leader of the Overmountain Men at the Battle of Kings Mountain. He cofounded the failed "Lost State of Franklin" west of North Carolina but was arrested for treason and extradited to Morganton, North Carolina, for trial. Fellow Kings Mountain soldiers and officials released him. The six-term Tennessee governor later served in the U.S. Congress and narrowly averted a fatal duel with Andrew Jackson in 1803.

Sevier moved his family across the Nolichucky River to Plum Grove at Telford, Tennessee, when he lost Mount Pleasant to Samuel Jackson in a court case. In 1967, Jackson descendants sold their property to Thad and Jack Wiseman, who sold it to the USFS in 1970; it is now part of the CNF. Archaeological evacuations at the site have revealed the remains of early Native American settlements.

The river continues north of TN-107 and the CNF boundary toward Clark Shoals. South of the river, a small road leads to the USFS Clarksville Iron Furnace and Sill Falls area. Near the community of Mount Carmel, where the river turns north-northwest, the ten-thousand-plus-acre, federally designated USFS Sampson Mountain Wilderness Area protects crystal-clear streams, seldom-seen waterfalls, a five-hundred-acre old-growth forest, prolific wildflowers and the largest East Tennessee black bear population outside the GSMNP. Washington, Greene and Unicoi Counties meet near the center of the wilderness.

South of the wilderness is CNF's Rocky Fork area, home to the Yonahlossee salamander (*Plethodon yonahlossee*) and other plant and animal species in need of conservation management. The river's pristine waters slide through a valley beneath Wilson Knob and Flint and Coldspring Mountains to flow under the Old Asheville Highway and join South Indian Creek, a tributary of the Nolichucky River. The decades-long land acquisition process, spearheaded by dedicated USFS and State of Tennessee employees, led to the protection of a large, unfragmented sanctuary for wildlife. After many years of obstacles and setbacks, they built solid relationships and support. "It was an incredible partnership," said Tom Speaks, the then CNF Forest Supervisor. "The Conservation Fund, Southern Appalachian Highlands Conservancy (SAHC) and the Appalachian Trail Conservancy, with the extraordinary political leadership of Senator Alexander, did the heavy lifting in regard to land purchases and political work," said David Arthur Ramsey, a Rocky Fork settler's descendant and a SAHC trustee. Ramsey was also the grassroots leader who rigorously persevered in raising public awareness and garnering crucial public support. The State of Tennessee acquired property to become the Lamar Alexander Rocky Fork State Park. If a visitor experiences Rocky Fork on "a spring day when bright green leaves twist in clear mountain air, or when summer swelter nudges you thigh-deep into one of the crystalline streams," wrote Ramsey, "then you are likely among the souls this rare place has claimed forever."

West of the wilderness area, the CNF manages the USFS Horse Creek Recreation Area. In the 1930s, men at CCC Camp Cordell Hull constructed a picnic pavilion and swimming area at the site. In 2022, funds from the Great American Outdoors Act enabled the USFS to improve its aquatic habitats and stabilize streambanks. The CNF also planned to repair damages caused by a 2001 flood. Two and a half miles away, on Jennings Creek, the primitive USFS Old Forge Recreation Area occupies the site of an early 1900s forge that provided iron for logging railroads.

Davy Crockett, a frontiersman and politician who ardently opposed the Indian Removal Act, was born in 1786 on the banks of the Nolichucky River near the mouth of Big Limestone Creek. He died in 1836 at the Alamo in San Antonio, Texas. Crockett's birthplace is now a state park. The Nolichucky River courses past Greeneville, Tennessee, the home of CNF's Unaka Ranger Station and the former home of the seventeenth U.S. president, now managed by the NPS as the Andrew Johnson National Historic Site. About fifteen river miles downstream from Greeneville, the Tennessee Electric Power Company built the Nolichucky Dam in 1912. Purchased by the TVA in 1939, it generated electricity until siltation filled the Davy Crockett Reservoir in the 1970s. The Nolichucky River then winds through pastoral landscapes to join the French Broad River near Newport, Tennessee.

FRENCH BROAD RIVER

The French Broad River begins its more than two-hundred-mile journey near Rosman, North Carolina, and enters the CNF near Paint Rock west of Hot Springs, North Carolina. The Tennessee State Scenic River heads north, picks up the Big Pigeon and Nolichucky Rivers and flows into TVA's Douglas Reservoir/Lake. At the Forks of the River Wildlife Management Area north of Knoxville, it meets the Holston River and becomes the Tennessee River. In Cocke County, the CNF provides recreational access to the river. Paddlers enjoy about thirteen miles of Class I–III rapids between Paint Rock and Del Rio, Tennessee.

In Hot Springs, northbound A.T. hikers cross the French Broad River and roughly follow the crest of the Bald Mountains to the CCC-constructed Rich Mountain Fire Tower, restored around 2018 by the USFS, ATC and others. Visitors can also access the structure by driving the graveled Hurricane Gap Road. The A.T. continues north toward the twenty-one-foot-high Camp Creek Bald Fire Tower, built in 1929. In 1948, when the A.T. directly crossed over the bald, Earl Shaffer, the first recorded hiker to complete the A.T. in one season, stayed overnight in the tower. Now, a short side-trail leads from the A.T. to the tower. In the 1960s, Bald Mountain Incorporated purchased Camp Creek Bald to build a ski resort but sold the property when the company suffered financial problems. In the 1970s, new owners built Viking Mountain Ski Lodge with round cabins, called "roundettes," but they, too, succumbed to economic hardships. A Georgia state senator purchased the property for a private residence but lost ownership when the court sentenced him to prison for bank fraud. After the USFS acquired the property, it removed the lodge structures and replaced the lookout tower's fourteen-by-fourteen-foot cab with a circular cab.

In November 1990, Max Lance drove his family along Viking Mountain Road to reach Camp Creek Bald. There they met a thirty-year veteran of the USFS, waiting to watch the sunset from the tower he had manned for eighteen years. Glad to share the evening with eager listeners, he pointed out Mount Pisgah, Mount Mitchell and the Rich Mountain Fire Tower. Wardens at Rich Mountain, he said, focused on the Tennessee side; Camp Creek Bald wardens watched North Carolina. They radioed one another if problems arose. "Ski lodge owners renamed the mountain Viking Mountain," he said, "and forced the A.T. organization to reroute the trail off their property." One October, he invited sixteen hikers in tennis shoes and no jackets to warm up in the tower. "They nearly froze to death. People don't realize the extremes in temperatures up here. I've seen six feet of snow in October." The A.T. leaves Camp Creek Bald, passes Andrew Johnson Mountain and slips through CNF's Rocky Fork tract to cut under I-26 at Sams Gap.

From Hot Springs, the French Broad River flows into the CNF past Paint Rock, where Native Americans drew illustrations about five thousand years ago. In 1826, seventeen-year-old Andrew Johnson and his stepfather led a blind pony pulling his mother's cart along an old wagon road beside the cliff. Johnson had left Raleigh, North Carolina, to move to Greeneville, Tennessee, and work as a tailor. Along Paint Creek, FSR-41 courses through the CNF past picnic areas, overlooks, hiking trails and Paint Creek Fishing Pond. Beyond Stephen, Dudley and Kelley Falls, visitors reach the USFS Paint Creek Campground, restored after a flood in 2001. Wildflower specialties, like the ashleaf goldenbanner (*Thermopsis fraxinifolia*), grow in the watershed. The rare pirate bush (*Buckleya distichophylla*), first collected by Thomas Nuttall in 1816 at Paint Rock, sinks its roots into the roots of other plants to steal nutrients.

Between 2010 and 2012, more than a dozen partners—including the USFS, conservationists, recreationists and loggers—participated in the Cherokee National Forest Landscape Restoration Initiative (CNFLRI) project, led by TNC. The project addressed complex ecological restoration issues within CNF's northern districts. The team studied past forestry practices and recreational use that had affected current forest health. They mapped nine broad forest types and conducted site surveys to identify sensitive species, restoration priorities, uncharacteristic growth patterns within the ecosystem, barriers to improvements and long-term goals. In 2012, TNC's Katherine

Paint Rock, 1947. *Tennessee State Library and Archives.*

Medlock compiled CNRLRI's restorative recommendations and presented them to the USFS. "The mission of the Forest Service is to sustain the health, diversity, and productivity of the nation's forests and grasslands," she wrote. "Our mission was to support the CNF through a public participation system that was scientifically sound and ecologically appropriate." The team then began presenting recommendations for individual watersheds in the north zone, starting with Paint Creek.

"This CNFLRI project was significant because it changed the project planning dynamics to include much more stakeholder ownership in the outcomes," said Mark Healey, retired CNF Fire and Natural Resource Staff Officer and current president and executive director of the recently formed nonprofit organization Friends of the Cherokee National Forest. "We copied this model on the south zone of the CNF. The collaborative process isn't easy, but it's worth the effort."

Beyond Paint Rock, the French Broad River slips into an S-turn at the Weaver Bend river access and passes the 2.5-acre Allen Branch Fishing Pond at the base of Brush Creek Mountain. A quarter-mile trail encircles the pond. Accessible piers welcome persons with special needs. Nearby, the Brush Creek Mountain Driving Route (US25/70, FSR-209 and TN-107) passes the USFS Houston Valley Recreation Area and the CNF Bubbling Springs Shooting Range. Equestrians, hikers and bikers share the region's trail systems. About a mile west of Houston Valley Recreation Area at Burnette Gap, FSR-142 travels three miles to the trailhead of a short, mountain-edge trail leading to 360-degree views from the Meadow Creek Fire Tower. The two-story, block-shaped structure is the fourth tower to replace the original 1926 platform held between three chestnut trees. The Gum Springs Trail from Houston Valley to the tower is a longer hike.

Early wildfire lookouts.
Tennessee State Library and Archives.

West of Allen Branch Pond, the French Broad River flows past the launch area near Wolf Creek Bridge. In 2021, the USFS acquired the 640-acre Huff Family tract in the Wolf Creek area from TNC and The Conservation Fund. Known as the "Tank Hollow/Buffalo Rock" area, this acquisition protects a one-and-a-half-mile segment along the river and a critical habitat for black bears and endangered bats.

The river courses along US-25/70 to its junction with TN-107 and flows by Del Rio. The Norfolk Southern Railroad also passes the community as it traces the French Broad River from Asheville, North Carolina, to Newport, Tennessee. In the early days, Del Rio was the railroad's water stop, known as Fairview Flats, replenishing water for steam locomotives from an elevated water tank.

In 1967, Catherine Marshall (1914–1983), the wife of the former U.S. Senate chaplain Peter Marshall, based her novel *Christy* on the missionary service of her parents, John and Leonora Wood, in the remote area of Del Rio. In 1909, Leonora, an Asheville native and schoolteacher, deboarded a train at Fairview Flats and later married the minister of Ebeneezer Mission. Her stories about the spirit of the mountain people inspired Catherine's book project and subsequent movies and television series. Today, Del Rio and Townsend celebrate ChristyFest, a mission homecoming.

"I am probably more knowledgeable about the people and locale in the *Christy* area prior to the construction of Interstate 40, connecting Newport and Asheville, than any other person," wrote the 1934–78 CNF employee B.W. Chumney. In the 1930s, Chumney worked with the CCC at an Allen Branch side camp. The men built a truck trail to Hall Top on Stone Mountain, constructed the Hall Top Fire Tower and strung a five-mile-long telephone line from the tower to the Hartford Warden Station. They also logged chestnut trees from Stone Mountain and processed them at a Denton sawmill for the construction of the Clinch Mountain Fire Tower, near Morristown, Tennessee. A rugged Forest Service road now climbs Hall Top past a cemetery dating to the 1700s. A challenging trail leads to the tower, but the USFS has removed the tower's steps.

In the 1940s, the USFS enlisted Chumney to organize a CNF fire warden system and fire prevention program. Since the Del Rio community lacked electricity, Chumney used a gasoline-powered generator to show USFS fire prevention films. "I showed the first motion picture they'd ever seen. Schools with no more than a dozen students would have 75 people show up for the shows." Chumney brought his personal copies of Mickey Mouse and Three Stooges films to show after the educational films to encourage residents

Railroad line along the French Broad River near Del Rio. *Tennessee State Library and Archives.*

to attend. Some parents instructed their children not to watch the sinful, entertaining films, but Chumney saw them peek anyway.

From the Pigeon River to the Gulf Creek and from Hartford to the French Broad River, Chumney walked every ridge, creek and trail to conduct timber stand mapping. Once, he counted twenty-seven bridges within three miles along Gulf Creek. He visited country stores, schoolrooms and backcountry homes and became a well-known, trusted Forest Service official. Each Thursday, he gathered with crowds around competitive checker games at a Grassy Fork Branch country store. Some men walked five miles to watch a game or challenge an opponent. The overall winner played the salesman, a checkers champion, who traveled there from Newport each week.

After the USFS noted increased incendiary fires in the Gulf Creek–Messer Branch area, a CNF law enforcement officer tracked a boy to the one-room cabin of two elderly sisters at the base of Hall Top Mountain. He escaped through the back door but later returned to murder one sister for money. The USFS transferred Chumney to become CNF's Air Tanker Dispatcher. Once, an Interstate 40 highway contractor, clearing brush along

Confluence of the Holston and French Broad Rivers, 1938. *Tennessee State Library and Archives.*

the right-of-way, lost control of a fire. The blaze quickly grew to sixty acres, so Chumney dispatched a B-26 tanker from the Knoxville airport. The pilot reported what he thought was a "spot fire," ignited by flying embers from the original fire. Chumney instructed him to release one tank of six hundred gallons and then circle around and drop another six hundred gallons. A ground crew at Cosby School was dispatched to the site to handle follow-up measures. When they arrived at Rabbit Branch, the water drop had doused the fire under a moonshine still and drenched the moonshiner. "An airplane tried to drown me!" he said. After he wrapped himself in a burlap bag and crouched down in a creek, "the darn thing attacked me again!"

———————•———————

AT THE COMMUNITY OF Bridgeport, the French Broad River departs the CNF and continues north of Newport. The CNF spreads west of the Pigeon River, envelopes a portion of the Foothills Scenic Parkway and borders the GSMNP. TN-32 follows the national park/national forest boundary from Cosby, Tennessee, to Davenport Gap. Northbound A.T. hikers leave the GSMNP at Davenport Gap, enter the CNF, cross over the Pigeon River and under Interstate 40, climb Snowbird Mountain, pass Max Patch Mountain and hike south of the 3,100-foot-elevation Round Mountain Campground, one of the highest CNF campgrounds. In November 2023, a tractor-trailer truck jackknifed on Interstate 40 and ignited a wildfire near this A.T. section. Firefighters arrived on scene, saw a bear fleeing the flames and named it the "Black Bear Fire" for reference in media and fire management communications.

Around 2000, The Conservation Fund purchased thousands of acres east of Interstate 40 and north of Snowbird Mountain from the International Paper Company (formerly the Champion International Corporation) for eventual transfer to the USFS and the State of Tennessee. Champion International had purchased the forested acreage, known as the "Gulf Tract," in the 1930s from the Lambs Gulf Company to supply wood for its paper products industry. Governor Don Sundquist dedicated the acquisition in 2002 and celebrated again in 2008 at the Hartford Welcome Center on I-40. Cosby, Del Rio and Grassy Fork students attended the event. A school principal reminisced about Gulf Tract field trips she took when she was a student at Grassy Fork. The USFS regional forester thanked the people who worked to save the scenic watershed. She welcomed the USFS partnership with the TWRA, Tennessee Department of Agriculture and Tennessee Division of Forestry in managing the region. The USFS acquired Gulf Tract acres that protected valuable bear habitat and six miles of the A.T. The state purchased Gulf Tract property that adjoined the CNF to become the Martha Sundquist State Forest, named after the governor's wife, an outdoor enthusiast.

In 2021, biologists with the National Parks Conservation Association (NPCA) and Wildlands Network completed a three-year study of wildlife movement patterns between the GSMNP and the Cherokee and Pisgah National Forests across a twenty-eight-mile stretch of Interstate 40. They used wildlife cameras, GPS collars and mortality surveys to assess when, where and how bears, elk, deer, bobcats and other species were attempting to cross and getting injured or killed on a highway used by twenty-nine thousand vehicles per day.

The USFS joined concerned citizens and two dozen federal, state, tribal and non-governmental organizations to organize "Safe Passage: The I-40 Pigeon River Gorge Wildlife Crossing Project" to address the

American black bear. *John Forbes.*

need for safer wildlife movement and vehicular travel. The group provides recommendations for wildlife crossing structures—like culverts, overpasses, underpasses and fencing—to the North Carolina and Tennessee Departments of Transportation. The Conservation Fund, NPCA, Defenders of Wildlife,

Great Smoky Mountains Association, North Carolina Wildlife Federation, The Wilderness Society and Wildlands Network formed the Safe Passage Fund Coalition to allow public donations at SmokiesSafePassage.org.

———•———

The literary journey ends. Go seek, find and connect. Watch and listen. Walk or ride. Drift or paddle. Energize the spirit. Soothe the soul.

BIBLIOGRAPHY

Akins, Bill. *The Unicoi Turnpike Trail: A Path through Time.* Etowah: Tennessee Overhill Heritage Association, 2008.

Alderman, Pat. *The Overmountain Men.* Johnson City, TN: Overmountain Press, 1986.

American Eagle Foundation. 2022–24. https://eagles.org.

Amman, Walter, Jr. "Outdoors Around Here." *Knoxville Journal*, May 9, 1954.

Appalachian Trail Conservancy. *The Appalachian Trail, 1921–2021 and Beyond.* Harpers Ferry, WV: self-published, 2021.

Appalachian Treks. 2008–present. http://appalachiantreks.blogspot.com.

Barclay, R.E. *Ducktown Back in Raht's Time.* Chapel Hill: University of North Carolina Press, 1946.

Bauer, Jennifer. *Roan Mountain: History of a Mountain Treasure.* Charleston, SC: The History Press, 2011.

BearWise organization. https://bearwise.org.

Belt, Gordon T. *John Sevier: Tennessee's First Hero.* Charleston, SC: The History Press, 2015.

Benton, Ben. "Cherokee Hotshot, Forest Service Crews Battle Wildfires." *Chattanooga Times Free Press*, April 21, 2021.

———. "Preserving a Path in History: Key Piece of the Trail of Tears Receives New Protection." *Chattanooga Times Free Press*, November 10, 2014.

Bierly, Michael Lee. *Bird Finding in Tennessee.* N.p.: self-published, 1980.

Blackburn, Marion. "Return to the Trail of Tears." *Archaeology* (March/April 2012).

Brewer, Alberta, and Carson Brewer. *Valley So Wild: A Folk History*. Knoxville: East Tennessee Historical Society, 1975.

Brooks, Cynthia. *Wagon Train and Cherohala Skyway*. Tellico Plains, TN: Tellico Publications, 2016.

Brown, Fred. *Coker Creek*. Coker Creek Ruritan Club, 1991.

Cavalcade. "Women Watch in Wilderness" (May 9, 1954).

Chumney, B.W., former CCC member/CNF staff. "Why My Interest?" Personal article, no date.

Clarksville Online. "Lamar Alexander Says Most Important Conservation Legislation in Half a Century Heads to President's Desk." July 25, 2020.

Coffey, J. Wallace, and John L. Shumate Jr. *Bird Study of Shady Valley, Tennessee, 1934–1999*. Booklet. N.p.: self-published, 1999.

The Conservation Fund. https://www.conservationfund.org.

Cox, Casper. *Snorkeling the Hidden Rivers of Southern Appalachia*. Corvallis, OR: Freshwaters Illustrated, 2020.

Depew, Jake. "Bald Eagles Returned to the Wild on South Holston Lake." *Jefferson County Post*, September 24, 2016.

Duggan, Betty J. *From Furs to Factory*. Etowah: Tennessee Overhill Heritage Association, 1998.

Dykeman, Wilma. *The French Broad*. Knoxville: University of Tennessee Press, 1955.

———. *Tennessee: A Bicentennial History*. Nashville, TN: American Association for State and Local History, 1975.

Ehle, John. *Trail of Tears*. New York: Doubleday, 1988.

Etowah Depot Museum. Exhibits, 2021.

Faulkner, Charles, ed. *The Prehistoric Native American Art of Mud Glyph Cave*. Knoxville: University of Tennessee Press, 1986.

Figart, Frances. "Moving in Harmony: The New Safe Passage Campaign." *Search WNC Magazine* (Summer 2021).

Fink, Paul. *Mountain Days: A Journal of Camping Experiences in the Mountains of Tennessee and North Carolina, 1914–1938*. Cullowhee, NC: Western Carolina University, 2019.

Fontenay, Blake. "Shooting the Rapids: How a Small East Tennessee Community Struck Olympic Gold." Tennessee State Library and Archives, April 22, 2016.

Freshwaters Illustrated. *A Deeper Creek: the Watchable Waters of Appalachia*, 2014.

———. *Hidden Rivers of the Southern Appalachia*, 2014.

Friends of Roan Mountain. https://friendsofroanmtn.org.

Giegerich, Carter. "Land Acquisition Will Bolster I-40 Wildlife Corridor Project." *The Mountaineer*, August 12, 2019.

Gove, Doris. *50 Hikes in the Tennessee Mountains*. Woodstock, VT: Backcountry Guides, 2001.

Graybeal, Johnny. *Along the ET&WNC*. 6 vols. Hickory, NC: Tarheel Press, 2001–5.

Gray, Gary Craven. *Radio for the Fireline: A History of Electronic Communication in the Forest Service, 1905–1975*. Booklet. Washington, D.C.: U.S. Department of Agriculture, U.S. Forest Service, 1982.

Gunn, Scott. "Recovery Plan for Ruth's Golden Aster." Document, 1992.

Guy, Joe. *The Hidden History of McMinn County*. Charleston, SC: The History Press, 2008.

———. *The Indian Boundary Fireside Companion*. Charleston, SC: The History Press, 2008.

Hall, Charles. *A History of Tellico Plains, TN, 10,000 B.C.–2,001 A.D.* Tellico Plains, TN: Tellico Publications, 2001.

Harvey Broome Group of the Tennessee Chapter of the Sierra Club. *Cherokee National Forest Hiking Guide*. 2nd ed. Knoxville: University of Tennessee Press, 2005.

Hasler, Vic, ed. *Appalachian Trail Guide to Tennessee–North Carolina*. 15th ed. Harpers Ferry, WV: Appalachian Trail Conservancy, 2016.

History of Johnson County. Wrightsville, GA: Johnson County Historical Society, 1986.

History of Tennessee. Nashville, TN: Goodspeed Publishing Company, 1887.

Homan, Tim. *Hiking the Benton MacKaye Trail*. Atlanta, GA: Peachtree Publishers, Ltd., 2004.

———. *Hiking Trails of the Joyce Kilmer–Slickrock and Citico Creek Wildernesses*. 3rd ed. Atlanta, GA: Peachtree Publishers Ltd., 2008.

Hsiung, David, ed. *A Mountaineer in Motion: The Memoir of Dr. Abraham Jobe, 1817–1906*. Knoxville: University of Tennessee Press, 2009.

Jones, Randell. *Before They Were Heroes at King's Mountain*. Winston-Salem, NC: Daniel Boone Footsteps, 2011.

———. *A Guide to the Overmountain Victory National Historic Trail*. Winston-Salem, NC: Daniel Boone Footsteps, 2011.

———. *Trailing Daniel Boone*. Winston-Salem, NC: Daniel Boone Footsteps, 2012.

Kazan, Elia. *Wild River*. 20th Century Fox, 1960.

Knoxville Journal. "Something New Has Been Added to Cherokee National Forest!" May 1954.

Knoxville News Sentinel. "Monroe Ruritans Save Magical Falls." August 15, 1988.

Markham, Doug. *Boxes, Rockets and Pens: A History of Wildlife Recovery in Tennessee.* Knoxville: University of Tennessee Press, 1997.

Marsh, Robert Clinton, III. "A Historical Overview of the Bumpass Cove Landfill Controversy, 1972–2002." Master's thesis, East Tennessee State University, August 2002.

Massey, Kevin, Director, Wild South. E-mails, 2022–23.

Masterson, Linda, and LaVonne Ewing. BearWise program. Website/webinar/e-mails, 2021–22.

Mathews, Pamela Hall. *A Pictorial History of the Tellico Plains, Tennessee Area (1849–1949).* Tellico Plains, TN: Tellico Publications, 2015.

Matlock, Gertrude (Karaivanoff). *The Rebirth of Parksville.* Booklet. N.p.: self-published, 1980.

McAllister, Glenn. *1001 Miles on the A.T.* N.p.: self-published, 2017.

McConnell, Owen Link. *Unicoi Unity: A Natural History of the Unicoi and Snowbird Mountains.* AuthorHouse, 2014.

McGuinn, Doug. *The Laurel Fork Railway of Carter County, Tennessee.* Boone, NC: Cook's Gap Press, 2016.

———. *The Lopsided Three: A History of Railroading, Logging & Mining in the Holston, Doe & Watauga Valleys of Northeast Tennessee.* Boone, NC: Bamboo Books, 2010.

McKinney, Frank. *Torment in the Knobs.* Athens, TN: McMinn County Historical Society, 1976.

Medlock, Katherine G. "Cherokee National Forest Restoration Initiative Steering Committee Recommendations to the Forest Service for the North Zone." The Nature Conservancy, 2012.

———. "Southern Appalachian Spruce Restoration Plan." The Nature Conservancy, 2014.

Millican, Mark. "The Heyday of Logging in the Cohuttas." Whitfield-Murray Quarterly Historical Society, 1955.

Molloy, Johnny. *Hiking Waterfalls in Tennessee.* Guilford, CT: Falcon Guides, 2015.

Moore, Debbie. *The History of Caney Creek Village, Ocoee River, Polk County, Tennessee.* N.p.: self-published, 2013.

Mountain Electric Corporation. "Where the World Ended and Tennessee Began." October 15, 1922.

Muir, John. *Writings of John Muir.* Vol. 1. New York: Houghton Mifflin Company, 1917.

Murray, Kenneth. *Highland Trails*. 4th ed. Johnson City, TN: Overmountain Press, 2004.

Myers, Robert, MD, comp. "The Ocoee Story: 75 Years of Changing Lives." Booklet, 2002.

Nash, John. "Elijah Embree and the Embreeville Ironworks." Jonesborough, TN: Washington County Tennessee Historical Association, 1997.

The Nature Conservancy. https://preserve.nature.org.

O'Connell, Kim. "Saving Islands in the Sky." Appalachian Trail Conservancy journal, April 2023.

Orr, Robert. *President Andrew Johnson of Greenville, Tennessee*. Knoxville: Tennessee Valley Publications, 2005.

Parish, Thurman. *Back to the Mountains*. N.p.: self-published, 2012.

———. *Mountain Memories: History, People, Legends & Tales of the Polk County Mountains in Southeast Tennessee*. N.p.: self-published, 2010.

———. *The Old Home Place: Pioneer Life in Polk County, Tennessee*. Polk County, TN: Newspaper Publishing Company, 1994.

People of Carter County, Tennessee. *Carter County, Tennessee, and Its People, 1796–1993*. Elizabethton, TN: Carter County History Book Committee, 1993.

Plumb, Gregory. *Waterfalls of Tennessee*. 2nd ed. Johnson City, TN: Overmountain Press, 2008.

Purser, Becky. "Alaskan Eagles Light in New Tennessee Home." *Kingsport Times News*, July 26, 1991.

Ramsey, David Arthur. *Rocky Fork: Hidden Jewel of the Blue Ridge Wild*. D.A. Ramsey Photography. N.p.: self-published, 2018.

Riddle, Ken. "The Cy Crumley Scrapbook." 1880s–1990s. http://www.stateoffranklin.net/johnsons/crumley/cyhome.htm.

Riggs, Brett. "Ft. Armistead and Unicoi Turnpike." Lecture on CD. Coker Creek Heritage Group/Barry Hodgin, 2010.

———. *Like a Distempered Dream: An Evaluation of Cherokee Deportation Routes through Monroe and McMinn Counties, Tennessee*. Chapel Hill: University of North Carolina Press, 2014.

Riggs, Brett, and Barbara Duncan. *Cherokee Heritage Trails Book*. Chapel Hill: University of North Carolina Press, 2003.

Riggs, Brett, and May Elizabeth Fitts. "Draft National Historic Landmark Nomination for the Fort Armistead Site (40MR708), Coker Creek, Monroe County, Tennessee." Non-published booklet.

Sakowski, Carolyn. *Touring the East Tennessee Backroads*. 2nd ed. Winston-Salem, NC: John F. Blair Publisher, 2007.

Sands, Sarah G. Cox. *History of Monroe County, Tennessee*. Vols. 1–4. Baltimore, MD: Gateway Press, 1989.

Satterfield, Jamie. "Cherokee National Forest Arsonist Soon to Be Freed After Earning Sentencing Break." *Knoxville News Sentinel*, October 27, 2011.

Sequoyah Birthplace Museum. https://sequoyahmuseum.org.

Smith, Christy A. *Lost Cove, North Carolina*. Jefferson, NC: McFarland & Company, 2022.

Sorrell, Robert. *Blue Ridge Fire Towers*. Charleston, SC: The History Press, 2015.

———. "The Day the Plane Crashed." *Bristol Herald Courier*, April 20, 2019.

Southern Appalachian Highlands Conservancy. Zoom meeting/virtual lunch and learn series/*View from the Highlands'* articles/online resources/YouTube videos/blogs/e-mails, 2021–24. https://appalachian.org.

Stansberry, Dan. *A Visit to Dry Hill*. Self-published, 2021.

The State. "The Boundary Diary" (May 1966).

Steen, Harold K., ed. *Jack Ward Thomas: The Journals of a Forest Service Chief*. Durham, NC: Forest History Society, 2004.

Tennessee Eastman Hiking & Canoeing Club. https://tehcc.org.

Tennessee Valley Authority. *The Scenic Resources of the Tennessee Valley: A Descriptive and Pictorial Inventory*. Self-published, 1938.

Tester, Herman. *Butler: Old, New, and Carderview*. Self-published, 2007.

Thompson, Jim. *Wagon Train*. Tellico Plains, TN: Tellico Plains Publications, 1988.

Tovar, Rosalind Dooly. "Conasauga from Records and Recollections." Booklet, 2000.

Trudge, Old. "Thrill of a Lifetime." *The State* (June 1966).

Tucker, Melanie. "Staging a Comeback: Local Scientists Work to Restore American Chestnut." *Daily Times*, May 9, 2021.

Unicoi County Heritage Museum. Exhibits/documents, 2022.

Up in Flames: The History of Forest Firefighting. Documentary film. Durham, NC: Forest History Society, 1984.

U.S. Department of Agriculture, U.S. Forest Service. "Environmental Assessment, Recreation Residence Standards, Cherokee National Forest." 2013.

———. Land acquisition forms/maps/websites/media releases/project documents, 2019–24.

———. "Mountaineers and Rangers: A History of Federal Forest Management in the Southern Appalachians, 1900–81." April 1983.

————. "Ocoee and Hiwassee Rivers Corridor Management Plans." 2008.

————. Ocoee River Project and 1996 Olympic documents/letters/newspaper articles/booklets/files/other resources, 1992–96.

————. Red Fork/Unaka Mountain Fire. Correspondences between forest supervisor, assistant supervisor, district forester and district ranger/wildfire reports/telegrams, 1925–26.

————. "Revised Land and Resource Management for the Cherokee National Forest." 2005.

U.S. Department of Interior. "Nolichucky River Wild and Scenic River Survey." Washington, D.C., 1980.

Valiunas, Andrius. "Camp Coker Creek." Honors thesis, University of North Carolina–Chapel Hill, April 25, 2012.

Waite, John R. *The Blue Ridge Stemwinder*. Johnson City, TN: Overmountain Press, 2003.

Whyte, Thomas R., and Larry R. Kimball. "Science Versus Grave Desecration: The Saga of Lake Hole Cave." *Journal of Cave and Karst Studies* (December 1997).

Williams, Samuel Cole. *History of the Lost State of Franklin*. Rev. ed. Johnson City, TN: Overmountain Press, reprinted 1993.

Wright, James. "Warriors Passage National Recreation Trail: A Short History." Document, November 2014.

Ziegler, Wilbur G., and Ben Grosscup. *The Heart of the Alleghanies*. Raleigh, NC: Alfred Williams and Company, 1883.

Correspondence/Interviews

Adkins, Anna Dugger, former Old Butler resident. Interview/e-mails, 2022.

Akins-McMillan, Mary Ann, relative of Beecher Colvin, USFS. Interview/e-mails, 2021–24.

Ammons, Chris, whitewater paddler. E-mails, 2022.

Arthur, Russ, USFS law enforcement officer. Interview/e-mails, 2020–24.

Barrow, Jerry, USFS engineer. Interview/e-mails, 2020–22.

Blassingame, Harvey, conductor, Hiwassee Loop Train excursion. Tennessee Valley Railroad, 2020.

Bradley, Wesley, Tweetsie Trail extension project advocate. Interview/e-mails, 2022.

Brocato, Sam, retired USFS timber, wildlife and fisheries staff officer. Interview/e-mails, 2021–23.

Caldwell, Linda, Tennessee Overhill Heritage Association executive director. Interview/article/e-mails, 2020–24.

Calhoun, Timothy, University of Tennessee–Knoxville graduate student/bog turtle researcher. E-mails, 2023.

Callahan, Jack, retired USFS engineer. Interview/e-mails, 2020–22.

Cameron, Sue, USFWS biologist. E-mails, 2022.

Card-Lillios, Amy. Interviews/e-mails, 2021–22.

Cloud, Kenneth, descendant of Dr. Warren Copeland Jr. family. Interview/e-mails, 2021.

Cox, Casper, former USFS snorkeling guide. Interview, 2021.

Dabney, Joe, former CNF wildlife biologist, USFS South Regional Office team leader, USFS Arkansas District ranger. E-mails, 2022.

Dalton, Kenneth, and Katherine Dalton, cofounder of Tennessee Overhill Heritage Association. Interview, 2020.

Davis, B.J., Camp Ocoee director. Interview/e-mails, 2021.

Dedeker, Jay, Whigg Meadow Bird Banding Station. E-mails, 2023.

Dickey, Joellen, Ocoee River Canoe and Kayak Association (ORCKA) executive director. Interview, 2020.

Dooly, Weyman, Jr., Conasauga River Lumber Company manager. Interview, 2020.

Drury, Matt, ATC associate director of science and stewardship. Interview/e-mails, 2023–24.

Elliott, Maryl, Parksville cabin owner. Interview, 2021.

Feehrer, Kelly, Parksville cabin owner. Interview, 2021.

Feehrer, Sammy, and Anne Feehrer, Parksville cabin owners. Interview/e-mails, 2021–22.

Figart, Frances. Great Smoky Mountains Association editor. E-mails, 2023-2024.

Forbes, John, hike/history guide. Interview/CNF tour, 2021.

Ford, Chris, President, ET&WNC Railroad Historical Society. Convention lectures/interviews/hikes/e-mails, 2022–23.

Ford, Kent, author/Ocoee River Olympic whitewater announcer/world champion whitewater competitor. E-mail, 2020.

Fritts, Jeff, Laurel Bloomery native. Interview/e-mails, 2022.

Fryar, Kevin, Eagle Boy Scout. Interview, 2020.

Gentry, Janis, Johnson County Welcome Center. Interview/exhibits/documents, 2021.

Gibbs, Dan, TWRA wildlife biologist. E-mails, 2022.

Gibi, Kathleen, Director, Keep the Tennessee River Beautiful. YouTube video/interview/e-mails, 2021–22.

Graham, Wallace, former CNF District Ranger, Tellico Ranger District. Interview/e-mails, 2021.

Griffeth, Robert, USFS contracting officer. Interview, 2020.

Hamby, Jerry, Lake Ocoee Inn and Marina owner. Interview/e-mails, 2020–23.

Harris, Richard, retired physician from the Cincinnati Children's Hospital pediatric bone marrow transplant center/CNF Trail maintainer. Interviews/e-mails, 2020–24.

Hasler, Vic. E-mails, 2023–24.

Healy, Mark, USFS fire and natural resources staff officer. E-mails, 2021–24.

Hern, Tyler, Supervisory Fish Biologist, Erwin National Fish Hatchery. Website/e-mails, 2023.

Herrig, Jim, retired USFS fisheries biologist. Interview/e-mails, 2021–24.

Holdbrooks, Kelly, Director, Southern Highlands Reserve. Interviews/e-mails, 2022–23.

Jones, Ken, former retired engineer, Tennessee's Benton MacKaye Trail, cofounder. Interview/e-mails, 2021–23.

Kearney, Lewis, CNF Lands and Minerals, Aviation and Fire and Cooperative Forestry staff officer (1990–2005). Interviews/e-mails, 2020–24.

Kelly, Josh, MountainTrue field biologist. E-mails, 2023–24.

Knoll, Ralph, Senior Project Coordinator, The Conservation Fund. E-mails, 2021–24.

Lee, Robert E., former USFS recreation residence manager. Interview, 2022.

Lemons, J.T., owner, Ocoee Outdoors. Interview, 2022.

Lynch, Gabrielle, The Nature Conservancy. E-mails, 2020–24.

Maddux, Sheryl, retired CNF district ranger, Watauga Ranger District. E-mails, 2022–23.

Massey, Kevin, Director, Wild South. E-mails, 2022–23.

Masterson, Linda, and LaVonne Ewing. BearWise program. E-mails, 2021–22.

Mathews, Pamela Hall. Interview/e-mails, 2020–24.

McDaniel, Larry, Friends of Roan Mountain. E-mails, 2022–24.

McGuiness, Joseph, former CNF biologist. E-mails, 2023.

McQueen, Kenneth, TNC's Shady Valley Preserves manager. Interview, 2023.

Milbourne, Mark, railroad historian. ET&WNC Railroad newsletter/guided Doe River train excursion, 2022.

Mink, Russell, Old Butler boyhood home. Interview/e-mails, 2022–24.

Mitchell, Bobby, CNF trail maintainer. Hike/interview, 2020.

Muise, Charlie, Whigg Meadow Bird Banding Station. Interview/e-mails, 2021–23.

Neuman, Sally Dooly, Weyman Dooly Sr.'s daughter. Interview, 2022.

Owen, George, founder/former president, Benton MacKaye Trail Association. Interviews/guided hikes/e-mails, 2020–23.

Pannell, Clayton, Tennessee's Benton MacKaye Trail section cofounder/designer. Interview, 2020.

Passmore, James, and Judy Passmore, descendants of the Higdon/Haskins families. Interviews/e-mails, 2021–22.

Presswood, Marian, Polk County Historical Society. Interview/resources, 2020–21.

Rakes, Patrick, Director, Conservation Fisheries Inc. Interview/e-mails, 2022.

Ramey, John, former CNF Forest Supervisor. E-mails, 2020.

Reece, Mary Jane, Treasurer, Coker Creek Heritage Group. Interview, 2022–23.

Reid, Tazz, Pastor, Cleveland Community Church, and former president of the Southern Appalachian Backcountry Horsemen. Interviews/guided hikes/e-mails, 2020–22.

Rhodarmer, Charlie, Director, Sequoyah Birthplace Museum, and Vice-President, Tennessee Trail of Tears Association. Interview/e-mails, 2022–23.

Rhodes, L.C., Jr., Parksville cabin owner. Interview, 2022.

Rogers, Jenny, Weyman Dooly Sr.'s granddaughter. Interviews/e-mails, 2020–22.

Rush, Scott, Mississippi State University professor/Whigg Meadow Bird Banding Station. E-mails, 2023.

Settle, Roy, USDA Appalachian Resource, Conservation and Development Council (ARCD) coordinator. Interview/e-mails, 2023.

Sherman, David, former NPS and USFS lands acquisition coordinator, Washington, D.C. Interviews/e-mails, 2020–23.

Sims, Lamar, Ocoee River Olympic whitewater announcer. E-mail, 2020.

Soehren, Eric, Whigg Meadow Bird Banding Station. E-mails, 2023.

Somershoe, Scott, former State Ornithologist of Tennessee. E-mails, 2023.

Spann, Laura, President, Tennessee Trail of Tears Association. E-mails, 2023.

Speaks, Tom, former CNF Forest Supervisor. E-mails, 2023–24.

Stiver, William, GSMNP supervisory wildlife biologist. Interview/e-mails, 2021–22.

Taylor, Granville, Nick Grindstaff descendant. Interview, 2022.

Turbyfill, Jerry, Avery County Historical Museum board member. Lecture/interview/e-mails, 2022.

Twaroski, Melissa, USFS Southern Regional Office Trail of Tears coordinator. Coker Creek presentation/e-mails, 2020–22.

Walker, Dean. "The Search for Flight 308." Blog/e-mails, 2024.

Ward, Shannon, Ocoee Division Boy Scouts of America volunteer commissioner/Hiwassee River race organizer. Interview, 2022.

Watson, Craig, former TWRA official, USFS researcher at USFS Francis Marion National Forest, USFWS migratory bird biologist. Interview/e-mails, 2022.

Webb, James Harold, Jr., Webb Brothers Rafting and General Store owner, cofounder of Tennessee Overhill Historical Association. Interviews, 2021–23.

Wilson, Chris, former Cherokee Type I Interagency Hotshot Crew member. Interview/e-mails, 2021–22.

Wilson, Juanita, Old Butler Museum docent. Interviews/e-mails, 2022–24.

Winter, Kim, PhD, USFS NatureWatch national program leader. Interview/e-mails, 2021.

Wright, Paul, Southern Region's Olympics liaison officer/CNF Ocoee Whitewater Project Manager. Interview/e-mails, 2021–23.

Zeller, Janet, USFS National Accessibility Program manager. Interview/e-mails. 2020–24.

ABOUT THE AUTHOR

 Marci is a retired nurse practitioner, medical missionary and author of *Clingmans Dome: Highest Mountain in the Great Smokies*, *Pisgah National Forest: A History*, *Nantahala National Forest: A History* and *Pisgah Inn*, published by The History Press/Arcadia Publishing. She also has written a children's book, essays for the Personal Story Publishing Project and an essay for Yosemite Conservancy, published in its book celebrating the National Park Service centennial.

Visit us at
www.historypress.com